Beyond Personhood

Beyond Personhood

An Essay in Trans Philosophy

Talia Mae Bettcher

University of Minnesota Press
Minneapolis
London

Portions of the text are adapted from "Trapped in the Wrong Theory: Rethinking Trans Oppression and Resistance," *Signs: Journal of Women in Culture and Society* 39, no. 2 (Winter 2014): 383–406, https://doi. org/10.1086/673088; copyright 2013 by the University of Chicago.

Published by the University of Minnesota Press
111 Third Avenue South, Suite 290
Minneapolis, MN 55401-2520
http://www.upress.umn.edu

ISBN 978-1-5179-0256-8 (hc)
ISBN 978-1-5179-0257-5 (pb)

A Cataloging-in-Publication record for this book is available from the Library of Congress.

Printed in the United States of America on acid-free paper

The University of Minnesota is an equal-opportunity educator and employer.

34 33 32 31 30 29 28 27 26 25   10 9 8 7 6 5 4 3 2 1

In Loving Memory of
Alexis Marie Rivera
October 28, 1977–March 28, 2012

Contents

Preface and Acknowledgments

THIS ESSAY WAS A LABOR OF LOVE that lasted a very, very long time. Some of the earliest ideas came to me midway through my graduate program at UCLA in 1993–94, when I was on the precipice of transitioning—ideas lodged in my bones and at the back of my throat, barely articulate. Most of the ideas were developed throughout my various adventures in trans communities and at Cal State LA over the past twenty years.

The ideas first found voice when I started to write about the murder of Gwen Araujo and the politics of (in)visibility surrounding that. Although I had had many deep conversations with Jake Hale as he was trailblazing what would come to be known as trans philosophy in the late nineties, this was the first time I sat down to do it myself. (Until this point, I had been trying to establish myself in early modern philosophy.) I was very much influenced by the community response in Los Angeles at the time. But my own experience with transphobia contributed deeply to the analysis—the analysis then providing soothing if not healing.

I was taken aback by how much sprang forth from me and the passion with which it came. The experience of writing philosophy that came from deep within my body, philosophy that had vibrancy and worldly significance, was transformative. By the time "Evil Deceivers and Make-Believers" was published, I had a lot of material left over and the idea for a book in my mind. I began to see how the ideas I'd developed in that article went deeper and even reached toward issues concerning "the self"—the very issues that had plagued me just prior to transitioning.

Over the course of the years, I published a series of essays that I felt were like "philosophical sketches"—attempts to approach the ideas from various angles, while also unfolding them cumulatively. Since I'm not the sort of philosopher who never changes their mind, the ideas didn't stay put. And since I'm not always a particularly patient philosopher, the ideas weren't always well expressed. Happily, many of the ideas that I developed between 2007 and 2016 find their home here, typically in new and hopefully better ways.

Unsurprisingly, by the time that trans philosophy arrived on the scene, I finally felt an increased urgency to finish the book. It was at that time, however, that I also found myself in leadership positions at Cal State LA. And now that trans philosophy showed up on the radar, the profession of philosophy itself started making demands—some of them thrilling, some of them not so much. The biggest problem was that the ideas were operating on their own timeline. I felt as if I had caught an enormous whale and that I was trying to reel it in, not even knowing how to fish. So, I inched along, finding time when I could, ever asymptotically toward the end, trying to do justice to what increasingly seemed to be one very huge, complex idea—an idea that had sought me out from the crowd, making me its inadequate translator.

As Paul Valery once wrote, "A poem's never finished, only abandoned." And I suspect the same is so for a philosophical idea. I had to birth it finally. Not only did I feel the increasing need for it as times seemed to darken around me, but I also had to get on with my life. It was only by convincing myself that this might be a beginning, rather than an end, that I could finally let it go in all its imperfection. So here it is. Yet another provisional attempt at articulating an idea that will have to be further articulated down the line.

I'd like to thank Mark Balaguer for his intellectual generosity, friendship, and feedback on so much of the work that developed and changed over the years. I'd like to thank Bill Wilkerson, Nancy Tuana, Hil Malatino, Andrea Pitts, Roberta Morris, students from my spring 2020 and fall 2023 metaphysics seminars, Jen Markewych, Sam C. Tenorio, Jules Wong, Omi Salas-SantaCruz, Andrea Miller, C. Libby, Jenny Saul, Jennifer De Clue, Jay Conway, David Pitt, the women of Lezerati (Jeanne Córdova, Lynn Ballen, Jane Ward, Judith Branzburg, Robin Podolsky, Claudia Rodriguez), and an anonymous reviewer for their helpful comments on some iteration or other of the manuscript. I'd like to thank Kathryn Hill and Isabella Rodriguez for their invaluable work as research assistants at some point during this extremely long process. I'd like to thank Schem Rogerson Bader,

Perry Zurn, Lou Pesce, Bonnie Bostwick, Carole White, and my parents, Dwight and Sandra Bettcher, for their continued support. And I'd like to thank Ann Garry for her mentorship. I'd also like to thank those from whom I have learned so much. There is no way I could have written this without your lessons. Valerie Spencer, Kellii Trombacco, Maria Roman-Taylorson, Alexis Rivera, Jake Hale, Shirley Bushnell, Sheila Blaise, Mother Karina Samala, Queen Victoria Ortega, Queen Chanel Chela Demuir, Masen Davis, Sabel Samone-Loreca, Christina Quiñonez, Jazzmun Crayton, Sondra Martin, Bambi Salcedo, Shirin Buckman, Miguel Martinez, Cathy J. Reback, Zulma Velasquez, Susan Forrest, Alyssa Bettcher-Forrest, Lexi Bettcher-Forrest, Hannah Howard, Christine Beatty, Reverend Bishop Carl Bean, Terri Tinsley, Ryka Aoki, Felix Montez, Maria Carmen Hinayon, Roy Lopez, Liz Gonzalez, Cheryl Hoffman, Emilia Lombardi, Jorge Uranga, Lena Chao, Drian Martinez Juarez, Michelle Enfield, Diviana Ingravallo, Alexander Yoo, Ashley Yang, Michelle Dennis, Ashley Love, Cristina Magalhaes, Ellen Magalhaes, Elise Turen, Miqqi Alicia Gilbert, Sonia Zambrano Rivera, Alva Santos Moreno, Frederick Smith, Dionne Espinoza, Melina Abdullah, Molly Talcott, Gayle Salamon, David Green, Eli Kale Likover, Dan Dumont, Cyan St. James, Lauren Steely, Sharon Brown, Francisco Dueñas, Rogers Albritton, Andrew Hsu, John Carriero, Hilde Lindemann, Shelley Tremain, Donald Carveth, Claudio Duran, Ann McKenzie, Kathy Watt, Virginia Prince, Robert Riley, Emma Sabean. It's sadly not possible to construct a complete list—my memory is too bad. If your name isn't here and it should be, I'm sorry and thank you.

Introduction

THIS ESSAY PROVIDES AN ACCOUNT of trans oppression and an account of so-called gender dysphoria. The latter arises and persists in a resistant tension with the former, I argue, and this tense relation between trans oppression and resistance is mediated through the complex social phenomenon of gender make-believe, located at the site of abusive personhood. My account of personhood is situated within the larger political context of European colonial expansion and the institution of race as we know it. I don't offer another basis for trans oppression as set apart from and privileged with respect to other forms of oppression, therefore. I offer, rather, a way for it to be understood within a much more expansive framework.

The philosophical innovations required to defend my view are by no means inconsequential, as I propose abandoning the notions of *person, self,* and *subject* that have been so central in the modern Western philosophical tradition. Less dramatically, I claim the deeply entrenched assumptions sustaining the deployment of these notions are both false and abusive. Only by short-circuiting these assumptions can a proper account of trans gender "dysphoria" and trans oppression be articulated.[1]

My concept of **interpersonal spatiality** is key. In introducing it, I mean to propose an interpersonal spatiality theory which I believe to have important, far-reaching implications in philosophy and more broadly. Because I'm charting new terrain, I have had to introduce new terminology to describe the phenomenon of interpersonal spatiality. While I have tried not to multiply new terms and phrases needlessly, I've had to include more terminology than I would have liked. To facilitate accessibility and comprehension, I've included a glossary at the end of the essay. (Note that only words unique to my views have been included. Other instances of jargon not of my own making have been left to their own devices.)

As I define it, *interpersonal spatiality* is the capacity of all sensory and discursive encounters between people to admit of **closeness** and **distance** as determined by boundaries. These boundaries, along with the various modes of access they define, are the mechanism by which **interpersonal objects** are determined. Although intimacy and distance depend upon the existence of some system of boundaries, which **boundary system** instantiates the demands of interpersonal spatiality is entirely contingent. Consequently, as interpersonal objects are immanent in the organized practices of interpersonal spatiality, there are different sorts of interpersonal objects constituted in different systems.

In the system governing many of us now—what I call the "*folk system of interpersonal spatiality*"—there's a differentiation in types of boundaries and in boundary structures that I call "***moral sex***" and likewise a differentiation I call "***moral maturity***." Thus, two types of interpersonal objects are given—male and female—each of which can be distinguished in terms of maturity. In effect, men, women, boys, and girls are the interpersonal objects provided for in the system.

While men and women are allocated differential modes of appearances in this system, these modes are falsely treated as existing prior to culture. This is achieved primarily through the **naturalization of nakedness**—whereby a mere sociomoral possibility is illicitly regarded as a brute biological and therefore precultural possibility. I say that men, women, boys, and girls possess **physical persons** (instead of "physical bodies") to capture this. And I call these objects "people" in the folky sense of terms such as *person* and *people* (in contrast with the technical, philosophical meanings). Because these people are interpersonal objects possessing morally saturated appearances for others, the difference between folk "people" and philosophical "persons" (in a technical sense) isn't merely one of equivocation, as interpersonal spatiality theory exposes and contests the underlying assumptions of the latter.

The key assumption among them is that objects of sensory and discursive access are morally equivalent and therefore fungible. Interpersonal spatiality theory, however, recognizes a distinction between interpersonal and **nonpersonal objects** where the former but not the latter are determined by boundaries on access. It's due to these boundaries that an interpersonal object is capable of self-presentation to others, and it's precisely this capacity that grants access to social agency.

To act upon this assumption of object fungibility is to violate boundaries and, when done so systematically, is to undermine an interpersonal object's capacity for *self-display* and therefore agency. Further, once objects are assumed equivalent, the capacity for *awareness of oneself as an object for others* and, therefore, the capacity for *interpersonal awareness* at all are foreclosed, leaving only awareness of oneself as a subject perceiving (presumed nonpersonal) objects as the sole site of self-awareness. That is, the whole model for the awareness of oneself in relation to the world is provided for by staring at a wall.

By giving (interpersonal) objects, rather than subjects, place of privilege, the modern equations *person* = *self* and *self* = *subject* shatter, and the concepts, at least as we know them, falter. Rather than selves, we're primarily beings with morally saturated appearances for others, and the central form of self-awareness, to the extent that we have it, is an awareness of ourselves as boundary-structured objects for others. Thus, this model situates the possibility of staring at a wall within a larger context—one that includes sensory and discursive access to other morally bounded objects like oneself. Once we recognize the falsity and abusiveness of the assumption underlying the deployment of the concepts *person, self,* and *subject,* we are ready to expose the historical emergence of these assumptions within the context of modern European expansion and racist domination. The *object fungibility assumption,* far from merely theoretical, is crucial in the dehumanization of those who were enslaved and colonized.[2] Trans theory and politics can then be properly positioned—"rightsized"—within the context of broader political struggle.

I call this work an "essay" because it's a sustained, cumulative argument in favor of a view. While I'll provide arguments for this or that position as I proceed, the central argument in favor of my theory of interpersonal spatiality—at least for the purposes of this essay—is this: it is the only way to illuminate both trans oppression and trans gender phoria adequately.

While my main idea is that interpersonal spatiality theory is uniquely able to achieve my two goals, the buried lede here is the rejection of the core assumptions sustaining the deployment of the concepts *person, self,* and *subject.* This constitutes the key argument—namely, to provide a satisfactory account of trans gender dysphoria and trans oppression, we need to adopt a theory that contests the underlying assumptions of the modern person.

The essay is divided into three parts—each given a structural title, as well as a more poetic one. Part I, "The Central Concepts: 'Worlds' Apart," provides the background necessary to understand this essay. Chapter 1 explains the two formal aims—namely, to provide an account of trans oppression and an account of trans dysphoria—in greater detail and then repositions them within a decolonial project. It also introduces the phenomenon of **reality enforcement**—a species of misgendering that is central to the essay. Chapter 2 unfolds the basics of interpersonal spatiality theory. Chapter 3 introduces the crucial notion of ontological pluralism, its relevance to misgendering and trans oppression and resistance, and, finally, its relation to interpersonal spatiality theory.

Part II, "The Main Idea: Between Appearance and Reality," provides an account of trans oppression and gender dysphoria in terms of interpersonal spatiality theory. Chapter 4 fulfills the first goal by providing an account of trans oppression. It then develops the related concepts of the physical person, **proper appearance**, and **intimate appearance**. Chapter 5 fulfills the second goal by providing an account of trans dysphoria. It explores the phenomenon of pretransition self-recognition in detail. Chapter 6 concludes "The Main Idea" and leads into "The Buried Lede" by focusing on the notion of **conscious gender identity** and its relation to theory and to resistance.

Part III, "The Buried Lede: The Liminalities among Us," intervenes in the deployment of the philosophical concepts of *person, self,* and *subject.* Chapter 7 situates the folk system within what María Lugones calls the "colonial/modern gender system," revealing how **folk personhood** was transformed in a racist vein for the purposes of colonial expansion.[3] Chapter 8 considers the emergence of the philosophical concepts *person* and *self* from within a colonial context, arguing that the underlying assumptions are both false and abusive. Chapter 9 exposes the key assumption—object fungibility—underlying the equivalence of *self* and *subject,* as well as its corollaries, demonstrating how interpersonal spatiality contests them through the concept of the **agent object.**

Note that in order to streamline the overall argument, important disputes, arguments, and theoretical engagements have been submerged into the endnotes. Because these will not stand out as much as they would were they located in footnotes, I want to expressly indicate their existence and encourage the reader to follow up with them to get a better sense of some of the moves that I am making below the surface of the text.

Since this essay explores philosophical questions about men, women, and personhood, and since the methodological approach used herein may be broadly described as philosophical, it's appropriate to describe the work as an exercise in philosophy.

Yet, it's also important to recognize that I locate this essay in a larger, multidisciplinary, and interdisciplinary context. First, it's situated within the broader multidisciplinary and interdisciplinary field of trans studies. Second, it's in dialogue with sociology, psychology, sexology, cultural theory, feminist theory, queer theory, critical race theory, and decolonial theory. As communication across different locations is a central aspiration, I'm reluctant to regard this work as bound to one unique discipline.

As a philosophical essay, it's best described as a work of *trans philosophy* specifically. By this I don't mean that it's a philosophical essay exploring "trans issues" (although it does do so). Rather, I mean that it is a resistant philosophizing in response to trans oppression and it is an instance of what I call "*ground-bound philosophy*." Briefly, by this I indicate, first, that rather than closing its eyes to it, ground-bound philosophy attends to the political work various philosophies perform, expressly incorporating that work as a topic of analysis. Further, it self-consciously engages in its own political work, often in coalition with other philosophical theories in the service of resistance. I mean, second, that it inverts common philosophical methodology. Rather than using philosophical practice to reveal philosophical problems and perplexity for a hitherto uncomplicated "common sense," ground-bound philosophy proceeds to address the philosophical problems and perplexity already there because this supposed common sense—more an oppressive atmosphere than anything else—never made sense to begin with.

Thus, I buried the lede. The standard philosophical approach

would have subsumed my trans work under the more general project of rethinking personhood. Trans issues and, indeed, trans people
would have become mere examples or sites of theoretical application. The goal would have been to unfold an abstract philosophical
vision that attempted to join "the grand philosophical conversation."
To understand my approach, however, one must imagine me as an
example—say, a philosophized desk of Edmund Husserl's phenomenology or of the composition problem—who has decided to speak
back. Or, rather, one must imagine me, as a trans person, reduced to
this status precisely through the fungibility assumption—precisely
through philosophizing trans people in the same way one might philosophize desks. My goal is not to join this grand conversation—it is
to resist it by exposing it to others and to itself as a project of violence.
My desire is to have conversations with the other "examples" qua philosophers who likewise speak back.

While I have learned from many philosophers and this essay is engaged in many conversations, I want to acknowledge my debt to María
Lugones and the importance of my ongoing engagement with her
work. It is no doubt odd that a white, Anglo-Canadian trans woman
should find such philosophical sustenance in work that might be
described as Latinx or Third-World or decolonial feminist but not in
any way trans philosophy. However, Lugones makes plain that her account of world-traveling applies to "all people who have been subordi-
nated, exploited, and enslaved."[4] And this account spoke to me in ways
that no other philosophy did. It spoke to me not only in its liberatory
capacity but also in its value as philosophy qua philosophy. Or, rather,
it spoke to me in both ways, indistinguishably. The fact is hers is just
a vastly superior philosophy. It is the deepest, most perceptive, acute,
vibrant, subtle philosophical work that I've ever encountered. Thus, I
engage as I do.

While I've endeavored (and no doubt failed) to philosophize in a
way that lives up to the standards set by Lugones, I've never tried to
imitate her as, hopefully, my different style and approach bespeak. I
do, however, continue to grapple with some of the central themes in
her work. Certainly, her decolonial feminist philosophy plays an important role in this essay. Yet, I should also make plain that her earlier work on selves and subjecthood has figured the most intimately,

and centrally, in my reflections. As will eventually become clear, both themes are intertwined in this essay, as I seek to bring to surface the dangerous assumptions in the rise of colonial philosophizing.

A final word. Recently there has been a notable turn to Lugones's theories as many philosophers doing work in resistant philosophizing —trans, feminist, queer, and the like—have come to appreciate the tools that she has left us. While I'm glad that more philosophers are discovering her work, I'm also concerned about an appropriation of her philosophy that somehow decenters race. As white, Anglo philosophers, it's imperative that we avoid this tendency. A failure to bring the act of philosophical theorizing into the living moment, where oppression and resistance meet in complex layers and levels, is a tragic failure to have understood her philosophy in the first place or, at least, a failure to have seriously engaged with it at all.

This essay originates in several Los Angeles trans subcultures, between the years 1994 and 2022. Since philosophy is often thought to be ahistorical and context-independent, to state as much is already to make an important move. First, this insistence on historical, cultural, and experiential location is an affirmation of a broadly empiricist philosophical methodology. Any philosophy, whether acknowledged or not, draws from a worldly experience that shapes intuitions and interests, and it's methodologically honest, in my view, to make plain the experiential basis of one's philosophizing.

Second, as a white philosopher writing from a globally hegemonic nation in a globally hegemonic language, I'd like to fight against the tendency toward self-universalization by marking the specificity and locality of my work. Let this essay therefore be marked as follows: a white, middle-class, more or less able-bodied trans girl from Canada living in Los Angeles, "Anglo" in a double sense of the word, transitions during grad school at UCLA, finds sustenance in the subcultural trans worlds of Los Angeles, finds a home at Cal State LA, and contributes to both, ever philosophizing along the way.

Third, this insistence stakes out limits. While I offer a theory that is broad, it comes from a particular place and time. In my view, a philosophical account functions more or less adequately for some particular purpose—a purpose that emerges under particular circumstances. Consequently, a difference or change in circumstance can require a different purpose and, therefore, a different theory. Whether or not this theory is useful, applicable, or even intelligible in other cultural locations remains to be seen. Rather than regarding this work as an attempt to present a total picture, it is far more accurate to regard it as a contribution to various ongoing conversations. In fact, rather than an account at all, in a pinch, what I present might be regarded as a box of new philosophical ideas—offered up in the hope that they might be of use.

Finally, this insistence is an acknowledgment and an expression of gratitude. The experiences from which the philosophy in this essay derives occurred in transformative interactions with many, many others. I was never some solitary philosopher thinking these issues through on her own. What fed my work, what forced me out of myself, what required me to respond to others, was trans community engagement. It was in learning from others, agreeing with others, disagreeing with others, understanding and misunderstanding others, and being challenged by others that I thought. And the thoughts were vibrant, living ones. And in working with others on vibrant, living issues, I was regularly forced to reassess who I was in relation to others and what I thought I was doing—particularly around matters of privilege, particularly around matters of race.

To be clear, I'm quite aware that the experiential origins of this essay don't erase the privileges I have and have had. Nor do these origins erase the various distortions inherent in this essay. To acknowledge these origins, however, is to clarify from whence this essay originates. It's to give credit where credit is due. The essay is the product of ongoing philosophical reflection through personal growth over a long period of time, in the crucible of conversation, cacophony, and struggle, across worlds, genders, generations, and cultures. It couldn't exist without the many people and experiences who have shaped it.

Part I

The Central Concepts
"Worlds" Apart

Chapter 1

Getting "Real"

IN THIS INTRODUCTORY CHAPTER, I formulate the two formal goals of the essay: to provide an account of trans oppression and to provide an account of so-called gender dysphoria. I explain why I reject a broad category-based account of trans oppression. Then, I introduce the phenomenon of reality enforcement, a form of misgendering and a structure of abuse the analysis of which is central to my goals. I then discuss the concept of intersectionality and its relationship to reality enforcement. Finally, I situate my project in terms of what María Lugones calls the "colonial/modern gender system," and I then conclude by discussing the notion of personhood.

Preliminaries

Sometimes things don't make any sense. Under the weight of oppression, the social world one inhabits can be so thoroughly saturated with perverse rationalizations and violent mystifications that up becomes down and down up while everything is turned inside out. The confusion isn't the effect of philosophical inquiry. It's there from the beginning in place of the much-touted "common sense" that traditional philosophy allegedly contests. As it shapes one's very life, this disorientation becomes existential in character. I call this perplexity the *existential WTF.*

This essay is a resistant sense-making exercise in the face of trans oppression, and for this reason it can be characterized as an instance of trans philosophy. I take for granted the presumptive validity of trans identities as a methodological starting point. Without it, one couldn't engage in sense-making that is liberatory for trans people—at least not to any meaningful degree. It is, to my mind, analogous to the claim that women aren't inferior to men—a claim that's obviously necessary for feminist philosophy to have place. And, certainly, any project designed to illuminate trans experience proceeding from the starting point that trans identities—unlike most identities—require defense of their validity isn't the sort of starting point that can provide any illumination for trans people. It could only perpetuate the confusion.

This isn't to deny that there can (indeed, should) be trans philosophical engagements with antitrans literature. It's crucial, however, that such interventions be understood—at least by those making them—as merely tactical. To lose sight of this is to jettison one's compass, is to leave oneself vulnerable to the machinations of a dominant ideology inherently hostile to trans and nonbinary people.

This is, however, to affirm that there must be another sort of trans philosophical work that does not cede such terrain—not even tactically. Here, the very endeavor of "making sense" is a resistant activity. It is resistant not only because the "common sense" of the dominant world tends to be disorienting for those who are oppressed but also because forces actively discourage trans people from undertaking this exercise in the first place (for instance, by attacking us so as to perpetually require our thinking be apologetic in nature or by leaving us vulnerable should we discuss our experiences in a nontactical way).

Since my work in trans philosophy has too frequently been misunderstood in this regard, I want to make sure that the following is clear: first, I only ever aim to provide illumination for trans people, nonbinary people, and friends. I do not believe in wasting my breath on transphobes. Second, the only other thing I attempt to accomplish through my work is to make new friends who are differently oppressed—a more edifying approach than begging for validation. Finally, while the attempt to alter the dominant practices of nontrans people may seem like a good idea—I'm frankly pessimistic—I am more interested in building new practices with new friends. If others want to give up their hostility and join us, that's great.

Two Aims

My first aim is to provide an adequate account of trans oppression—one that does not reduce to the **beyond-the-binary account.** Roughly, the latter claims that the oppression of trans and nonbinary people can be explained by appeal to a binary—a binary between man and woman, male and female, and masculine and feminine. Trans and nonbinary people are oppressed, says this view, by the cultural insistence on these binaries and by the mandated alignment of the three binary pairs.[1]

I want an account that makes room for trans people who self-identify as men (male, masculine) or women (female, feminine). I don't want to exclude those who don't. Rather, I take misgendering as the precondition for most other forms of abuse directed toward trans and nonbinary folk alike. I understand *misgendering* as synonymous with *gender identity invalidation*. It includes not only referring to individuals with pronouns and gender terms in misalignment with their own self-identity but also deadnaming. It includes the violence and abuse that often attends such discursive actions. Finally, it includes not only overt behavior but also the very regarding of an individual in ways inconsistent with their own gender identity. All of us confront the persisting phenomenon of misgendering and the violence that attends it, and the trick, surely, is to illuminate the phenomenon without falling prey to its perpetuation.

I understand *gender identity* as a reflexive sense of belonging to a sex or gender category. This can include "male," "female," "woman," "man," "nonbinary," "genderqueer," "trans," "transsexual," "transgender," and so forth. Further, I take gender self-identification as necessary to ascribing a sex or gender category to an individual. If an individual doesn't self-identify with a category, it doesn't apply to them, and if an individual does self-identify with it, it does.[2] A corollary to this is that the exact meaning of a category cannot be fixed without avail to an individual's self-identification and their own understanding of its meaning and relevance to them. Here, the sharing can take the form of intimacy. (I say all this drawing on my experience of trans subcultures. I discuss these practices in greater depth in chapter 6.)

I ought to be clear that trans people who identify as trans men or trans women needn't identify as men or women, respectively. Such identifications may sometimes involve self-positioning in complex tension with the binary. Moreover, trans folk who identify as men or women needn't position themselves within some binary, as these folks may not believe in a binary at all, welcoming a plethora of self-identifications. Happily, this undermines the view that any trans person who self-identifies as a man or a woman is a friend of the binary and therefore an enemy of those contesting it.[3]

The issue, rather, is that while useful, the beyond-the-binary account is insufficient to capture all forms of trans oppression. The presumption that it's sufficient, alas, requires all trans men and women to be positioned outside the categories "men" and "women" and says that they're both deluded and complicit in their own oppression in case they identify as men and women, thereby threatening a radical form of misgendering. Surely, trans folk who attempt to live their truth in a world that denies it must be regarded as resisting oppression. The goal, then, is to elucidate this oppression and resistance among other forms of oppression and resistance.

My second aim is to provide an account of trans *gender phoria* that doesn't reduce to the well-known *wrong-body account (WBA)*. I've coined *gender phoria* (using *phoria* in departure from the original Greek meaning "carrier") to capture both dysphoria (unhappiness) and euphoria (happiness) since there isn't a term that already does so. I'll often speak of "negative gender phoria" rather than "dysphoria" since the latter is deployed officially as a diagnostic term.[4] And I'll often speak of "positive gender phoria" rather than "euphoria" since the latter sounds just a little too happy to be believed. One benefit of the neologism *phoria* is that it admits of degrees of positivity and negativity, as well as complicated mixtures of valences.

While there are many variations, I'll take the wrong-body account—at least the version that is most trans friendly—to consist in three claims: namely, that negative trans phoria derives from an incongruence between internal sense of self and external appearance; that the internal sense of self is innate; and that the innateness of this sense validates trans claims to belong to a particular sex.

I seek an account that, in contrast to the WBA, avoids a sharp and artificial phenomenological divide between those experiencing bodily phoria and those who, while content with their bodies, experience various forms of phoria with their sex-differentiated self-presentation. The WBA, in my view, erases or downplays the latter sort of phoria even among those who aren't content with their bodies, as if the body alone were the problem.

Happily, the move toward greater inclusiveness places pressure on any account that regards gender phoria as innate. I say "happily" since I want an account that doesn't run contrary to feminist insight that "one is not born a woman."[5] I want an account of gender phoria that doesn't depend upon an appeal to an innate gender identity or bodily sense. Instead of an account framing trans gender phoria as a pathology in search of a cure, I frame it as a form of resistance to an oppressive system.

Certainly, the intimate relation between dysphoria and trans invalidation is painfully obvious: the constant rejection and violence to which we're subject frames our dysphoric experience in a very significant way. The stronger claim I make is that this likewise characterizes gender phoria not only after an express trans self-identity has developed but instead at the very outset, from the very inception. In this way, the two aims are related. On the one hand, I articulate an account of trans oppression. On the other, I articulate an account of trans phoria as resistant to oppression.

Oppression and Categories

I avoid formulating oppressions in terms of category-based vectors. In that approach, oppressed individuals are identified according to a set of common features by which they belong to a particular identity category and are then subject to various forms of oppression on the basis of membership within that category. Instead of focusing on broad identity-based categories of oppression, however, I consider organized practices of violence and domination—rape, for instance. I analyze instances of forms of abuse and violence, grouping them together in terms of structural similitude. I see such a project as operating at a different level of analysis since it does not proceed with a more abstract formulation of category-based oppression. Instead of talking about the oppression of women, for instance, I talk of "sexist oppression," by which I mean various forms of violence and abuse—such as rape—that exhibit a similar structure.

In saying this, I reject the view of social constitution as the mere act of social naming whereby some presocial entity is selected on the basis of criteria and then named and thereby assigned a status and allocated to some social set of norms. Rather, I regard discursive practices as intertwined with extradiscursive ones. By the time some entity gets named, it has often already been put to work in some extradiscursive social activity, and what gets named is thereby already social in character. Terms like *banker* and *fashion model*, for example, cannot be extricated from the extralinguistic practices that effectively constitute bankers and fashion models.

Indeed, even the deployment of a word to name must be regarded as one of many possible discursive deployments. Consider how the term *bingo*, while naming both the game and a winning state, is also required as a move in the game (namely, saying "bingo"). Rather than viewing "woman" and "man" as categories (of gender), for instance, I prefer to think of various discursive practices in which the terms *woman* and *man* are deployed with some significance. Here, the terms themselves can have different uses that are not always even descriptive. For example, they can be used to hold somebody accountable to norms governing gender expression (e.g., "Be a man!"). I'll mention another shortly.

One reason I avoid the appeal to category-based vectors is that this approach cannot accommodate misgendering as a form of oppression. Trans people are typically not oppressed because we are placed into the category "trans"—or, if we are, there is a much deeper move afoot. Misgendering is the practice where all self-identities—man, woman, trans man, nonbinary, genderqueer, etc.—go to die. Rather than being oppressed on the basis of belonging to a certain category, one is oppressed, in part, by having one's identity eradicated. Consider that trans men are oppressed through placement within the category "woman" and trans women are oppressed through placement in the category "man." In these cases, the term *trans* may not even be salient. To put it crudely, it doesn't usually go down like this: "Hey, look, a transgender person! Let's go harass them!" It typically goes down like this: "Hey, look, a man in a dress! Let's go harass him!" Further, the very interpretation of *trans* is up for grabs in case the expression is actually salient. To some, the expression *trans woman* may mean "man who lives as a woman," while to trans women, the expression will typically mean something quite different.

The point is this: one cannot, on the one hand, formulate the vector as the oppression of "mere men claiming to be women" and "mere women claiming to be men." Such a formulation is itself a form of invalidation and hence is useless for liberation. On the other hand, one cannot say that we are oppressed because we are trans since we are not oppressed because we are situated in that category— "trans"—and then oppressed and since there is no one single category with which those subject to misgendering self-identify anyway.

The second reason I reject an appeal to categorical vectors is more general. It's highly plausible that concepts themselves are oppressive and, indeed, multiply so. To the extent that the dominant concept of *woman* has heterosexuality as an ideal built right into it, for example, it can function to marginalize or even exclude lesbians. To the extent that the dominant concept of *woman* has white femininity (e.g., fragility) built right into it, it can function as a vehicle for racist marginalization. Further, given the multiple ways in which the deployment of *woman* can function to oppress or marginalize, there are invariably multiple resistant resignifications of the term—reclaimings that contest various modes of oppression and marginalization. Consider, for example, the resistant resignifications inherent in the lesbian separatist term *womyn* and the open-ended and coalitional *women of color*. This suggests that taking terms like *woman* as the firm starting point for a feminist analysis, with the meaning fully fixed, is a questionable move. Given the multiplicity of meaning, what meaning is one presupposing? By fixing it in advance, one forecloses the necessary political analysis, negotiation, and therefore possibility of coalition-building.

Reality Enforcement

To achieve my ends, I focus on the phenomenon of reality enforcement as a structured form of violence and abuse. Not only do I regard the phenomenon as easily the most life-shaping form of transphobia, but I also regard it as the tip of an enormous philosophical iceberg— one that I hope to reveal a little more deeply in this essay.

To be clear, I don't think that all trans oppression reduces to reality enforcement. However, I do believe that reality enforcement is easily the most prevalent and ubiquitous threat to most trans people today.[6] First, it provides the basis for almost all other forms of violence, discrimination, and marginalization against us. Consider, for instance, the trans woman who is assessed as flouting norms of masculinity and punished accordingly. Such assessment is possible only because she is regarded as a man ("really a man") in the first place. Second, as we'll see, it concerns the very respects in which we are relationally positioned with regard to others in terms of intimacy and distance. Finally, it conditions the very issue of passing in the lives of trans people. Reality enforcement, I maintain, is easily the most significant form of oppression that trans and nonbinary people face.

It's a form of misgendering characterized by an appearance–reality contrast whereby a trans person is viewed as *really* a so-and-so *disguised* as a such-and-such. This contrast can be manifested in two ways: namely, one may be regarded as engaged in deception or else one may be regarded as merely playing at make-believe. The two main forms of the appearance–reality contrast—deception and pretense—then constitute a double bind: either risk exposure as a deceiver or else come out as a make-believer.[7] A trans woman, for instance, will be constituted either as a man trying to mislead others into believing "he" is a woman or else as a man engaged in a sort of pretense or role-play.[8] Following Marilyn Frye, I recognize the double bind as a hallmark of oppression—being constrained, immobilized on all fronts. We can see it as a foreclosure of liberatory agency through the foreclosure of any meaningful choice.[9]

The appearance–reality contrast depends upon a perceived misalignment between gender presentation and sex. By *gender presentation* I mean the way a person appears and behaves so as to be read as a man/male or woman/female or something else. This is different from gender expression, which likewise includes appearance and behavior but, in this case, is characterized and assessed as feminine or masculine. The latter presupposes a read on the basis of which there is then an assessment according to norms. Thus, it is possible for a butch to present (and be read) as a woman but to have her appearance and behavior still assessed as masculine.

As I mentioned in the introduction, what I mean by *sex* is *moral sex*—that is, the differentiation in types of **interpersonal boundaries** and boundary structures that regulate sensory and discursive access to each other. While this notion will be developed throughout this essay, let me say now that it is something like anatomical sex as governed by differentiated interpersonal boundaries—a sort of moralized morphology, if you will. This is evident in the phenomenon of reality enforcement, which, it turns out, is bound up with abuse. Specifically, there is a disturbing connection between the "reality" part of the appearance–reality contrast and **boundary violation** through genital verification. In cases of literal genital verification, trans people may be forcibly exposed or touched to determine what's between our legs. Not only are these sexual violations, they're also attempts to cut through mere appearance to expose "the reality." The violator transgresses a boundary on sensory access to a person's anatomy to determine "the truth." This is also apparent in less extreme forms of genital verification that, rather than sensory transgressions, involve invasive questions, typically posed in euphemistic form where, once again, the "truth" is equated with genitalia and access to it is secured through a boundary. For instance, "Have you had the surgery?" "How far along are you in your transition?" And, as I promised earlier, we find a peculiar variant that uses gender and sex terms euphemistically to communicate genital status—for instance, "was discovered to be anatomically male" or "was found to actually be a woman."

Inspired by these facts, my account of reality enforcement posits a representational relation between gender presentation and sex or, as I originally put it in "Evil Deceivers and Make-Believers," "genital status."[10] One can take the gloss of gender deception as genital communication through gender presentation and run the logic backward. If trans people are deceivers through a public gender presentation that inaccurately communicates the form of genital status, it follows that those who align a gender presentation with their moralized genitalia must, therefore, be telling the truth: they must be honestly communicating their genital status through their public gender presentation on a regular basis.

From this, I've also concluded that this **sex-representational system** is inherently abusive. If one agrees that the genital inquiries discussed above are invasive, one should conclude that this entire system of genital communication is likewise so. It compels a truthtelling about information that this system itself also registers as intimate. Truthful disclosures are mandatory: failure to comply leads to punishment. Since compelling or manipulating a person into sharing intimate information about themselves is violating, we should surely conclude that the system is abusive.

Reality Enforcement 2.0

In this essay, I focus on an aspect of reality enforcement that I have, for the most part, left undertheorized in previous work. Reality enforcement constitutes trans people as either deceivers or make-believers. Offering a friendly critique of my account, Loren Cannon proposes a third possibility that he takes not to be included by the deceiver and make-believer constitutions. Cannon writes:

> Yes, we are often negatively viewed as deceivers or make-believers, but the third option is something far more positive. For those wishing to display their *Progressive* credentials we become a vehicle with which to do so. We are like the new exotic animal whose acquisition is boasted about by the zoo managers.[11]

What Cannon misses, however, is that reality enforcement can often appear "far more positive" and the treatment of a trans person as "the new exotic animal" is likely predicated on the individual *playing along* with them. The constitution of a trans person as a make-believer needn't result in ridicule and rejection. It can, on the contrary, result in this corresponding form of make-believe. Sadly, this is often the case. It's certainly come to pass, for many of us, that friendships we thought were close turned out to be based on a confusion in which a friend viewed us as something that we weren't, something that made us feel like fiction. Here, there was a painful failure of intimacy.

The problem is that while playing along can be evident through tone, attitude, and pronoun slips, often it is not. Often, it's more subtle. In these latter cases the "player" has a strong interest in being accepting of trans people because they have a strong interest in being a good person. This may even lead to a player's self-deception about their beliefs and motives.

In such cases, the fact that this is merely playing along won't be apparent. One will have to wait until certain other contexts arise (or don't arise). Specifically, different forms of pretense are associated with different harms that can arise in taking the game too far. For instance, while pretending to be a brain surgeon at a masquerade party is fine, operating on somebody's brain is more than a little risky. It is in these contexts of calamity, I say, that the pretense will become plain. Otherwise, the self-deceived player will simply arrange it so that such contexts never arise in the first place. That is, such contexts will be unconsciously foreclosed.

It is notable, if not unsurprising, that the imagined harms in the case of gender make-believe concern sexual intimacy. One involves the fear of sleeping with the "wrong sex." For instance, a heterosexual (nontrans) man willing to treat a trans woman as a woman within a nonintimate context may be unwilling to sleep with her on the grounds that she's "really a man." The other involves sexual violation in cases of sex segregation. For instance, a (nontrans) woman willing to treat a trans woman as a woman within a nonintimate context may feel violated when the latter uses women's changing rooms. Both calamities can therefore stay out of sight in nonintimate contexts. But as soon as the possibility of intimacy comes to the fore (or even almost does so), these calamities can suddenly become pertinent. Now, of course, we are concerned with what the trans person is "really," and the pretense has to end, lest it go "too far."

There is another variant worth mentioning—one that runs in the opposite direction, one blocking the movement from the intimate to the public, rather than from the public to the intimate. As trans women know all too well, many straight-identified men are actually quite happy to have sex with us in secret—where we function as a convenient substitute for the real thing. As mere performers in a sexual role-play, however, trans women become "dirty little secrets," relegated to a hidden sexual domain, with no access to the typical route from sexual encounters to the publicly recognized heterosexual relationships available to many nontrans women.[12] Often, one does not find out about one's relegation to secret status until he refuses to introduce one to his friends or family.

Understanding the playing-along phenomenon is crucial. It suggests several related lessons. First, it highlights why transition requires more than name and pronoun changes, changes in public gender presentation and private body, the use of medical technologies, and the like. Transition further involves integration in systems of interpersonal spatiality. Without this uptake, gender presentation remains nothing but a disguise (more on this anon).

Second, any presumption of so-called happy social progress needs to be called into question. While it might seem that people are adopting more inclusive language, these new practices may be nothing more than playing along by another name and therefore no progress at all. Third, the elimination of misgendering cannot be obtained merely by focusing on getting names and pronouns right in any given context. Nor even is it enough to afford trans people access to the appropriate restrooms. Such adjustments won't constitute a genuine inclusion of trans people until the underlying conditions that give rise to misgendering are remedied. Finally, the undue focus on categories, terms, and pronouns that has so concerned advocates and philosophers alike gives way to social possibilities of social interaction—that is, of relations of distance and closeness.

While the make-believe side of the ***deceiver–make-believer bind*** serves a significant purpose in the oppression of trans people, however—and this is a key dimension of this essay—it also provides a site of resistance for us as well. Indeed, it provides a way to reframe trans phoria as a form of resistance or, if you will, resistant tension with trans oppression. I attribute particular import to the experience of recognizing oneself in a state of make-believe prior to transition. I explain this as a form of otherworldly self-awareness, an experience of ***dignity*** or ***self-collection.*** By appealing to the techniques of make-believe, the artificial prioritization of bodily dysphoria (over gender presentation, say) can be mitigated and a more integrated account provided.

In this view, resistance takes the form of ***realization***—the attempted movement from gender pretense to gender reality. Formally, it's the process by which the pretransition experience of self-recognition is made actual through integration in ***interpersonal space.*** Thus, my account connects my two formal goals by explaining trans oppression in terms of relegation to the state of structural make-believe and characterizing trans phoria as emerging in the liminal state of make-believe. Rather than occupying a space in between man and woman, these beings occupy a space in between appearance and reality.

Let's now return to my point that not all forms of misgendering are forms of reality enforcement. If it was not obvious before, it should be obvious now. The crucial difference between reality enforcement and other forms of misgendering is that while all types of misgendering involve the (mis)application of categories, reality enforcement also involves distinctive extradiscursive social practices surrounding the representational feature of gender presentation.

This means that while somebody who is not taken to misalign gender presentation and genital status but simply self-identifies in nonnormative ways (e.g., nonbinary) may be vulnerable to misgendering and other normative judgments, they are not vulnerable to reality enforcement. By contrast, for those who have come face to face with their own apparition, for those who have been called by this liminal being, achieving realization will likely be transition's guiding end. The tension between the forces of derealization, on the one hand, and the attempt to self-realize, on the other, is absolutely central.

Thus, returning us now to an earlier point, while the fact that I typically speak of "trans women" and "trans men" throughout this essay (where the expressions require self-identification to be applicable) might seem to limit the scope of the essay unnecessarily, the essay is intended to be applicable to whomever finds it applicable. If there is an applicability, it will require a similitude not in categories of self-identification but, rather, in susceptibility to violent social practices—and, in particular, reality enforcement. As such, the phenomenon of reality enforcement helps me specify those central to this essay in ways that self-identifying terms like *trans man* and *trans woman* never could. It better enables me to witness forms of resistance that are otherwise obscured—forms that strive for realization.

To be clear, this is not to say that this project concerns only those we might call "apparitionals." While the WBA is overly exclusive in this respect—it concerns only "transsexuals," those who seek medical transition—my account is not limited in this way. Rather, in attempting to explain reality enforcement and pretransition self-recognition, I appeal to my general theory of interpersonal space as well as my specific account of the folk system of interpersonal spatiality. This new approach affords much-needed resources to illuminate other forms of trans oppression—oppression through the binary mandate, say—as well as other forms of trans phoria that don't concern apparitionality or the drive for realization. Indeed, my theory of interpersonal spatiality and account of the folk system illuminate multiple forms of oppression and resistance—as we shall eventually discover. It is to say that the attempt to explain this tension between gender appearance and reality is precisely what necessitates the development of this new account. It is what justifies it.

Intersectionality

While Kimberlé Crenshaw's term *intersectionality* has come into theorical and political prominence, it is worth remembering that the insights she articulates—and as she herself would be the first to admit—have a long history before her as is evidenced, for instance, by the Combahee River Collective's Black feminist statement.[13] It is also important to keep in mind that while the term puts into play the metaphor of a street intersection, the issues motivating Crenshaw's move actually undo the appeal to streets altogether (and this is not news to Crenshaw!). On the face of it, the point of the metaphor is that when we focus on only one vector at a time, we don't notice that sometimes these oppressions can intersect with each other. We end up leaving out the fact that some people are standing in more than one street and can therefore get hit by different cars from different streets.

Crenshaw's concept goes well beyond the metaphor, however. Consider, first, the phenomenon of blended oppressions.[14] Sexual violence, for example, has historically been used as a form of racial subordination (as white men were able to rape enslaved Black women with impunity). In such cases one cannot distinguish or separate the racism and sexism into discrete parts. There's one thing (rape) that is at once both an instance of sexist oppression and an instance of racist oppression. As Angela Y. Davis points out:

> Sexual coercion was, rather, an essential dimension of the social relations between slavemaster and slave. In other words, the right claimed by slaveowners and their agents over the bodies of female slaves was a direct expression of their presumed property rights over Black people as a whole.[15]

These phenomena are not captured in the metaphor of intersecting streets. In addition to being hit by racist cars on one street and sexist cars on another, one would have to imagine "racexist" cars falling from the sky, hitting only those in the intersection.

Consider, second, the blending of oppression and privilege. White women's experiences of sexism aren't untainted with race; they're just untainted with racial *oppression*. Black men's experiences of racism aren't untainted with sex, after all; they're just untainted with sexist *oppression*. One thing this means is that there's a sort of blending that occurs outside of the intersections of oppressions. So, once again, the street metaphor collapses. And this, in turn, has consequences for how we understand blended oppressions (discussed above).

Returning, then, to racialized rape, we find that not only are racism and sexism inseparable but that to try to separate them into "racism" and "sexism" already involves an abstraction shot through with privilege. That is, vector categories (like "racism" and "sexism") abstract from the reality of blended oppressions. There are no such things as "pure racism" and "pure sexism." On the contrary, these vector categories build in an implicit privilege that is not acknowledged (e.g., "pure sexism" = sexism experienced by those who are racially privileged; "pure racism" = racism for those privileged by gender, etc.).[16]

On the face of it, this might seem to yield a problem. Since sexist and racist oppressions and privileges are blended, we end up with different forms of sexist oppression and therefore seem to forfeit the thought that there might be a common oppression. Yet, while Crenshaw is deeply concerned about blended oppressions and privileges, she still recognizes the possibility that women of color can be subject to double damage and that they can also be subject to sexism alone and racism alone.[17] Indeed, that is specifically why she introduces the metaphor of the intersection in the first place. Following Crenshaw, it seems important to keep this possibility of double damage and "sexism alone" in play.

My own approach involves recognizing that once blended instances of abuse are centralized, we can nonetheless note structural similitude in abusive practices that track away from the center. For instance, sexual violence against white women bears structural similarity to the racialized rape of Black women. Likewise, racial subordination of Black men bears a structural similarity to the subordination of Black women. However, the structural similarities in the two cases are distinct, and so we may differentiate these similitudes by speaking of "sexism" and "racism" separately.

Instead of grounding the similitude by appealing to the notion of a categorical vector, however, we appeal to what can be called "a trajectory of privilege." Along a trajectory from the center to the margins, we find sites of oppression/resistance that have lost key features in which consequences become both less likely and less severe.

That is, the increasing clarification of a distinct "vector of oppression" is simply a movement along a "trajectory of privilege."

Intersectionality and Reality Enforcement

Although Crenshaw herself encourages expansive application of the notion of intersectionality, caution is still required. The concept emerged specifically as an intervention in the erasure of (nontrans) women of color and, more specifically, Black women. And it should not be assumed in advance that it will work just as effectively in other cases. I say this especially since an abstract model that posits vectors creates facile analogies among various forms of oppression as if they were somehow interchangeable. In the case of reality enforcement, this is particularly so when considering sexual violence.

Trans men, for instance, are likewise subject to the blending of reality enforcement and sexual violence. One way of punishing trans men for deception and for proving that they are "really women" is just to rape them *as women*. Here, rape is at once an instance of both reality enforcement and sexual violence. Thus, it makes little sense to understand trans men as located on a trajectory of privilege away from the blending of reality enforcement and sexism, in the way that is analogous to racialized sexual violence discussed above. Instead, it seems that the character of sexual abuse depends on the modality of reality enforcement. While trans men are subject to sexist violence because they are viewed as actually being women, trans women are subject to it because they are viewed as pretending to be women. Privilege, if there is any to be had in this case, surely has more to do with passing so as not to effect a read as "really a man" or "really a woman."

It is also worth noting the prima facie difficulty in fathoming the interblending of relegation to pretense and subjection to sexist abuse. If the sexist abuse is merely the effect of playing along, how can it be serious? Isn't it just pretending? It turns out, however, that this relegation to pretense ends up enabling and then trivializing the abuse. One example of this is the phenomenon of sexual assault as "forced feminization" and "forced feminization" as sexual assault. By abusing someone "as if they were a woman," one can abuse in a way that is structurally the same as abusing them "as a woman" while denying them comparable recourse to intervention or aid—such as the right to leave sex work.[18] Another example of this is the relegation of trans women to "dirty little secrets" (mentioned earlier). While many women can be subject to this relegation—on the basis of appearance, body size, and social status, among other things—this specific relegation of trans women is exercised precisely on the basis of them being "really men pretending to be women," and it's precisely this relegation that helps constitute them as pretending as well.

In addition to cases of single acts of blended forms of abuse, there are other cases that involve something like a complex system. For instance, the manipulative character of heterosexuality is grounded in numerous double binds. Once he buys the drink or strikes up a conversation, she can terminate the discussion immediately (be a bitch), allow for some movement down the pathway to avoid rudeness and then opt out gracefully later (be a tease), or glide down the slide and have unwanted sex.[19] Now, when a trans woman finds herself in a (hetero) sexualized context (or one that is leading there), it is highly likely that if she is "exposed," the trans woman will be viewed as "really a man trying to seduce unsuspecting straight men." This risk of exposure and violence creates a pressure to maintain a certain form of presentation and conduct that continues the nonverbal exchange. Trying to terminate the sexual interaction may lead to exposure. As the nonverbal communicative exchange continues, however, it is likely that she will also become more and more an object of sexual interest and therefore scrutiny (increasing the chances of being "read" as "really a man"). Moreover, the longer the exchange continues, the greater the risk for extreme violence, since the man's own sexual desire, and therefore sexual identity, is increasingly implicated as the path to intimacy is further traversed.[20]

One of the most important instances of this form of intersectionality is trans sex work. Let's begin by noting how thoroughly reality enforcement shapes it. To the extent that trans sex workers operate in a niche market, demand for the service hinges on various permutations of the eroticization of gender pretense. For instance, trans women may be constituted as "real women" in the fantasy (and therefore as role-players without). Or else as "really feminized men" both within and without. Or else as "a (nontrans) chick with a dick"—that is, a mystical unicorn-like creature who exists only in fantasy.

Meanwhile, supply is made possible through coercive conditions saturated with reality enforcement. The lack of meaningful employment for trans women, for instance, is made possible by the view that they are "really men."[21] Crucially, any right to exit for trans women is specifically foreclosed as programs, services, shelters, and the like are typically closed to trans women on the basis of the imagined calamity grounding sex segregation discussed earlier.

Further, while supply and demand are the forces that press trans sex work into existence, there are likewise forces that press it out of existence. Certainly, criminalization is key—again, for trans women this can involve being housed with nontrans men, being invasively searched by men, and so forth. Beyond officially sanctioned abuse, maverick freewheeling also occurs. Some examples include the use of strip searches to perform genital verifications or transphobic forms of sexual abuse, the denial of access to basic technologies of personhood (e.g., wigs, bras, hormones) for the purposes of humiliation or other transphobic reasons, jail and prison housing itself (in isolation, in general population, or in some specialized unit), and, of course, rape. And in addition to criminalization itself, let me further add that trans women who engage in street-level commercial sex provision are left vulnerable to harassment and violence from transphobic men who control or at least operate on the street—gang members, for instance, who spray the working women with bleach or urine as they drive by.

Indeed, trans sex workers are vulnerable to potential clients, who always have at their disposal the claim "I didn't know that was a guy! He tricked me!" offered either as cover story or else in earnest. This is because the provision of commercial sex by trans women constitutes a paradigm case of reality enforcement on the deceiver side of the bind. The moral structure of intimate appearance is explicitly relevant to the encounter: genitals probably matter. And as gender presentation may be taken not only to advertise sexual availability but also as a signal of commercial availability, it is easy to see how trans women can be taken to engage in deception—in this case, false advertising. Here, the actions of trans women are not merely reduced to sexual motives, they are reduced to economic ones. And this has specific consequences for trans women in general—namely, the phenomenon of harassment for "walking while trans." Trans women who walk the streets, visibly trans, are taken to be looking for clients.

The point is that in the case of trans sex work, we find the complete integration of reality enforcement, sexist violence, and economic exploitation. And in the United States, this is more correctly understood as a species of racist domination as well. Certainly, conditions such as poverty that help create the supply of available trans women are heavily racialized. More than that, however, the criminal justice system is clearly one of the main instruments of racial oppression in the contemporary United States—particularly against Black people. And criminalization is arguably constitutive of the sex work itself.

Rather than viewing the forces that push trans sex work into existence (supply/demand) and the forces that push it out of existence (criminalization/violence) as oppositional, we really ought to regard them as operating in tandem. Consider the way that police involvement serves less to prevent commercial sex than to destabilize workers and keep the costs low. It seems to me that delocation of commercial sex from the traditional wage-labor model, the allocation of commercial sex to "underground" or "black market" activities, helps constitute it as such in many cases.[22] That is to say, rather than regarding economic exploitation solely in terms of a wage-labor model, we ought to include, following Aníbal Quijano, "all forms of control and exploitation of labor and production"—among them, "slavery, serfdom, petty-commodity production, reciprocity, and wages."[23]

It's therefore unsurprising that those trans women in jail or prison, those most vulnerable to violence, are largely women of color. This issue isn't merely that racial oppression exacerbates the conditions of trans sex work. Rather, race is just as interwound with it as is the economic component. Indeed, the depth to which the phenomenon is saturated with reality enforcement, the degree to which it is everywhere a condition, everywhere a danger, suggests that rather than an instance of a more general structure of violence—reality enforcement—the system that creates trans sex work is a fundamental and concrete form of violence where *reality enforcement* merely designates one possible form of structural violence and trajectory of privilege away from it.

The Colonial/Modern Gender System

In an essay such as this in which trans oppression and resistance are expressly central and the trans woman who writes it is a white, middle-class, English-speaking resident of the settled Global North, the intersections are still inevitably marginalized, a limited vantage point is enshrined, and the risk of falling prey to a necropolitics all too common in the literature looms large. In effect, the work becomes an instance of "trans studies."

As Treva Ellison, Kai M. Green, Matt Richardson, and C. Riley Snorton ask, "Will the canonization of transgender studies proceed via the abstraction of race as a modern global signifier? Or, more accurately: in what ways does transgender studies always already depend on an abstraction of the racialization of space as foundational to the production of gender and sexuality?"[24] And as Mauro Cabral writes, "The very label of 'trans studies' seems to be intrinsically associated not only with the academy but also with an academy that reads, writes, and speaks in English—and that colonizes the rest of the world in pursuit of 'cases.'"[25]

These concerns don't merely attend to the inclusion or exclusion of race in trans studies. They point, rather, to the foundational presuppositions that allow *trans* to be pulled into prominence in the first place. They point to both the distortions and the material conditions that make such distortions possible. For instance, Snorton points to the use of enslaved Black women in the development of surgical techniques. And he also shows how the resistant redeployment of racist fungibility in escape from slavery often involved practices of passing and cross-dressing.[26] Such developments, he argues, paved the way for what is now called "transgender." In effect, transness in the United States is inextricably bound up with anti-Blackness and resistance to it.

The trajectory of this essay, therefore, is to reveal some of the ways in which what we call "trans" itself is saturated with, built through, the gendered racialization of a historically contingent system. That is, I want to provide some tools by which to subsume (white-inflected) trans politics and theory into a much larger political-theoretical complex.

Since I first began theorizing reality enforcement, in "Evil Deceivers and Make-Believers," I have been intent on showing not only how reality enforcement inhabits more complex structures of oppression but also how it is inherently a form of racism, every bit as much as it is a form of transphobia and sexist violence. My opening move in that essay was to argue that since reality enforcement is of a piece with sexist violence, it is ipso facto an instance of racism. To make this move, I cited the racist mythology that so thoroughly shapes sexual violence in the United States—namely, the myth of the Black rapist and the myth of the oversexualized Black woman.

Francisco J. Galarte insightfully expands on this approach by pointing to the symbolic association of Chicana sexuality with deception:

> The rhetoric of deception and betrayal also has a history
> within the sexualization of Chicanas. Chicana feminists such
> as Norma Alarcón and Cherríe L. Moraga have identified
> the trope of betrayal as central to patriarchal construction of
> Mexicana, Mexican American, and Chicana womanhood and
> sexuality.[27]

However, I also recognize that my effort—while correct—is also fast, inviting a deeper and more sustained analysis. One of my hopes is to provide a more thoroughgoing analysis here. On this head, Andrea J. Pitts shows some ways in which reality enforcement can be of some use in thinking about Indigeneity. Specifically, they've shown how these features of reality enforcement—identity invalidation, the deceiver–make-believer bind, and genital verification—can be useful in understanding some forms of Indigenous oppression and resistance. Pitts points to the ways in which Indigenous communities were subject to renaming through violent practices, subject to accusations of deception (e.g., the slur "Indian giver"), and scrutinized about their sexuality and in this way were forcibly "intimized."[28]

Further, Pitts points out that, like resistant trans subcultures, "a number of Native communities have historical, cultural, and linguistic forms of existence that likewise do not enforce relations between gender presentation and genital status."[29] They continue, "While, as Native scholars like Wilson note above, Two Spirit, queer, and trans Native peoples still experience colonial enactments of reality enforcement in their home communities, for many, such enactments constitute the perpetuation of colonial violence within their communities."[30]

To deepen this conversation, then, I want to situate the phenomenon of reality enforcement within what Lugones calls "the colonial/modern gender system" and reveal how the sex-representational character of the system is thoroughly interwoven with gender, race, and sexuality. I want to do so in a way that illuminates features of the social institution of slavery as well as the practices of land theft. To do this, I engage with Sylvia Wynter's notion of the coloniality of being/power/truth/freedom and the work of Hortense J. Spillers, Charles W. Mills, C. Riley Snorton, Deborah A. Miranda, and others. The key, for me, is to understand, in greater depth, the process of colonization that has led up to the global capitalist system as one that imposed a system of race, gender, and sexuality where these elements were thoroughly integrated. Lugones explains:

> In "Heterosexualism and the Colonial/Modern Gender
> System" I proposed to read the relation between the colonizer
> and the colonized in terms of gender, race, and sexuality. By
> this I did not mean to add a gendered reading and a racial
> reading to the already understood colonial relations. Rather I
> proposed a rereading of modern capitalist colonial modernity
> itself. This is because the colonial imposition of gender cuts
> across questions of ecology, economics, government, relations
> with the spirit world, and knowledge, as well as across every-
> day practices that either habituate us to take care of the world
> or to destroy it. I propose this framework not as an abstraction
> from lived experience, but as a lens that enables us to see what
> is hidden from our understandings of both race and gender
> and the relation of each to normative heterosexuality.[31]

I want to show how this colonial/modern gender system is sex-representational in a way that gives rise to reality enforcement. And I want to reveal how the very constitution of the system as sex-representational is thoroughly racialized. To do so, however, we must move beyond gender to something more basic: namely, intimacy and distance—that is to say, interpersonal space.

Crucially, the concept of interpersonal space is a rival of the philosophical concept of personhood. As I announced at the outset of this essay, interpersonal spatiality theory undermines the very assumptions sustaining the philosophical deployment of the terms *person*, *self,* and *subject.* In this respect, my essay might be described as—at least with regard to philosophy—nothing short of revolutionary.

A Farewell to Personhood

Let me conclude this chapter, then, with a few remarks about personhood, thereby setting the stage for further discussion over the next several chapters. Post-Lockean philosophers commonly recognize a distinction between two notions: the philosophical (roughly Lockean) sense of *person* (as in *self* and *subject*) and a more ordinary one. Consider, for instance, the following *Oxford English Dictionary* definitions of *person* and *people*: "An individual human being; a man, woman, or child. In ordinary usage, the unmarked plural is expressed by the word *people*; *persons* emphasizes the plurality and individuality of the referent" and "Men or women; men, women, and children; folk."[32] I will call this the **ordinary notion of personhood** as opposed to **Lockean personhood,** which identifies personhood with selfhood.

Philosophers regard the ordinary notion as uninteresting from a philosophical point of view. As Harry G. Frankfurt writes:

> There is a sense in which the word "person" is merely the singular form of "people" and in which both terms connote no more than membership in a certain biological species. In those senses of the word which are of greater philosophical interest, however, the criteria for being a person do not serve primarily to distinguish the members of our own species from the members of other species. Rather, they are designed to capture those attributes which are the subject of our most humane concern with ourselves and the source of what we regard as most important and most problematical in our lives.[33]

As we shall discover in chapter 3, however, the ordinary notion can itself be distinguished into two different ones: **people-as-human** and **people-as-folk** (men, women, boys, and girls). The latter is far more interesting than these philosophers might imagine. To explain it, I will propose that men, women, boys, and girls are interpersonal objects constituted within the folk system of interpersonal spatiality—differentiated through moral sex and moral maturity. The system is sex-representational insofar as the physical person is constituted through sex-differentiated proper appearances that represent and provide information about sex-differentiated intimate appearance. It is here that reality enforcement finds place—namely, in the very constitution of the physical person. And the system is racialized, in part, because the meanings that enable sex representation are thoroughly racialized. The consequence of this is that in addition to being sex-differentiated, physical persons are race-differentiated where both differentiations are of a piece. The colonial/modern gender system can then be understood to include the imposition of a specific system of interpersonal spatiality on those who were colonized and enslaved and an abusively differential positioning of them within that system, facilitating theft of land and physical person. It is precisely through this imposition that indigenous land is appropriated at the most fundamental level.

Within this colonial context, I then examine the philosophical concept of personhood. In addition to revealing its underlying assumptions and thereby dislodging the taken-for-granted character of the concepts underwritten by them, I show how the philosophical concept of *person* emerges within the context of the colonial/modern gender system—specifically, the development of the English version of chattel slavery.

This requires examining both the folk and philosophical notions, as well as the relation between them. Through colonialism, the former is transformed to incorporate race as a central feature in the operations of moral sex. Meanwhile, the philosophical concept of personhood is introduced—the term *person* pulled away from its ordinary use—to allow for the possibility that there are individuals who look human but who fail to possess the cognitive depth to achieve the **moral status** the colonizers and enslavers afford themselves. The transformed version of folk personhood provides the basis for the racist claims undergirding denials of moral status, while the philosophical concept of personhood allows for an abstraction from moral sex—an abstraction that obscures the operations of racial oppression in folk personhood altogether, one crucial operation being land appropriation.

Of course, we have much ground to cover before we get there. What needs to be said also needs to be said slowly and methodologically (as the previous few speedy paragraphs probably demonstrate).

Before we do anything else, then, we must turn to the notion of interpersonal spatiality in chapter 2. That will then prepare us to discuss folk personhood as a feature of a specific system of interpersonal spatiality in chapter 3. Then, we will be able to turn to an analysis of trans oppression and of trans phoria in part II. Only then we will be truly ready to turn part III to "unbury the lede" and expose the colonial legacy of personhood.

Chapter 2

On Intimacy and Distance

IN THIS SECOND CHAPTER, I introduce and elucidate the key concepts in interpersonal spatiality theory. The overarching argument in favor of the theory—for the purposes of this essay, at any rate—is its unique ability to achieve the two main goals of the essay: namely, to provide accounts of trans oppression and of trans phoria. The more general argument is simply the theory's philosophical fecundity and explanatory power—that is to say, the transformative power of the new concept of interpersonal spatiality itself.

The theory is expressly grounded empirically, designed to accommodate actual experiences. The point is to elucidate these experiences, show how they connect systematically. To be sure, this is hardly a scientific theory. The data haven't been collected rigorously through formal experimentation. They have, rather, been collected over the course of a life, in the shape of a life. But that, perhaps, is well suited to my professed aims.

As my theory is charting new ground, it's to be expected that what I have presented is incompletely developed, imprecise, and likely mistaken in some details. In moderation, these failures oughtn't invalidate the basic ideas advanced here. Indeed, all of this is to be expected in charting a new direction in which critique and correction constitute contributions to the development of a theory that needn't belong to a single individual.

I do feel clear that this direction heads some place of value. Interpersonal spatiality saturates our encounters and relations with each other. It is a taken-for-granted aspect of our everyday experience of the world. And yet it has not been examined theoretically in any serious detail. I see interpersonal spatiality as a new point of departure for philosophical investigations much in the way that phenomenology and the linguistic turn have, in their times, served as points of departure.

I should note that what follows is not a full elaboration of interpersonal spatiality theory. Rather, the discussion has been tailored to the overall needs of the essay. This means that certain details had to be postponed or removed altogether to provide an overall picture useful for this project.

Further, because in some ways this chapter constitutes an interruption in the overall flow of the essay, I present the reader with the option of reviewing a specific section prior to a specific chapter, rather than reading the whole chapter at once. "Interpersonal Space" should be read before chapter 3. "Interpersonal Objects" should be read before chapter 4. "Interpersonal Awareness" should be read before chapter 5. "Interpersonal Identity" should be read before chapter 6. And "Final Thoughts" should be read before chapter 9. If the reader opts to read the whole thing now, this breakdown may still prove useful in case a return to this chapter is required at subsequent stages.

Interpersonal Space

If you think about it, you'll notice that some encounters between us are intimate and some are not. In fact, all encounters, through sense perception and through discourse, can be characterized in terms of degree of intimacy or lack thereof. I call this "interpersonal spatiality." Interpersonal spatiality is the capacity of all sensory and discursive encounters between us to admit of closeness and distance. Another way to put it is to say that all our encounters occur in interpersonal space.

Now, of course, the appeal to space is often—although not always—merely a metaphor. However, this metaphor is very useful. Think of intimate space like actual space—suppose we are planets or spheres of some sort. We move in space. We can move closer together or farther apart. Now, suppose two spheres are in some sort of engagement—moving closer to each other. There are different ways this can happen. First, sphere A can move closer to B or sphere B can move closer to A. Second, A can pull B closer (using a tractor beam, say) or B can do this to A. I call self-movement closer "self-display" and pulling closer "*attention.*"

Let's now return to a more familiar example. Suppose Jaydin and Alaynna are watching Netflix. Jaydin puts his hand on her thigh. He has gained intimate access to her—he has pulled her in closer through intimate attention. Suppose Alaynna says, "I want you to kiss me." Here, she has shared a feeling discursively—she has engaged in a form of self-display, moving closer to Jaydin.

Imagine that the process by which A and B move closer to each other is accomplished in stages. For example, first A moves closer to B a bit. Then B moves toward A. Then B immediately uses its tractor beam to pull A closer a bit. And so on. I call the movement at each stage a *"gesture of intimacy."* Obviously, there are plenty of combinations possible. However, we can also imagine that the movement closer follows a preset pattern (or set of patterns)—a structured increase in intimacy—a well-organized progression that I shall call a *"pathway."*

Gestures of intimacy can then be understood as communicative when done intentionally because the gesture/movement is an invitation for the other to move down the pathway a bit by moving on to the next stage. When Jaydin puts his hand on Alaynna's thigh, he is communicating that he would like intimacy, and there is the suggestion of moving further. When Alaynna says, "I want you to kiss me," she indicates that she is likewise interested in intimacy. Note, also, that when gestures of intimacy are organized in structures of increasing intimacy, skipping stages will constitute jumping ahead and can lead to a violation. So, should Jaydin begin by placing his hand on Alaynna's crotch rather than her thigh, he would have jumped ahead and, depending on the context, outright violated her. We would say that Jaydin violated a boundary—*her* boundary.

These interpersonal boundaries are inherently tied up with communicative gestures—they're presupposed by the gestures and made possible through them. In other words, these boundaries are immanent in the gestures themselves. Without them, self-display and attention would not be possible. For instance, to display to another something of oneself, that something has to be held back. And this means that the other can't already be accessing it. Indeed, it has to be something that they typically don't access in a way that is normatively regulated. This is secured by a boundary on access that is to be observed (i.e., respected). Similarly, it is precisely through this

boundary that attention is made possible as an intimate gesture—
that is, as a **boundary traversal**. In this way, interpersonal boundaries are very different from boundaries that are supposed to protect artifacts in museums, say. Interpersonal boundaries are permeable in that they are meant to be crossed either through traversing attention or display. Indeed, that is their very point: to make interpersonal space possible. The wrong of violating them is ultimately the wrong of undermining interpersonal spatiality itself. This is a key point to which I'll return at the conclusion of this section.

Before that, however, I want to introduce a second way of undermining interpersonal spatiality—namely, *intimate disregard*. To understand it, we need to have the concept of **vulnerability**. By *vulnerability* I mean something akin to emotional vulnerability—although physical intimacy, even though it does not necessarily involve the expression of profound emotions, can itself be a site of vulnerability in this sense. Basically, you're in a vulnerable state if somebody else has more intimate access to you than you have to them and you're aware of it.

For instance, Sheena makes her move by inviting Germaine on a date. At this point, she is vulnerable to Germaine because she has exposed her intimate interest. Another example: when Silvia spills her plate of food all over herself, she becomes an object of attention—others feel drawn to stare at her, to cross her boundaries, and she is aware of this. She is vulnerable to the others.

What makes vulnerability so important is that it makes intimate dialectic possible. By this I mean that through making oneself vulnerable to another through a gesture of intimacy, one can exert a moral demand of reply. To fail to reply is, all things being equal, to engage in intimate disregard. Consider that there's a sort of formal vulnerability inherent in any gesture of intimacy. To engage in a communicative gesture—including traversal—one reveals an intimate intention, thereby effectively sharing with another. For example, suppose Germaine asks Sheena how she is feeling (and means it). As this is an intimate request, Germaine has made herself vulnerable to Sheena. This vulnerability is what generates a prima facie requirement to reply—if only to acknowledge the gesture.

To be clear, the fact that one shares an intimate intention that another engage in self-sharing scarcely requires that the other engage in that self-display. It requires a mere acknowledgment of the intimated intention—and this can include a declination. I will also acknowledge that it's entirely possible that gestures of intimacy be deployed cynically and for manipulative purposes. It would be entirely appropriate to ignore the gesture when one knows that another is engaging this way. After all, manipulations are abuses of *intrinsic intimacy* and as such are themselves wrong. All things being equal, however, to deliberately fail to acknowledge an intimate gesture is to demonstrate disregard toward the other's vulnerability. And ultimately, what makes it wrong is that it undermines the possibility of an intimate dialectic and, therefore, interpersonal spatiality.

With this in mind, I want to conclude the section by bringing to the fore the crucial moral implications of the notion of interpersonal space. While we could easily say that, by definition, it's wrong to violate a boundary *because* it's a boundary, and we could also say something similarly trivial about intimate disregard, we have something far more important to which we can appeal—namely, the very values of intimacy and distance themselves. In the theory that I'm proposing, intimacy and distance are supreme values, much in the way that one might tout free will or the life well lived as a supreme value. This is to say that, in my view, they are overarching and of fundamental importance. To be clear, I am not claiming that all morality can be reduced to a theory of interpersonal space. For instance, the mitigation of suffering would surely ground important moral considerations.

What I am positing, however, is that intimacy and distance are fundamentally what make us who we are. As we shall soon recognize, interpersonal objects are constituted through boundaries—we could not exist without interpersonal space. More than this, the very way we experience ourselves in relation to the rest of the world is grounded in interpersonal awareness. Indeed, without interpersonal spatiality, we could not experience ourselves in the everyday world at all. This is to say, interpersonal spatiality is a fundamental condition of how we experience ourselves in the everyday world. Without it, our lives would be unrecognizable.

One reason the supremacy of interpersonal space is so important is that there can be different systems of interpersonal spatiality. This means that what's a boundary violation in one system may not be a boundary violation in another. If we just said that the violation of a boundary was wrong, by definition, then we would be unable to judge entire systems as being abusive. The entire account would be relativistic. And this would be useless from a political point of view. Because we can appeal to the guiding values of intimacy and distance, however, we can judge systems of interpersonal space as undermining those values. For instance, if a system were arranged so that a certain group of individuals was invariably subject to forced exposure, in contrast to another group, then we could say that this system was abusive because it undermined the ability of the first group to engage in intrinsic intimacy where intrinsic intimacy, after all, is the point of the system.

In light of this, it is worth emphasizing the respect in which I depart from social constructionist positions. While I recognize that there are different boundary systems in different cultural locations—specific boundary systems are contingent—I also recognize that the demand that there be some such system is transcendentally required in the sense that who we are—how we experience the world—requires some such system. In this way, violation and disregard become wrongs not merely of a particular system but of the very values of intimacy and distance themselves. Further, while a boundary system is contingent, one's very experience of oneself and others in the world is fundamentally structured by that system. Consequently, when confined to only one system, it becomes virtually impossible to recognize that the structure of one's experience of oneself in the world is contingent (albeit binding).

To capture these considerations, I will say that boundaries and gestures are morally constituted. By this I mean to play on the double sense of *moral*. On the one hand, it is synonymous with *ethical*, while, on the other, there's the association with *mores* (customs, manners).[1] As we shall eventually see, this term is also useful in avoiding the contrast between nature and culture that will play an important part of our discussion of the colonial/modern gender system.

Interpersonal Objects

Interpersonal objects are the participants in a system of interpersonal space. They're like the spheres or planets that can move closer together or farther apart. We might have called them "people" if the word wasn't so tainted. The key thing about interpersonal objects is that they are defined as objects of sensory and discursive access—where that access is determined by boundaries.

To be clear, I do not claim their *esse* is *percipi*. For instance, being alone is an interpersonal configuration defined against other interpersonal configurations. I do, however, claim that these objects are determined by their perceivability within a system. They are objects determined by boundaries on sensory and discursive access. They contrast with other beings—nonpersonal ones—that, while also perceivable, are not subject to these boundaries. This means that some interpersonal objects need not even be sentient (although the overall constitution and management of a system of interpersonal spatiality admittedly requires that there be some significant portion of interpersonal beings that possess a cognitive capacity to sustain the system). By contrast, I regard subjection to interpersonal boundaries as a precondition for recognizable cognition within the system. I say this since I take being constituted as an agent object as a precondition and subjection to interpersonal boundaries is necessary for constitution as an agent object.

SUBSUMPTION

The perception of interpersonal objects comes in the form of a **boundary observation** (or **boundary crossing**) from the start. One doesn't begin with some neutral sensory perception of nonpersonal objects such as tables and chairs, say, and interpersonal objects such as men and women, say, and then determine whether what one perceives is to be regulated by boundaries. Instead, one simply perceives the latter through observation or crossing and the former not.

Rather than a formal application of criteria, there's an "if-can" test stipulating that if one can be so perceived, then perceive them that way.[2] By this I mean that, instead of criteria, there are cues smoothly tracking perception into default positions. I call this process *"subsumption."*[3] This process applies to nonpersonal objects as well as interpersonal ones. That one perceives nonpersonal objects in ways that don't involve observing or crossing doesn't mean that they aren't conditioned by boundaries. They are conditioned at least as boundaryless, in contrast to bounded, so that both interpersonal and nonpersonal objects can be integrated into a single experience.

In this way, both interpersonal and nonpersonal objects possess a morally determined sensory appearance, since there are specific cues enabling this boundary-conditioned perception.

STRIPS

One of the characteristic features of interpersonal objects is that access to them is ordered by boundaries. First, boundaries are typically ordered in terms of moral force. By this I mean that some boundaries are more morally weighty than others. To violate them is to engage in a worse wrong than the others; to traverse them is to achieve a greater closeness. For instance, the boundary on genitals is weightier than the boundary on buttocks, so a violation of the former is worse than the latter, and a traversal of the former is more intimate than a traversal of the latter.

Second, this moral ordering is usually a temporal ordering. By this I mean that the dialogically accepted traversing of one boundary can be a precondition for the dialogically accepted traversing of a morally weightier one. In other words, there are constraints on jumping ahead. (This isn't to say one can't jump ahead, of course. It is to say that this is precisely why it would count as jumping ahead.) When boundaries on access to a single interpersonal object are ordered in this way, I call them a "*strip.*"

As a first, provisional move, strips can be regarded as short pathways. However, they are pathways in which increased access is one-way. In typical pathways, there is a dialogical play of intimate gestures and through this a sort of mutual **intimization.** For instance, suppose that Sheena touches Germaine intimately. Germaine, in turn, touches Sheena intimately. Both Sheena and Germaine are intimized, and one supposes that throughout the course of the pathway, intimization will go back and forth. In the case of a strip, by contrast, there is only increasing access to a single object by another. Suppose, for instance, that Germaine performs a striptease for Sheena. Sheena's access to Germaine increases throuhout Germaine's intimate self-display, while Germaine's access to Sheena does not. I call this increase in visual access a "strip."

Let's suppose now, however, that Sheena slowly strips Germaine where the stripping follows the same pattern as above. In this case, Sheena gains increasing access to Germaine not through Germaine's self-display but through her own engagement in boundary traversal. This sort of engagement is a different pathway because there are different intimate gestures involved—namely, increasing self-display in the one case and increasing attention in the other. To put it in other terms: the erotic significance can be quite different in the two cases.

By contrast, the strip is the same in both cases. In both cases, the increase in access is determined by a pattern—and it is the same pattern, the same moral and temporal arrangement of boundaries. To differentiate *pathway* and *strip,* we can say that the former is something like a script—a preset arrangement of intimate gestures, something analogous to a dance—while the latter is simply a pattern of boundaries arranged by increasing moral force and temporal ordering—a pattern that can be found in different pathways.

This pattern ought to be viewed as an abstraction from the pathways. Boundaries, after all, are immanent in intimate gestures. Similarly, strips are immanent in pathways. Despite it involving an abstraction, the notion of a strip is of particular importance in understanding interpersonal objects as such. As interpersonal objects have cues for subsumption, they also have boundaries on access, and these boundaries are arranged in a pattern.

AGENCY AND SELF-DISPLAY

When I was talking about vulnerability in the earlier section, I noted that every gesture of intimacy involves a kind of self-display in the sense that one reveals an intimate intention. This sort of self-display must be distinguished from the primary sort. The primary sort is more obvious. One shares a deep feeling. One shows oneself off to another. One tells an intimate story about oneself. One displays a little flesh.

What's unique about primary self-display is that the gesture making one vulnerable in revealing an intention for intimacy uses self-intimization to effect that revelation. For instance, in sharing one's feelings of sadness with another, one makes oneself vulnerable, thereby also communicating an interest in a degree of intimacy with the other.

In this respect, I call the interpersonal object an "agent object." The object displays themselves as an agent insofar as the gesture is an intentional act undertaken by the agent, it reveals this intimate intention, and the gesture draws on the object's own boundaries to make the gesture.

Self-display is fundamental in that it is linked to the nature of the interpersonal object as a boundaried being in a way that other intimate gestures are not. For instance, the very wrongness of violating an object's boundary derives from the fact that undermining it undermines an object's capacity to engage in self-display, and therefore the capacity to reveal itself as an agent, and therefore to engage in any gesture of intrinsic intimacy.

PRESENCE AND COMPORTMENT

Interpersonal objects can be present to each other. When one object observes or crosses another's sensory boundaries, the other is present. So, of course, objects can also be absent from each other. And it's entirely possible for an interpersonal object to be all alone. This state of being alone (e.g., in one's apartment, car, etc.) ought not be set apart from states of interpersonal interaction. It is an interpersonal configuration understood within the framework of interpersonal space.

Presence can be distinguished into two kinds. First, one can have a *passive presence*—for instance, as one is in a waiting room among others, reading a book. Here, one's boundaries on sensory access are observed and that's it. Second, one can have a *dialogical presence* with another. This involves having one's actions called by another and, likewise, the capacity to call another through the play of vulnerability.

Crucially, passive and dialogical sensory presence aren't cut off from each other. Instead, *comportment* is a special form of self-display through which the agent object can move from passive presence into dialogical presence, the latter of which is required for any other form of intimate gesture, including self-display, to have place. Because of this, I regard comportment as a fundamental kind of self-display. Without it, it would be impossible to display oneself as an agent object to others because movement from passive to dialogical presence would also be impossible.

Suppose, for instance, we observe each other's boundaries as we sit together, not interacting, on a bus. We don't look at each other, except sometimes covertly. We try not to stare, as this is to cross a boundary. Likely, we play with our phones. It is, nonetheless, an access determined by boundaries. We are passively present to each other.

For one to engage with another is just to traverse a boundary, as one looks at the other—perhaps, even, in the eyes. What makes this a friendly dialogical engagement, rather than a rude intrusion, is, in part, a self-display. One maneuvers oneself into the sensory field of another by speaking, waving, smiling. In attempting to move from one configuration to a more intimate one (boundaries have been crossed), one signals to the subject that it's okay to look, it's okay to traverse some of the boundaries on sensory access to oneself. In this way, comportment is closely bound up with passive presence, therefore bound up with the initial conditions by which one is subsumed, and therefore bound up with one's sensory appearance. Without a morally bounded sensory appearance in the first place, one could not engage in the comportment. And without comportment, one could not have a dialogical presence and therefore could not be recognized as an agent object.[4]

AVOWALS

While comportment is necessary for agential self-display, it is not sufficient. To be recognized as a social agent, one must have social reasons for acting that can be shared with other social agents. As these reasons require a broad psychological repertoire, a social mechanism by which thoughts and feelings are shared is necessary. Because of this, I consider the capacity for avowal as equally fundamental as the capacity for comportment.

Like other instances of self-display, the sharing avowal has the effect of reflexively constituting a boundary on access to thoughts or feelings shared. It likewise presupposes an observation of boundaries on this access prior to the sharing. This is exemplified by deferential questions such as "How are you feeling?" To such a question, the first person always retains the right to refuse ("I don't want to talk about it now"). One must respect their right to privacy—a privacy that would be violated were it possible to read their mind. Such privacy can also be violated when one shares information with others that had been shared with one in confidence. Finally, as an act of self-display to another is a gesture of vulnerability, a particular response is demanded that witnesses and thereby completes the intimacy.

This, I believe, may shed some light on what philosopher's call "first-person authority."[5] While, in one view, first-person authority over one's mental states concerns an epistemic privilege that at least comes close to incorrigibility, I am more inclined to believe that part of the seeming authority derives from the illocutionary force of such avowals. Because they are constituted as a kind of sharing—not of fact but of feeling—to respond to a person who says, "I'm really sad," by saying, "No you aren't," is to be confused about what the first person is doing.

I am also inclined to suppose a sort of ethical authority that derives, in part, from the boundaries on privacy governing mental states discussed above. More deeply, this ethical authority is grounded in the fact that to undermine the capacity of an interpersonal object to avow is to undermine their very capacity to be recognized as a social agent within the field of interpersonal spatiality.

Let me conclude this section by pointing out that comportment and avowal mutually require each other. For one's comportment to constitute agential self-display, the interpersonal object must be capable of avowing feelings and thoughts. However, to avow feelings and thoughts, one must be capable of moving from passive to dialogical presence to another. That is, one must be able to comport oneself. This isn't a vicious circle. Rather, the capacity for comportment and the capacity for avowal are integrally linked together as the fundamental condition for agential self-display. That is, they come in together as the essential correlates of the agent object.

Interpersonal Awareness

While this might seem perverse, I call any awareness "interpersonal" —even the sort of awareness one has when one is alone. After all, one is aware that one is alone. What's important to me is that we prioritize interpersonal awareness in the obvious sense—one is aware of oneself with another, either passively or dialogically. In this obvious sense, one is aware of both another and oneself, and so such interpersonal awareness includes both self-awareness and awareness of another. In addition to this, we can throw in all the nonpersonal objects. In this view, they're secondary. This is why I speak of "interpersonal awareness" even when one is alone staring at a chair.

To better understand what I have in mind, recall that interpersonal spatiality theory holds that sensory perception is already bifurcated into perception of interpersonal and of nonpersonal objects, the first being subject to boundaries and the latter not. An important corollary of this is that sensory perception of interpersonal objects is likewise already bifurcated into the perception of oneself and of other objects.

Whatever sensory awareness one has of oneself, it cannot be an access governed by boundaries (one can't violate one's own boundaries). Yet neither can this awareness amount to no more than the nonpersonal access one has to things such as tables. After all, if one couldn't tell the difference between oneself and some nonpersonal being, one couldn't tell the difference between any interpersonal object and some nonpersonal one. Consequently, one must have a sensory awareness of oneself as an interpersonal object that is not subject to boundaries. That is, one must have a distinctive awareness of oneself.

Sensory self-awareness, I maintain, is part of the same process by which other interpersonal objects and nonpersonal objects are subsumed. One might say that any awareness of another as an interpersonal object requires that one have—or at least be capable of having—a distinctive sensory awareness of oneself as an interpersonal object. Surely to perceive another as determined by boundaries restricting one's own access, one would have to have awareness of oneself as a potential traverser of that restriction. For instance, to be aware of another as determined by a restriction on being stared at, one would have to be capable of an awareness of oneself as staring. And for that to be so, one would have to be aware that one had an appearance and what staring would look like.

Certainly, one can be sensorily aware of oneself. For instance, one can look down at oneself, see one's legs and hands and belly, or squint to see one's own nose. One can look in a mirror. And this sensory awareness of oneself is distinctive. Further, through the coordination of vision and proprioception, one can acquire an awareness of one's appearance even when one cannot see oneself. Consider learning to dance before a mirror. With practice, one learns to move one's body so that it looks a particular way through that movement. One is thereby aware of one's visual appearance to others. What this requires, however, is that one's proprioceptive awareness of one's body already have basic coordination before this fine-tuning. Otherwise, it's not clear why one should take the use of a mirror to help.

VULNERABILITY AND INTERPERSONAL SENTIMENTS

The basic form of self-awareness is an awareness of oneself as an object (or potential object) for others. Since participants in a system are essentially interpersonal objects, object self-awareness will be the most crucial, revealing form. To be clear, awareness of oneself as an object is awareness of oneself not as any sort of object, such as a table, but rather as an object governed by boundaries on access—an interpersonal object. More than this, one is aware of oneself as an active object. That is, one's awareness of oneself as a bounded object is always with regard to one's capacity for self-display or lack thereof.

Properly speaking, awareness of one's presence to another involves the experience of vulnerability or one of its variants. The experience of vulnerability introduces an affective dimension into interpersonal awareness. When somebody is staring, for instance, one can suddenly become acutely aware of oneself—aware of one's appearance and one's presence before another. One becomes awkwardly self-conscious, in the nontechnical sense. This is a sort of vulnerability that one experiences—in this case, unwanted. Specifically, one becomes aware of oneself as exposed to another.

The feeling of vulnerability is more basic than embarrassment or shame. The latter are unpleasant feelings, while vulnerability can be either pleasant or unpleasant—embarrassment and shame are, rather, modalities of vulnerability. I speak of different ways of experiencing vulnerability—different modes. While I think that there are actually a great number of variations to be investigated, let's note a few dimensions that can be used to differentiate these modes.

First, vulnerability admits of degrees of intensity relative to the degree of exposure. This is just to say that where the boundary is located in a strip is typically registered in degrees of vulnerability. The further down the strip, the greater the exposure, and the greater the experience of vulnerability.

Second, vulnerability admits of a kind of negation-reversal. By stopping this exposure from happening—by psychologically pulling inward—one can reverse this vulnerability into a sense of *self-containment*. For example, upon noticing that somebody is staring at one's breasts, one might experience vulnerability, and upon turning away, experience the negation of vulnerability. This contrastive experience can also occur in case one is aware of another as vulnerable. One sees another as vulnerable—perhaps they are the object of some ridicule—and one, in contrast to this, feels self-contained.

Third, vulnerability can be agential or nonagential. That is, it can be experienced in conjunction with the sense of a capacity for self-display as exercised or withheld, or it can be experienced with the sense of a lack of capacity for self-display. For instance, in case one is exposed to others and can do nothing about it, there is no sense of agential capacity that would require the ability to pull within and to experience self-containment (*intimate hemorrhaging*).

Similarly, one might feel so entirely closed off that one is not capable of sharing with another—that is, as if one were sealed within one's own domain (*intimate deadening*). The specific experience of agential self-containment I call "self-collection," and it is required for agential vulnerability to be possible (just as agential vulnerability is necessary for it). While the experience of self-collection might be characterized as a sense of dignity, I am worried that the term is freighted with unwanted history and significance and, besides, is not even expansive enough. Another word that comes to mind is *poise*.

Fourth, vulnerability admits of temporal variations. It can either be anticipatory (future-oriented) or in-the-moment (present-oriented). In thinking about impending attention from another, for instance, one may already experience a kind of vulnerability, and then a greater degree of vulnerability once the act has been executed. This is made possible by the emergence of the *intimate meaning* into awareness without the actual *intimate movement* upon which the meaning is conferred having occurred yet. Further, one may experience both future-oriented and present-oriented modes of vulnerability at once due to the ordered character of boundaries and gestures.

Fifth, in dialogical presence, vulnerability is experienced as gestural. To experience oneself or another as vulnerable is one thing. To experience another as making themself vulnerable to me or me making myself vulnerable to them is quite another. Intrinsic intimacy involves the communicative interplay of attention and self-display and therewith the experience of demand or call—both calling and being called. This is because gestures of intimacy minimally yield a formal vulnerability, thereby requiring a reply on pain of disregard. Note, also, that as passive presence is continuous with dialogical presence, passive interpersonal awareness can include an awareness of the absence of this demand, as well as the anticipation of dialogical experience.

One key feature of this interpersonal awareness is an awareness of one's capacity for avowal. Upon experiencing a feeling or thought, one will experience it as capable of being avowed and as subject to boundaries. That is, one will experience these thoughts as shareable. Crucially, the alignment between one's experiences and the discursive repertoire of avowable states is not something that need always be assumed. For instance, upon experiencing an intense state, I might avow that I feel bereft. Whether this is the exact right characterization is unclear. It may not be, for instance, that the feeling wears "bereft" like a badge. On the contrary, the avowal would seem to function as something like an interpretation—and, in light of my remarks earlier about first-person authority, an authoritative interpretation whereby the feeling is retroactively constituted "bereft."

Finally, it also ought to be acknowledged that while the affective modalities discussed here concern presence to others, it is also possible to experience some of them—or something analogous to them—when one is alone. For instance, one might experience shame upon viewing oneself in the mirror as the consequence of constant disregard in the company of others. Or, precisely because one is alone, one might experience oneself as self-contained as a sort of limit case of the negation-reversal discussed above. Certainly, one might experience thoughts and feelings as potentially avowable to others. While these instances can't properly be described as awareness of one's presence to another, they are deeply connected to that awareness.

DISPOSITIONS

Let me conclude this section by noting that boundary-regulated interpersonal perception is a habituated one. This is most obvious in the case of implicit boundary observation in which there's no express holding back. Rather, one simply doesn't look at someone a particular way or in a particular place. This means that whether one is observing a boundary, say, depends not upon where one looks but upon why one looks only here and not there. And that requires training. This can also be said of gestures and intimate meanings. One becomes vulnerable in a particular interpersonal configuration, for instance, precisely because one has developed the habit of responding in that way. In much the manner one understands a native language, one understands a native system of interpersonal spatiality, understands how to negotiate it.

We must also allow for idiosyncratic dispositions—dispositions that, while largely facilitating negotiation of interpersonal spatiality, also yield or fail to yield *interpersonal sentiments* in system-appropriate contexts. One imagines that as one learns the system—as it is in-culcated—it is never mastered perfectly. Moreover, certain sorts of subsequent experiences may yield certain sorts of habits to experi-ence things a particular way—for example, by being habitually self-conscious.

Interpersonal Identity

PRELIMINARIES

Whenever we access an interpersonal object sensorily, we access them as having a past and a future and a capacity for existence independent of this one encounter. This presupposition needn't require that we know them or have access to extensive details of their life. It requires, only, that we impute an *interpersonal identity*—however thin it may be—for instance, "the woman sitting at the bus stop, talking on her phone."

Interpersonal identity can be understood as something like a bio-graphical account that determines a character. It determines a *"who"* by providing an answer to the question "Who is so-and-so?" This "who" is the protagonist or star, if you will, of the biography. One can view such an account as composed of various situations, events, and actions the "who" was involved in over time, the others with whom the "who" has interacted, and, often, the "who's" thoughts and feelings.

In case the "who" is living, the biography constantly unfolds through uptake. That is, whenever the "who" does something or some-thing happens to the "who," this event is then taken up into the bi-ography so that the object is now understood through the expanded biography. For instance, the woman at the bus stop now screams and then drops the phone on the ground. This expands the biography while allowing the "who" to both change over time while remaining one and the same "who."

Interpersonal identity isn't merely biographical, however. It is susceptible to what I shall call *"existential depth."* It affords the question "Yes, but who is she *really?"* Here we're invited to a portrait of some individual up close and personal. This capacity for existential depth is important for the purposes of intrinsic intimacy, of course. For it is presumably through intrinsic intimacy that one is enabled to know better who somebody is, really, and through displaying who one is, really, that one can foster intrinsic intimacy.

As the identity is interpersonal, I don't mean strictly or solely a self-identity (or self-conception)—that is, an account that one tells oneself or by which one conceives or experiences oneself. The identity I have in mind can be accessed both by oneself and by others. It can be shared with others. And it is thereby subject to boundaries on informational access. That is, an interpersonal identity, like a sensory appearance, admits of degrees of access. Some aspects of the biography are private and some can be shared, and when they are shared by the "who" themself, they can count as a gesture of intimacy. Indeed, this is what distinguishes an interpersonal identity from a nonpersonal one.

In characterizing interpersonal identity, neither do I mean an express discursive narrativization. To be sure, the latter can articulate the former. Indeed, the possibility of such express discursive narrativization is a condition of the existence of the biographical account, and it is one of the important practices of interpersonal spatiality. However, it is preferable to view the interpersonal identity as an intelligibility-conferring interpretive framework.

This allows us to make sense of the way in which one can gain access to information about an interpersonal object while in their presence even though discourse is not used to share that information. It can be gained through sensory access alone, for instance. In the presence of an interpersonal object, we may notice what they look like or what they are doing without it having to be said.

We can therefore also distinguish two ways in which an object might share who they are with us—namely, through telling or showing. The former involves narrating various intimate facts about oneself—recounting incidents within one's life. The latter involves doing something of an intimate character, making an intimate gesture toward another that is then taken up into one's interpersonal identity. In a sense, then, the former is also an instance of the latter, since sharing intimate details about one's life is an intimate gesture. However, the latter also includes instances of sharing that are non-discursive in character—one might show who one is during sexual intimacy in a particularly profound moment, for instance. While there are degrees of intimate display, what I shall call *"self-revelation"* is marked as the deepest or end limit of intimate displays. One shows who one is, really. This can occur when one bares one's soul in words or it can occur when one shows who one is through action—particularly of an intimate character.

THE "WHO"

The **imputation** of an interpersonal identity is a constitutive feature of the specific practices of interpersonal spatiality. In observing, traversing, or transgressing the boundaries of an interpersonal object, we necessarily impute the identity. That is, the identity is imputed through the practices of sensory access. We must therefore be careful not to take the "who" as somehow prior to these practices, as somehow independent from them. The "who" is nothing more than a feature of the practices or, if you will, an effect of them.

For instance, to attribute the sensory appearance to the "who" obscures the nature of the relationship between them. Where the appearance is provided for by the cues that enable observations and traversal, the "who" is nothing but the content of the interpersonal identity, the necessary temporal dimension imputed in cases of such perception. To put it crudely, both appearance and identity are features of the structure of boundary-mediated perception, and it would be a mistake to take the former as a characteristic of the content of the latter.

Similarly, while the act of self-display will be attributed to the character of the imputed identity, as though the "who" themself did the deed, that a "who" is put in play at all is because self-display, as a gesture of intimacy, requires as much. One might say that the character is the effect of the act, rather than the other way around, were it not for the fact that self-display also requires a prior boundary observation and, therefore, a prior imputation. I call the process by which self-display allows the interpersonal object to inhabit the character and to that extent become the "who" the process of *"animation."* And in light of the fundamentality of comportment/avowal, we can say that it is, in the first instance, the movement from passive to dialogical presence that enables animation. And, of course, this animation is a constitutive part of the process by which we become recognizable as social agents.

Now, while there might be a respect in which various social activities can be truthfully attributed to a "who" (they're included in the bio), there is also a respect in which this attribution is misleading. It is more correct to attribute the activity to the agent object where the "who" is merely the content of an interpersonal identity possessed by this agent object. It is, rather, merely a constituent in the overall structure of the agent object that enables the attribution of social activity to it.

This means we should distinguish between the interpersonal object as viewed from the inside and from the outside. Consider, by way of analogy, the social practice of prayer or holy monuments such as temples. From the inside, prayer is a form of divine communication and temples are inhabited by gods. From the outside, prayer and monuments such as temples can be considered social practices located within a broader network thereof where various false beliefs about these practices are part of that network—beliefs about Zeus, say, or Athena. In examining the practices, we do not need to commit to the existence of Zeus to recognize that prayers to Zeus might well exist and that, further, false beliefs in this deity are essential to the practice itself. Similarly, the beliefs that determine the "who" are typically false and yet part of the constitution of interpersonal objects within a given system. That is, strictly speaking, the "who" does not exist even though the agent object does. Interpersonal objects, after all, aren't typically considered interpersonal objects within a given system. Rather, interpersonal objects are viewed in ways provided for by the specific system.

SELF-IDENTITY

If sensory awareness of one's appearance is necessary for—part of the process of—the subsumption of nonpersonal and other interpersonal objects, then it should be unsurprising that the same is so with respect to the imputation of identity. To impute an interpersonal identity to another requires that the postulated "who" be positioned with regard to oneself. And that requires that one have a conception of oneself as well. For instance, imputing the interpersonal identity "the woman over there, looking at her phone" requires an awareness of oneself as likewise on the bus, and so forth.

To a large extent, by *self-conception,* I mean what many other philosophers might mean—it's a sense of who and what one is. As such, this conception includes an overall understanding of the world in general, to position oneself within it. Further, a self-conception is temporal—one remembers one's past and anticipates one's future. Finally, rather than being passively received, a self-conception can be the partial product of challenging the picture of the world one has been presented with.

The distinguishing feature of my views about self-conception, however, concerns interpersonal spatiality. In this account, the distinction between oneself and others again concerns boundaries. Just as I am aware of my sensory appearance as subject to boundaries on access by others, but not access by me, I am aware of details about my interpersonal identity as subject to boundaries on access. I am aware that sharing certain details with another will constitute a gesture of self-display. I am also aware that the details of another's interpersonal identity are likewise subject to boundaries. I know that to ask certain details about an individual's life is to make an intimate gesture, and so forth.

This means that interpersonal identity must be prioritized over one's own self-conception of it. By this I mean, for instance, that the temporality of a self-conception is not used to determine personal identity over time in neo-Lockean examples. Nor do I think that a self-conception provides an answer to the question of who somebody is, really—as is common in narrative conceptions of self.[6] Rather, I view a self-conception as answering the question of who somebody *thinks* they are. It's important, I maintain, to capture the dissonance between an egotist's conception of who they are and who they *actually* are—as plainly evident to those with whom they interact. To be sure, the self-conception is part of who they are (a self-deceived egotist). But that is not the same thing. This therefore also means that identity places constraints on self-conception. If one is too far from the mark—for instance, one believes oneself to be an attack helicopter or Napoleon—one's self-conception is discredited. One cannot simply conceive of oneself however one pleases and have that make sense.

Final Thoughts

Rather than call the central participants in a system of interpersonal spatiality "people" (in either the ordinary or the philosophical sense), I call them "interpersonal objects." This technical expression is deployed to describe the general features of interpersonal spatiality in any system, while terms like *person* and the like are deployed specifically within what I call the "folk system of interpersonal spatiality"—a particular system of boundaries—which I shall analyze and critique in chapters 4 and 7. This shift in terminology is useful given the overall project. It will allow us to examine the various meanings and deployments of the more traditional terms without having to take the words for granted. An account that took the notions for granted would, of course, make it difficult to notice the underlying assumptions that we want to question.

That said, there are a few exceptions to this approach. First, consider my strategy of using the corelative terms *object* and *subject*. Happily, even here, however, there is a departure, as will become evident in chapters 5 and 9. I'll say now that I only use *object* and *subject* to designate the structural positions provided for by the perceptual relation. I don't mean—as is sometimes meant—"the subject" as accessed from the inside in first-person experience such that "the subject" could never be perceived by another. Rather, I do mean that the perception of interpersonal objects (and thereby nonpersonal objects too) must be conditioned by a boundary in a broad sense. Crucially, this overlap in terminology will allow me to put pressure on the assumptions that I ultimately want to critique. To put it crudely, I elevate objects over subjects, instead of the other way around. This means that while our philosophical tradition may incline us to posit interpersonal objects primarily as beings that are in some way cognitively sophisticated—minimally, beings that can perceive in this system—I posit them primarily as beings that *are perceived* in a system.

The other exception concerns the word *personal*—an exception that is a bit more troubling. Because of its close relation to the word *person*, it might seem that I am relying on the notion of personhood in my overall account of interpersonal spatiality, rather than analyzing it as a feature of the folk system and as a concept within that system. Here I had the choice between *intersubjective* and *interpersonal*, and the former seemed worse because it promotes a radical confusion about how we relate to each other (as I'll explain in chapter 9). Meanwhile, *personal* signifies the intimate and/or subjection to boundaries. So, it seemed apt.

Regardless of its aptness, in using it in this way, the risk of drawing too much on the folk system remains. (Actually, the risk remains even if I don't use *personal* in this way.) The worry, of course, is that my account of interpersonal spatiality might be infected with specifics of a particular system. And no doubt it is to some degree. I hope it is not too much, however, and I do think the fact that my theorizing comes not from the folk system per se but, rather, from a multiworldly access to the folk system, as well as subcultural systems of intimacy developed in trans communities, helps mitigate this worry somewhat.

At any rate, on this head, there is an odd thing worth noting. There are many uses of *person*, most of which predate the Lockean one. One of the curious features of my theory of interpersonal space in general, and the folk system in particular, is that it seems to illuminate many of these senses. Consider, for example, the French *personne* as "presence, appearance" (ca. 1135).[7] One of the earliest senses of *person* in English is "a role or character assumed in real life, or in a play, etc.; a part, function, or office; a persona; a semblance or guise" (ca. 1230).[8] And consider the following:

An individual considered with regard to his or her outward appearance; a figure of a man, woman, etc.[9]

A man or woman considered as a physical presence at some place or event. Now only in *in person. . . . One's proper person*: oneself, in person (*obsolete*).[10]

The living body or physical appearance of a human being; *spec. (a)* the body regarded as distinct from the mind or soul, or from its clothing, etc.; *(b)* the body regarded together with its clothes and adornments. Usually with *of* or possessive.[11]

Law. The human genitals; *spec.* the penis. Originally in legislature relating to the crime of indecent exposure. It has been contended that the term as used in the Vagrancy Act of 1824 refers to any part of the body normally clothed, but specific reference to the male genitals is usually understood.[12]

The aptness of my interpersonal spatiality account in illuminating these different senses suggests I may well be unearthing something that underlies our various ordinary uses of *person,* something that is reflected in the way basic social practices are culturally organized in the folk system. As I shall contend in chapter 8, the emergence of the philosophical concept of *person* during the Enlightenment successfully obfuscated the notion of *people* as folk. And with it, any of these senses were deserted while the Enlightenment notion of *person* moved philosophers away from outward appearance toward inward subjecthood. In this respect, my theory might be regarded as, in part, a philosophical illumination of these various lost meanings of *person* and their relation to what I call "folk people."

Chapter 3
The Multiplicity of Meaning

I'VE PROVIDED A GENERAL SENSE of where we're headed as well as
the theory guiding our journey. In this chapter, I'll bring out a concept
shaping everything that follows—namely, ontological pluralism—and
I'll propose that it be understood in terms of interpersonal spatiality.
In the first part, I introduce María Lugones's version of ontological
pluralism and argue that the validity of trans identities is grounded in
resistant worlds and undermined in hegemonic ones. In the second
part, I elaborate the relation between ontological pluralism and interpersonal spatiality, and I begin a discussion of the folk system.

In Favor of Ontological Pluralism

THE MULTIPLICITY OF WORLDS

In describing ontological pluralism, Lugones posits multiple "worlds."
She writes:

> Worlds are all lived and they organize the social as heteroge-
> neous, multiple. I think of the social as intersubjectively con-
> structed in a variety of tense ways, forces at odds, impinging
> differently in the construction of any world. Any world is tense,
> not just in tense inner turmoil but also in tense acknowledged
> or unacknowledged contestation with other worlds.[1]

What holds a world together, for her, is a sufficiently self-coherent
"logic" that can be distinguished from other worlds through its inconsistency with them. She also says worlds overlap; they're intertwined semantically and materially. I take this as including the claim
that the very meanings of words are under contestation between
worlds and that the underlying social practices and other material
features that provide the background for the contested meanings of

those terms are likewise contested. And, for her, worlds often stand to each other in relations of power: the contestation over semantics/practice can involve the push of oppression (from one world) and the pushback of resistance (from another). To capture this, I will often use the relative expressions *overworld* and *underworld,* ever remembering they are provisional simplifications.

Crucially, Lugones distinguishes worlds through personhood: one is in a different world just in case one is a different person there. And she says one travels to another world just in case one becomes a different person.[2] This raises deep questions about what, exactly, Lugones means, and as should be obvious, these questions are particularly pressing considering my own project.[3] Because these questions also connect closely to Lugones's later views about the coloniality of gender, I will not be in a position to take them up fully until the end of the essay.

I will, however, propose that we understand Lugonian personhood here in terms of interpersonal objects. To be a different Lugonian person in a different world is to be a different interpersonal object in a different system of interpersonal spatiality. To be clear, this is not a direct translation of what Lugones is discussing into my own theory. Rather, I think there is a lacuna in Lugones's account that my own addresses. I will return to this at the end of this chapter. At present, however, let's keep matters relatively simple.

Lugones doesn't mean to belabor the truism that one expresses different parts of oneself in different contexts. Of course, one may act one way with a friend, another way with one's parents, and another way with one's lover. We all have different sides. But this doesn't mean each one of us is many persons in the way Lugones has in mind. For Lugones, world-travel involves a shift in contradictory character-central properties. She isn't simply saying that there are different social contexts in which one shows different sides of oneself. She is saying that there are some worlds in which one possesses a displayable side and others in which one completely lacks that side altogether.

We can begin with properties that concern what one is. She says she finds herself constructed as "stereotypically Latina" in Anglo worlds, while in Latin worlds she finds herself constructed as (nonstereotypically) "Latina."[4] It seems impossible for one person to be both stereotypically Latina and not stereotypically Latina, both actually Latina and not actually Latina. What's under contestation is what it means to be Latina.

Due to this conflict over what one is, we also get different renditions of who one is. And this, I take it, is core to her claim that we are multiple people. For example, Lugones says in some worlds she isn't playful at all, while in other worlds she is.[5] She doesn't mean that in some social contexts she expresses her serious side while in others she expresses her playful side. She's claiming that in some worlds she's a mostly serious person who wouldn't know fun if it fell on her—a person who doesn't even have a playful side. She's claiming that in other worlds she's a well-balanced, fun-loving person—a person who does possess a playful side that she can show with ease whenever appropriate.

We all know serious people—people defined by their seriousness, people who rarely crack a smile. Here, seriousness and nonseriousness are character-defining features. Obviously, it's impossible to be both an entirely fun-hating, serious person who doesn't even have a playful side and an entirely fun-loving, well-balanced person who does. That's a contradiction. Lugones's solution is to say that the different predicates are true of the being in different worlds. And given that these "character-central" predicates mark a difference in who one is, Lugones says that one is a different person in these different worlds.

THE APPEAL TO ONTOLOGICAL PLURALISM

Lugones's main reason for endorsing ontological pluralism—one I find compelling—is just that it best captures the experiences of outsiders to the mainstream.[6] She wants an ontology of the social that squares with everybody's experience of the social, and she sees no other choice than to commit to it.

In line with this, I suggest ontological pluralism best captures the truth of trans and nonbinary misgendering. There's a multiplicity found in the tension between dominant and trans underworlds. For some of us, we're both women and not women, men and not men. For others, we are nonbinary in resistant worlds while men or women in dominant ones. And what's under contestation here is what it means to be a man, a woman, or nonbinary.

Any trans woman who's been in a social situation in which they are viewed by everybody around them as a man knows what it is like to be socially constructed as a man. One must walk through the world wearing that representation, being treated according to that representation, being expected to act according to that representation. What else could it mean to say that one is "socially constructed as a man"? When somebody insists on repeatedly calling a trans woman "sir," they are not merely reminding her of "the facts." There's a force to such assertions—an attempt to *make* her a man. And it's through such social force that she *becomes* a man in dominant worlds.

This is, in some ways, like racist constructions. When one must move through the world encased in stereotypes, it doesn't matter whether the stereotypes are true. Rather, one simply finds oneself inhabiting a social world in which one just is that thing (socially), regardless of one's own thoughts on the matter. That racist claims are empirically false simply doesn't matter. One still finds oneself constructed in a particular way, read in a particular way. That's what it means to be constructed in a racist way.

Ontological pluralism is therefore a bitter pill to swallow. At worst, it suggests trans men *are* women and trans women *are* men in overworlds. At best, it suggests that some trans men are only marginally men and that some trans women are only marginally women there. The bite may be lessened by formulating the thought more precisely: in the dominant world, trans women are *constituted* as men and trans men are *constituted* as women. Yet this doesn't open the door to "anything goes." Learning that chess is socially constructed, for instance, doesn't mean that rules can now get changed so that a bishop can, under certain specified conditions, become a queen.

To provide an account of trans oppression and resistance—one that includes misgendering—we need an account that is realistic. We must have an account that fits with the facts. And this means we mustn't underestimate the force of oppression we face. We mustn't confuse tactical maneuver with truth. As Lugones writes, "It is a desideratum of oppression theory that it portray oppression in its full force, as inescapable, if that is its full force."[7] And I do see trans oppression, in some worlds, as inescapable.

To return to one of the opening themes of this essay, one of my concerns with an apologetic approach to trans philosophy is precisely that in aiming to validate trans identities, one will obscure the actual realities of the situation by undercharacterizing the depth of trans oppression. One may, for instance, confound the resistant discursive practices that one has embraced with the discursive practices of a much larger society. One may then go on to suppose that the oppressive practices must be wrong—a misapplication of the correct way of speaking. But this is simply a mystification of what we're up against. This will become even clearer in the section that follows.

What bestows full centrality, full womanhood or full manhood, upon us instead are the resistant subcultures, the alternate ontologies that we can inhabit. As Lugones writes, "I also consider it a desideratum of oppression theory that the theory be liberatory. . . . If oppression theory is not liberatory, it is useless from the point of view of the oppressed person. It is discouraging, demoralizing."[8] Resistance can still occur; it occurs, however, in resistant worlds of meaning. Or, better, the very multiplicity of worlds is what makes resistance possible at all.

Because of this, Lugones recommends "contradictory desiderata for oppression theory, desiderata that are in both logical and psychological tension."[9] She sees ontological pluralism as the key to resistance. This requires, alas, that we abandon the view that trans and nonbinary folk are who we say we are, period, in favor of one that has us correct in one world while incorrect in another. Moreover, it requires abandoning the view that the validity of trans identities is secured by an ontological priority of the resistant one over the dominant ones.

To be sure, I do allow for an ontological priority of the resistant over the dominant in the following sense: worlds that endorse the view that there is only one world, worlds that treat their own social phenomena as if they were somehow prior to culture, are simply committing to falsehoods. For example, insofar as the dominant world treats men and women as natural entities, it's making a mistake. And I do think that our resistant underworlds don't err to the degree that the overworld does. Indeed, we have insight into its mistakes that are invisible from within that world itself. Yet I don't think that our own worlds are immune to these types of errors. Certainly, the idea that trans people are "naturally" men or women isn't an uncommon thought in these worlds.

Regardless, this type of ontological priority means nothing when it comes to the question of what we are ultimately. Trans invalidation isn't about transphobes "getting it wrong." They do get it wrong in our resistant underworlds. But there's an oppressive overworld in which they "get it right." What we're up against isn't a few bad apples. What we're up against is an entire world of meaning—a system of interpersonal spatiality—that is ultimately annihilating to us. In attempting to formulate the full depth of trans oppression, then, I show that the very fabric of sociality, its social ontology, can be oppressive.

The central priority I assign, instead, is an ethicopolitical one. I do recognize the ontology that invalidates trans people as given by an oppressive world and, more specifically, by an abusive system of interpersonal spatiality. Further, I regard the oppression of trans people as a feature of a more broadly abusive system—one that is likewise sexistly, sexually, and racistly abusive. While a trans woman may not count as a woman in an overworld, the consolation is that there are good reasons for not wanting to be that sort of thing in the overworld anyway. After all, it would involve acquiescing to oppression, perpetuating it, or likely both. Who would want that? As we have seen, while ontology may be multiple and contingent, the various systems of interpersonal spatiality that undergird those ontologies can be assessed according to the values of intimacy and distance that they purport to make possible.

TARRYING WITH THE CONCEPTUAL

To defend my appeal to ontological pluralism as the best strategy for validating trans identities, I want to consider two possible trans-friendly analyses of the meaning of *woman* in mainstream practice. In this section, I show that even if either analysis were true, trans identities would still be marginalized. In the subsequent section, I show that, even worse, both fail to capture the dominant discursive practices accurately by minimizing the importance of sex and, consequently, the dominant practices turn out to be more invalidating than even these analyses would have us believe. In sum, I argue that these trans-friendly analyses are not nearly trans-friendly enough.

Clarifications

Before proceeding, let me preempt a few possible misunderstandings. First, my appeal to ontological pluralism shouldn't be understood as an analysis of the meaning of terms such as *woman*. Pluralism is, rather, partly a claim about the ordinary discursive and extradiscursive practices determining the meaning, and the appeal says there are different discursive and extradiscursive practices that stand in a contestatory relation with each other and that, consequently, there are different meanings at stake. It says, furthermore, that the only way to ground trans identities is precisely through the resistant discursive and extradiscursive practices that already exist. This leaves it entirely open how the meanings of the terms should be analyzed in either world. Thus, an appeal to ontological pluralism is not the same as an appeal to semantic contextualism (explained below) as an analysis of a particular discursive practice in a given world.

Second, I am not proposing an ameliorative approach—an approach I find particularly unrealistic.[10] If this project is to change the way all feminists speak or even to change the way feminist philosophers speak—as it advocates—then one must wonder whether the ameliorationist has actually met any such people. More importantly, given the fact that the meaning of *woman* is contested in multiple and complex ways (as I pointed out in chapter 1), it's not clear what role the philosopher has to play in mitigating these disputes.

By contrast, my descriptions of underworld practices are merely that—descriptions. My reporting the deployment of terms such as *woman* and *man* in certain trans underworlds isn't a philosophical innovation or an instance of conceptual engineering from on high. Neither are the practices themselves. The practices of which I speak are specific, local, idiosyncratic, spontaneous, organic, and quite real. Indeed, their locality, their formally unregistered history, is crucial in understanding my appeal to ontological pluralism.

When I transitioned, I was welcomed into Los Angeles subcultures that had existed for many years and that had long-standing practices that had never even shown up on the radar of mainstream culture. There I learned from trans women of color that it was possible to be a full and complete woman without surgical or even hormonal intervention. This flew in the face of the beyond-the-binary account that would have characterized us as in-between. And it's a plain example of what C. Riley Snorton calls "other ways to be trans."[11]

My goal is not to make everybody conform to these practices. A philosophy genuinely invested in resistance will understand itself as a work of philosophy. It will understand how it is itself positioned socially as an endeavor. It will therefore undertake work that is doable and appropriate to itself. The project of changing the way people—or even just theorists—speak is not an example of such work. The work of this essay is merely to provide some intelligibility—shed some light—for trans people where possible and to make friends with other ground-bound philosophies that reflect different forms of oppression and resistance. While this project may seem meager, I believe that it is a realistic and valuable undertaking.

This isn't to deny that change in the overworld is possible. Although I doubt that the overworld practices can themselves be changed so radically to eliminate all abuse, I do think it is possible for individuals engaged in overworld practices to adopt underworld practices instead. In fact, I think it is already happening. Such changes occur—if they occur at all—locally and organically through human connection, not philosophical pronouncements. And while such changes are possible, I'm skeptical about the pace and extent of the change. As we've seen in chapter 1, often what might appear to be a recognition of trans identities turns out to be a mere instance of playing along. Considering this, I'm also worried about the wisdom in making such a project the central strategy for positive transformation.

Family-Resemblance Concepts
On the face of it, dictionary definitions of terms such as *woman* seem highly uncongenial to trans people. The claim that *woman* means "adult female human being" would seem to rule out many trans women and rule in many trans men. Because of this, there have also been alternative analyses that seem far more congenial to trans people. Ludwig Wittgenstein proposes the notion of a "family-resemblance concept" according to which there needn't be one feature or set of features that all members of a category have in common; there needn't be easily specifiable necessary and sufficient conditions for membership.[12] Rather, they can possess several overlapping features; some members might have some, some might have others,

some might have all. In providing a family-resemblance analysis, one can list the features that are part of the meaning without being able to have an easy recipe for membership. Many philosophers offer analyses that draw on this idea.[13]

The analysis has a benefit in elucidating how *woman* contains some content besides sex—features such as sexual orientation, gender self-identity, and gender expression (appearance, behavior, psychological attitudes characterized as "feminine" or "masculine"). Moreover, such a move may appear to support a trans political project by broadening the analysis of gender terms away from the standard definitions: at least some trans women will count as women, since they'll possess enough of the relevant features. The invalidation of their identities can be understood as the wrongful insistence on a traditional definition that, in centralizing sex characteristics such as genitalia, leaves out the other content relevant to the meaning of the term.[14]

Yet, the analysis is still problematic.[15] Trans women will nonetheless be viewed as marginally women, in the best-case scenario. Since we may lack some relevant supposedly biological features, we couldn't count as paradigm instances of womanhood. Moreover, according to this analysis, there may sometimes be no fact of the matter whether a trans woman is a woman. (While some features may count in favor of her being a woman—identity, expression, orientation—others will count against it—namely, sex or sex characteristics. Indeed, the latter counts in favor of her being a man. What should we say then? One is inclined to say there's no real answer to the question since the concept itself provides no recipe for settling the matter.) The problem, at any rate, is the marginalization of trans women in the best-case scenario.

Semantic Contextualism
A second candidate for a trans-friendly analysis is semantic contextualism. According to this view, features that determine membership vary depending upon the context. In such a view, a term can operate like an indexical for which content is determined by the specific context in which it is used as the standards for correct application of the concept contextually vary. Despite this variability of content, however, the meaning is still fixed insofar as there's a single rule-governed way in which the content is determined. By analogy, while the indexical *I*

changes its referent when different people utter it, the indexical still has a fixed meaning insofar as the referent is determined by the rule: *I* refers to the person who utters it. Crucially, then, semantic contextualism concerns the operation of a term within a single linguistic community, unlike ontological pluralism.

Jennifer Mather Saul considers a semantic-contextualist account of *woman*.[16] In such a view, there are multiple contexts that select multiple membership-determining features. There can be a context in which the relevant feature (for correct application of the term *woman*) involves "sincerely self-identifying as a woman," and there can be another context in which the relevant feature involves "having XX chromosomes."[17] Thus, whether a trans woman counts as a woman depends on which standards are relevant in a given context. One of the benefits of this move is that it makes it possible for any trans woman (regardless of whether she has undergone medical procedures) to count as a woman. It does this by allowing for contexts in which the standard of self-identification is salient in determining correct applicability.

Saul herself raises some problems with this proposed account, however. One concern is that it does not do justice to trans women in a nontrivializing way, since claims that trans women are not women are also true in certain contexts. Indeed, claims Saul, questions around trans women using women's public restrooms, for example, will have to be settled by extrasemantic moral and political considerations. And this surely seems to be a marginalizing consequence.

Esa Díaz-León, however, refines Saul's contextualist account to address this concern.[18] To accomplish this, she distinguishes two different kinds of contextualism—namely, "attributor-contextualism" and "subject-contextualism." In the former, factors that determine context depend on the person making the claim and include the attributor's own beliefs about relevant standards. In the latter, the factors concern the "objective" features of the context in which the subject of the claim is located. Díaz-León argues for the latter, claiming that "the relevant standards at issue in a context are those *that are relevant for practical purposes* (where these are broadly conceived to include theoretical, prudential, moral, political and even aesthetic values)."[19] Thus, the moral and political considerations that Saul deems extrasemantic are actually included within the analysis of how the contextually shifting term *woman* operates. And with regard to use of public restrooms, argues Díaz-León, trans women will count as women since identity, rather than supposed biological sex, is most relevant for those practical purposes, and antitrans claims ("She's not a woman") won't be true after all, since their beliefs aren't relevant to the assessment of the claim. By contrast, there may still be other contexts in which sex determines membership such as the medical screening for vaginal disease.[20] (In this context, not only would some trans women not count as women, but some trans men would also count as women.)

Concerns remain, however. In some ways, semantic contextualism is not that different from (or indeed incompatible with) a family-resemblance account. In both, there are various features that play a role in the determining of womanhood. It's simply that semantic contextualism allows that different contexts will bring different features into prominence.

Consequently, my worries about the resemblance account play out here as well. Insofar as this account still allows for contexts in which trans women don't count as women (i.e., when sex is salient), it's still vulnerable to charges of invalidating trans identities. This also means that an analogous asymmetry will remain in full force. Unlike trans women, most nontrans women are going to count as women in any context and on almost any reasonable standard. Thus, the failure of the semantic-contextualist account is similar to that of the family-resemblance account. In both cases, even if they were correct analyses of dominant discursive practices, trans identities would still be marginalized.[21]

An Underworld Practice

If, rather, we embrace ontological pluralism, we have the validating practices of trans subcultures to which we can appeal, and in these worlds trans women can count as women paradigmatically. While trans women will only count as women in some worlds and not others, unlike those nontrans women who count in all, recall that I have not aimed to provide an analysis at all. I am merely maintaining that there are different discursive practices and hence different analyses required for each. This matters since while I can describe trans invalidation in certain worlds as oppressive—something to be contested—

both family-resemblance and semantic-contextualist accounts effectively endorse this oppression through their analyses.

To better appreciate these points, consider the following example of a discursive practice that can be found in some trans subcultures.[22] It can be represented as a two-step process. First, *trans woman* is taken as a basic expression, not as a qualification of the dominant meaning of *woman*. Whether someone is a trans woman doesn't depend on questions about the applicability of the terms *man* and *woman* (i.e., the criteria for the correct application of *trans woman* don't depend on the criteria governing the application of *woman*). Rather, the criteria are roughly equivalent to the criteria governing *male-to-female trans person*. Roughly, a person counts as a trans woman just in case she was assigned to the male sex at birth and has either transitioned or has the desire to transition. *Transition* means adopting a public female gender presentation for most of the time, including going by a female name (or a name that can pass as female) and using female pronouns. *Nontrans woman* is taken as a basic expression that is, by contrast, applied to individuals who are assigned female at birth and who don't transition or desire to transition.

The second step is that being a trans woman or a nontrans woman is taken as sufficient for being a woman. Thus, in resistant trans worlds *woman* applies to both trans women and nontrans women alike, and consequently, we get entirely new criteria for who's a woman and a new extension of *woman*. Indeed, we get a concept of *woman* in which a trans woman is paradigmatic. She's not marginal. She's not arbitrarily stipulated into the category. There's a fact of the matter whether she's a woman. And the fact is *she is*.

Crucially, it's a different practice. It's given by the following type of trans logic inherent in resistant trans worlds: since trans women are paradigmatic women, it follows that possession of a penis, and so forth, goes absolutely no distance at all in detracting from womanhood any more than does wearing a blue hat. It's such a significant departure from dominant sociolinguistic practice that we must speak of two sets of meanings rather than one: once penises are no longer invalidating to one's womanhood at all, we're not in Kansas anymore.

While such a practice and my superficial analysis thereof bring out the usefulness of an appeal to ontological pluralism, however, it's crucial to recall that neither this discursive practice nor this analysis thereof are specifically necessary in an appeal to ontological plural-ism. (This is fortunate since this practice invalidates the identities of some trans people in order to validate the identities of others—in chapter 6, I'll explore a more inclusive practice.) The appeal consists merely in the view that such validating countercultural practices exist. The basic claim I'm making is that such an appeal is necessary to ground trans self-identifies in a nonmarginalizing way.

SEX AND PRETENSE

Both trans-friendly analyses considered in the previous section mis-leadingly downplay the centrality of sex. This is unfortunate since sex is hardly irrelevant to trans identities. Many trans women self-identify as female every bit as much as women, and many trans men self-identify as male every bit as much as they self-identify as men. Unsurprisingly, this centrality isn't a problem in trans subcultures, since there is likewise a shift in meaning with regard to the terms *female* and *male*.

This failure to centralize sex is also unfortunate because it un-dercuts even the pretensions of these analyses to eke out at least marginal validations in the dominant world. That is, in getting the dominant practices wrong, they distort the oppressive force of mis-gendering. The family-resemblance analysis, for instance, treats sex and other features such as gender expression, gender presenta-tion, gender identity, and sexual orientation as on par semantically. They're alike regarded as criteria for determining the application of the term (although it is admitted that sex is likely to be weighted the most). This is a mistake.

Gender expression and sexual orientation are all subject to evalu-ation as feminine or masculine. Let's call the basis for these evalua-tions "gender norms."[23] The norms are evaluative in the sense that femininity and masculinity come in degrees. One can be feminine but less feminine than another. In cases of evaluation, of course, an assessable range is to be expected.[24]

If this is right, then it is one thing to be evaluated as conforming to norms associated with some concept and quite another to be placed under a normative status in the first place. And whether one's evalu-ated according to norms governing womanhood and manhood de-pends on the category within which one is situated in the first place.[25]

Consequently, conformity to evaluative norms governing woman-hood can't be used as a criterion for membership since prior assignment to a status category is necessary for the appropriate evaluation to take place. Most features listed in the family-resemblance analysis can then be dispensed with as instances of conformity to evaluative norms and hence as presupposing the prior assignment of a gender category, and we're left with sex alone as the determining feature.[26]

This mistake yields a misdescription of how misgendering operates. Specifically, it positions a trans woman who doesn't alter her body but who self-identifies, self-presents, and self-expresses as a woman as in-between categories or at least close to the edges. What happens, however, is that this trans woman is situated firmly and squarely within the category "man." The misdescription has it that while supposed biological sex may pull her toward "male," her self-identity, self-presentation, and self-expression can pull her toward "female." What actually happens is that her public gender presentation is viewed as misrepresenting her supposedly biological sex, her self-identity is viewed as mistaken, and her efforts to behave in accordance with feminine norms of gender expression are regarded as simple violations of masculine norms of behavior. Not only would the family-resemblance analysis fail to center trans identities, if correct, it simply isn't correct and instead distorts the process of misgendering by making it seem less bad than it is.

The problem with the semantic-contextualist analysis, by contrast, is it makes it seem that sex isn't going to be particularly relevant for trans people except in cases of medical exams and other rarefied contexts. Yet consider contexts in which sexual activities occur. Penises and vaginas are presumably pertinent in these contexts. And claiming that the standards at issue in this context—the ones "that are relevant for practical purposes"—somehow don't include them is a tough sell, to say the least.

Regardless, many trans women who haven't had bottom surgery regard themselves as women—indeed, females—entering into heterosexual relations with men. Alas, it's precisely such contexts that often yield the greatest violence against trans women (along with misgendering and accusations of deception). Rather than validating trans identities, unfortunately, the analysis would have to agree with the verdict of the transphobe in such contexts. Rather than identifying and explaining misgendering, it would, in these contexts, merely endorse what trans folk regard as misgendering as correct gendering.

The failure to take seriously sexual contexts, however, now becomes the basis of a further difficulty—specifically, it's not clear whether those cases in which trans people are taken to count as their self-identified gender are genuine in the first place. This returns us to the problem of "playing along" introduced in chapter 1. Insofar as the semantic-contextualist approach requires misgendering the trans person in these intimate contexts, it must misgender the trans person in *all* contexts. That is, what appear to be cases of gender validation are, in fact, cases of invalidation when properly considered within a comprehensive view.

It's not enough to focus on this or that context. The interrelations among them matter. Any given context must be taken within a larger, holistic view to determine whether a term is applied veritably or in pretense. And so, my worry with semantic contextualism, here, is that it wrongly treats each context as if it were discrete, disconnected from the rest of the social order. One must understand how the extradiscursive practices are related to the discursive ones, and one must understand how the former allow or forbid movement from one context to the next. This helps further underscore the differences between semantic contextualism and ontological pluralism. The error of the former, to repeat, is precisely that it treats each context individually and as separate from the rest. And when I say that trans women are women in some worlds and not others, I mean in different social fabrics of interconnected social and discursive contexts and not others.

The Interpersonal Spatiality Hypothesis

THE SUPERMAN ARGUMENT

One of the nice things about the pluralist approach is that we are now free to analyze dominant meanings without the need to make them appear to validate trans identities or to be, in other ways, less oppressive than they are. On the contrary, they can be exposed in all their oppressive force. In this section of the chapter, therefore, I'll argue for my own analysis of the terms *man* and *woman* as they circulate in the overworld. And in doing so, I'll demonstrate the surprising irrelevance of biological sex, biological maturity, and biological species to those meanings. Instead, I'll propose that terms like *man* and *woman* name kinds of interpersonal objects differentiated through boundary structures. I'll start with species and then move to what I call "moral sex" and "moral maturity."

Let's begin by considering two views. The first is that "being human" is analytically included in the concepts *man, woman, boy,* and *girl.* In such a view, it would be a contradiction to suggest that some man might not be human, just as it would be a contradiction to posit a triangle that isn't a polygon. The second view is when we're talking about men, women, boys, and girls, we're talking about a natural biological kind, say, *Homo sapiens,* where both sex and maturity concern biological differentiations. In this view, *man, woman, boy,* and *girl* rigidly designate adult male humans, adult female humans, child male humans, and child female humans, respectively.

In both views it is impossible for there to be men and women, boys and girls, who are not human. But this, it turns out, is false. It's common in *Star Trek* to speak of Vulcan and Klingon men and women.[27] Superman (Kal-El), while from the planet Krypton, is a man—in fact, the Man of Steel! And in *The Lord of the Rings,* there are nonhuman dwarf-women and dwarf-men.[28] Indeed, it's not even clear that animality is a necessary condition in case androids, such as Lieutenant Commander Data from *Star Trek: The Next Generation,* get to count as men, and so forth. This means that it's possible for there to be nonhuman men and women. So, the positing of a Kryptonian man is not a contradiction in terms. And the terms *man* and *woman* don't rigidly designate members of the species *Homo sapiens* or even the genus *Homo.*[29]

Now, to be sure, as far as we know, human men and women are the only men and women that exist. And this is presumably why it is falsely supposed that this restriction is a necessary truth. But the fact that only human men and women exist simply doesn't yield this restriction.[30] And it should be stressed here that, happily, this result does not depend upon the potentially corrupted intuitions of philosophers, either. On the contrary, examples like this abound in literature and film created by nonphilosophers and therefore show something important about the overworld concepts.

This argument has another upshot that will be important as

we proceed with the essay—one concerning the ordinary notion of *person* (and *people*) introduced in chapter 1. The *Oxford English Dictionary*, recall, defines *person* and *people* as follows: "An individual human being; a man, woman, or child. In ordinary usage, the unmarked plural is expressed by the word *people*; *persons* emphasizes the plurality and individuality of the referent" and "Men or women; men, women, and children; folk."[31]

What the **Superman argument** shows is that components in these definitions can be pulled apart—specifically, a human being, on the one hand, and a man, woman, boy, or girl, on the other. Since *person* (and *people*) would, presumably, be appropriate in either case, we might speak of both the *human* sense of *person* and the *folk* sense of *person*—that is, *person* as in "man, woman, boy, or girl."[32] The latter shall, of course, occupy us at length in this essay. After all, once people-as-folk has been distinguished from people-as-human, the former cries out for explanation. Just what *are* men, women, boys, and girls if not humans?

No doubt there are various possibilities. What I shall propose, however, is that *folk* are interpersonal objects constituted within what I shall call the "folk system of interpersonal spatiality." In this view, men and women (and boys and girls) are different kinds of objects—ones differentiated by boundary structures—within this system. And I shall call the differentiations "moral sex" and "moral maturity," respectively. We can call this proposal the "interpersonal spatiality hypothesis."[33]

MORAL SEX

By *moral sex* I mean the difference between the interpersonal objects *men* (and *boys*) and *women* (and *girls*) in the folk system of interpersonal spatiality. To be clear, I mean the basic difference. As we saw above, norms governing gender expression are assigned on the basis of already belonging to the category. So, if these norms are part of the concepts *man* and *woman*, they aren't part of the criteria on the basis of which they're assigned. Moral sex, by contrast, is precisely the criterion on the basis of which they're assigned. And as the criterion on the basis of which they're assigned, moral sex isn't itself assigned on the basis of further criteria. Rather, it's cue-differentiated in the very process of subsumption. The difference in moral sex is then reflected by a difference in cues and strips (i.e., a difference in specific bound-aries and their moral and temporal ordering), as well as a difference in position within any given pathway.

Although moral sex can be regarded as a difference in kind of in-terpersonal object, it can also be viewed as a difference in the very way our interpersonal awareness is structured. Not only are folk people and tables differentiated, male and female people are likewise differentiated via cues, strips, and pathway position. Further, one's own self-awareness relative to others is itself structured according to moral sex. In short, the very modality by which the world—including oneself—is given is structured by these differences. Moral sex consti-tutes the very form of interpersonal intimacy in the folk system.

I do not, therefore, consider moral sex an aspect of gender (what-ever "gender" is). First, as the basic, morally binding structure in the way we so much as experience the world, it is a mistake to associate it with something that suggests mere social construction. Second, since moral sex is not assigned on the basis of biological sex but is, rather, itself the basis on which gender norms are assigned, it's pref-erable to keep the distinction between moral sex, on the one hand, and gender (norms), on the other, in play.

By *biological sex* I mean whatever it is that actual biologists mean. For instance, biologist Joan Roughgarden points out that in sexual re-production the only binary to be found concerns sizes in gametes (large and small).[34] She says that the only sense to be made of *male* and *female* is in terms of the production of small and large gametes, respectively.

What I'm claiming is that this is not what everyday people typi-cally mean when they speak of sex as the difference between men and women. To put it differently, whatever biologists are talking about when they talk about sexual reproduction is disconnected from what ordinary folk are talking about when they talk about men and women. While folks may hold views about how reproduction works for men and women, not even these views are relevant to an under-standing of what men and women are essentially. Instead, moral sex is often confused with biological sex. Indeed, I think it's passed off *as* biological sex by being treated as "natural." Because of this, it is falsely supposed that gender norms are assigned on the basis of bio-logical sex. It turns out, however, that biological sex has little to do with men and women at all.

To see why, let's ask which biological features are necessary for men and which are necessary for women. It certainly can't be an XX or XY chromosomal configuration, since there is no reason to suppose that Vulcan women must have XX chromosomes to be female and that Vulcan men must have XY chromosomes to be male. What else could this feature be? While not all men and women produce gametes, one could tell some sort of biological story that would permit grouping into biological kinds. Regardless, it seems just as possible to suppose some alien men and women, from the planet Ziggle IX, produce large and small gametes, respectively, as it is to suppose that there exist men and women who are Zigglian in the first place. Indeed, it seems entirely possible that men and women from Ziggle IX switch back and forth with regard to large and small gametes, alike produce both, or even fail to produce either, reproducing, rather, through asexual means.

Certainly, none of this is analytically foreclosed. Nor must *man* and *woman* name producers of small and large gametes, respectively, in all possible worlds. What this shows is that the distinction between men and women does not turn on any biological notion of sex. Whatever sex folks have in mind when they're talking about men and women, it's not the sex that biologists have in mind. It is, under the *interpersonal spatiality hypothesis*, moral sex.

To be clear, this isn't to deny that "being female" is analytically included in the concept *woman*. It may or may not be. But, if it is, the concept of *female* in question is not the one deployed by biological scientists. Consider, for instance, that *male* and *female* are colloquially used to simply mean "man" and "woman" (whereas a biologist would presumably use them to speak of other animals, as well as plants). Further, the terms can be used to refer to specific morphological differences concerning genitalia alone ("insy" and "outsy"), leaving out, say, chromosomal and gonadal differences. Indeed, the terms are even commonly used to refer to plugs and sockets and the like—suggestive of the role insy and outsy play in heterosexual coitus. Consider, also, that the very distinction between *man* and *woman* scarcely depends on the related words *male, female*, and *sex* in the first place. While *man* and *woman* were used in Old English, *male* and *female* weren't used until later in Middle English.[35] Presumably, the words operated just fine before this development, as there was already a distinction between men and women without an appeal to sex. The conclusion, to repeat, is that the basis on which men and women are distinguished—moral sex—is, rather than a biological characteristic, a feature of (folk) personhood itself.

MORAL MATURITY

In addition to moral sex, folk people are differentiated by moral maturity. Consider that besides the biological notion of sexual maturity, there's a cultural-moral notion. This is evidenced, in part, by legal notions deployed in age of majority laws. Further, it's clear that the notion of maturity operative within the concepts *man* and *woman* is itself at least partially cultural in character. A female human who reaches sexual maturity at age twelve, for example, is simply not a woman according to the dominant concept of *woman*. To be sure, her sexual maturity may well permit her mother to say, "My little girl has become a woman now." But it's also clear that she's not culturally a woman yet. She's still a kid.

That this sense of maturity is moral in character is evidenced by the rationales for segregating adults and minors at public school restrooms—rationales that cite concerns about inappropriate, boundary-violating interaction. And because these boundaries concern sexuality, moral sex is brought into salience here.[36] Although a full discussion of moral maturity is beyond the scope of this essay, let me note now that a normative basis grounding such boundaries is precisely the fact that children have not yet been sufficiently inculcated in the system to have mastered it. Boundary-traversing behavior exploits this lack of mastery while interfering with the process by which they are instructed into the system in the first place.

Ontological Pluralism and the Agent Object

At the outset of this chapter, I said I would return to Lugones's account of ontological pluralism in terms of interpersonal objects. This concluding section makes good on this promise. Specifically, I address what I take to be a lacuna in Lugones's account, and I propose interpersonal spatiality to address it. This culminates in a discussion of interpersonal spatiality across multiple systems and what I call *"complex intimacy."*

Agency (or lack thereof) plays a crucial role in Lugones's understanding of personhood. Let's say that to be an agent is to act for reasons, where "acting for reasons" entails that one possesses a complex repertoire of psychological, motivational states. Then, given that all possible actions, along with the reasons for engaging in them, are provided for and thereby constrained by culture, we can speak of distinct agents in distinct cultures. This is just to say that in one culture, certain actions and reasons may exist there that do not exist in another. Or, if agency is given within a system of actions and reasons, then different systems yield different agents. For Lugones, to be a different person, in part, is to be a different agent, and to be a different agent is to be in a different agential structure.[37] The key here is that in dominant worlds, the oppressed individual is an agent in only the faintest of senses: all their actions are self-defeating as they navigate a system of double binds.

One might wonder why there couldn't be one and the same agent who operates in different agential systems. After all, while it's clear the structural role of the agent will be different, nothing here prohibits the agent themself from remaining the same. That is, we can easily distinguish between structural agency (the agency provided for by a given system) and the prior agency that is required to operate within said structure. On the face of it, this would likewise appear enough to deliver one sense in which we can speak of different persons—namely, there would be different biographical identities in these different worlds. This is trivially so in that the activities recognized in one world would differ from those recognized in another. And, of course, the background conception within which such activities made sense would likewise differ.

However, Lugones worries about this very positing of an agent outside of these structures. Does the agent have psychological states? And if so, what are they about and where do they come from? Lugones thinks—rightly, I believe—that psychological states are going to require immersion in agential structures and that, consequently, immersion in different agential structures will yield different psychological profiles. Thus, she writes, "Structures construct or constitute persons not just in the sense of giving them a façade, but also in the sense of giving them emotions, beliefs, norms, desires, and intentions that are their own."[38]

Lugones sees oppression as involving the foreclosure of resistant intentions within dominant worlds. One can only intend to do something that can occur in that world; the action one undertakes must be a possible move in the game. One cannot play chess and, in full knowledge of the rules, intend to move one's rook diagonally. Of course, one could pull such a stunt in the middle of a game. But then it would become clear that one was not intending to play chess, that one was doing something else (e.g., pulling a stunt). "Just what, exactly, is this individual doing?" one might wonder. One would need some explanation, otherwise the behavior would cease to be intelligible. So, if the dominant world is set up such that the only available social moves lead to one's downfall, it becomes impossible to intend a liberatory action there. At best, one's behavior will be read as unintelligible. Thus, the existence of alternative worlds becomes indispensable—not only for the existence of resistant action but for resistant thoughts and intentions.

This recognition can be expanded to include all thoughts, feelings, desires, and so forth: One cannot have a mental life that is not provided for socially, goes the argument. One cannot be angry about an action that isn't even intelligible in that world. One cannot think about some entity that isn't even provided for in the culture—isn't something that could be so much as imagined. Resistance requires the existence of different agential possibilities and, therefore, different psychological profiles, different cognitive-affective lives.

While this is all quite convincing, it does seem to me that Lugones's position leaves something out—namely, the appearance of the agent themself. We have different actions in different agential systems, yes. And within those different systems, we have different psychological profiles, yes. And we can place these different actions and profiles into contestation, yes. But what is the thing that *has* those profiles—that shows up to undertake those actions? A ghost?

One possible response is to posit an animal organism—a member of the species *Homo sapiens*—that can then be socially constituted as having different agential possibilities, different psychological profiles in different worlds. The problem, however, is that any appeal to an animal organism that is prior to being worked up socially simply doesn't get to the issue at hand—namely, the organism must somehow be made manifest socially. Merely positing some animal organism won't suffice. What we need, in addition to this, are the specific practices that enable it to be appear culturally. Otherwise, there's a gap. We'll just have a bunch of social actions done by *what?* And we'll have those culturally determined psychological states possessed by *what?* Worse, we'll have some precultural animal wandering around that hasn't even been picked up on the cultural radar.[39]

What need to be centralized, it seems to me, are the practices of interpersonal spatiality that constitute the appearance of the agent and that make possible self-display. It is precisely this that allows for an interpersonal object to present itself as an object, to move from passive into dialogical presence through comportment—the condition under which it is possible to avow feelings and thoughts as further intimate agential display.

To begin to develop this proposal of understanding Lugonian persons to be interpersonal objects, I need to develop interpersonal spatiality theory in ways that I have not yet discussed. Specifically, I haven't examined the fact that systems need not be isolated from each other and that individuals can occupy different systems over time and even at the same time. This requires that we advance interpersonal spatiality beyond the structural to the in-the-moment processual negotiation of interpersonal spatiality in ways that exceed the constraints of any one system. It requires the introduction of *infraintimacy*.

For Lugones, one can be aware of one's multiplicity both at a given time during which one occupies two worlds and over time by remembering oneself as a different person in a different world.[40] This awareness, in Lugones's view, is a kind of achievement, as some people can lack it. It requires cross-referencing between worlds. And it fosters the development of an internal mental life exceeding anything given by any one given world. It can allow for multiworldly thoughts, feelings, and intentions that implicate both worlds—that transcend the structural limitations of these different worlds. One can then gain a critical perspective on both worlds that one couldn't get just from looking at one world from the perspective of the other (and conversely).

To be clear, this is not some sort of God's-eye view prescinded from all earthly experience. Rather, there's a third perspective afforded by the unification of multiple worlds within a singular consciousness—

the sort of perspective that a multicultural person can have that exceeds the sum of the perspectives of any one given world.[41] As Lugones writes, "That the liminal state is structurally invisible does not necessitate that liminal states not be sociohistorical states. The social transcends the structural without metaphysical transcendence. The historical subject is multiplicitous and something liminal."[42]

Such an awareness is crucial for resistance, says Lugones. To not have it—to lose connection to this multiplicity—is to forget oneself as different in a different world and to effectively become trapped in a single world. It's to have oneself sized to that world so that no liberatory intentions can be formed at all. One simply becomes—internalizes—that thing one is constructed to be.

To better understand this notion of resistance, we must turn to Lugones's distinction between different orders of meaning.[43] The first order concerns mental states (intentions, anger, etc.) that occur within a single world. For example, Lugones identifies a sort of anger that makes a claim on respectability within that world. The second order concerns mental states that move across worlds. One may experience and express anger about the fact that a world of sense forecloses the possibility of one's respectability within it. Here, one doesn't use anger to claim respectability within that world; rather, one expresses anger toward the world itself. As such, this anger is experienced in a resistant world and is expressed about and toward the dominant one.[44] In the dominant worlds it isn't even intelligible. Lugones also recognizes a third order of meaning—one that involves a sort of metacommunication across multiple oppressions (we won't return to it until chapter 6; at present, we'll stick with first- and second-order meaning).

Here's another example, which Lugones draws from the work of Alfred Arteaga.[45] On the one hand, a resister may be confronting an oppressor—addressing them in their language, on their terms, in a single-worldly way. Meanwhile, however, a second-order and infrapolitical communication is made among those who share a resistant world of meaning, who acknowledge each other as together supporting the resistant significance of the intervention. In this multiworldly conversation, the oppressor isn't the addressee but, rather, the topic of conversation. The colonized monologue of Anglo-American oppressors, for Arteaga, is thereby "dialogized" through the polyglossia of Chicanismo.[46] One of the central features of this multiworldly conversation involves the recognition of the communal support and creation of this resistant meaning. One's intentions to resist are grounded in and backed up by the collectivity. That is, one's action wouldn't be possible without the resistant community.

With all this in mind, I posit a future-oriented mode of experiencing multiplicity, in addition to both the present and past modes recognized by Lugones—one that turns on *anticipatory vulnerability* as a complex form of interpersonal awareness. In opening oneself to another, one is always open to disregard. However, in complex vulnerability, one is open to different receptions in different worlds, and one does not know in which world one will be received. For instance, disclosing that one is trans to another may either constitute a gesture of intimacy or constitute the admission that one is "really" a man or woman. In such cases, as one makes oneself vulnerable to another, the vulnerability in question is not given within a specific system of interpersonal spatiality. Rather, there's the recognition of multiple worlds of meaning, multiple systems of intimacy. There's the serious possibility that one will find oneself subjected to a dominant reading. And there's the awareness of this fact. In this awareness, one is aware of oneself as one or, rather, a potential one that has yet to be received.

One of things this means is that for this complex gesture to be completed, it must be witnessed in a way that appreciates this complexity. One who does not understand the complex vulnerability inherent in trans self-sharing is in no position to engage in complex forms of intrinsic intimacy with trans people at all. This, in my view, is at the root of the bulk of intimacy failures confronting trans people: the other is aware of only one system of intimacy—or rather, simply takes the system for granted—and hence is incapable of giving or receiving vulnerability in precisely this way.

One important consequence of foreclosure—a saving grace, if you will—is that intimacy failure through obliviousness yields a sort of privacy by which one's gesture turns out not to have been a self-revelation after all. Since one could never truly be fully "got" by this monocultural perception, one could never be truly exposed to the oblivious perceiver in the first place. I call the intimate that is hidden to single-worldly perception through foreclosure the "infraintimate."

Crucially, the infraintimate allows for a way to understand awareness of oneself as two interpersonal objects at the same time in the present and over time in memory. On the one hand, one can be aware of oneself as violated in the overworld. And yet, on the other hand, one can also be aware of oneself as concealed from this disregard through the very obliviousness by which it is effected. Similarly, one can remember oneself as abused and experience oneself as now untouched by the abuse as if by way of some sort of dignifying counterresponse. To be clear, this is not to deny the abuse—one is subsumed into a hostile overworld and one's self-display is rendered meaningless. It is, however, to understand that something remains beyond the reduction—something is left untouched, unexposed, precisely due to the obliviousness itself.

Part II

The Main Idea

Between Appearance and Reality

Chapter 4
The Politics of Pretense

HAVING PUT THE PRELIMINARIES BEHIND US, I undertake my two aims. In this chapter, I focus on the first—to provide an account of trans oppression that doesn't reduce to the beyond-the-binary account. In the first half, I introduce the related notions of physical person, proper appearance, and intimate appearance to explain the relegation of trans people to gender make-believe. In the last half, I show how the beyond-the-binary account of trans oppression fails to elucidate this phenomenon, while my account succeeds at explaining the binary. To do so, I focus on the classic works of Harold Garfinkel and Judith Butler. (In chapter 5, I then undertake the second aim—to provide an account of trans phoria that doesn't reduce to the wrong-body account.)

The account in this chapter goes beyond the account of gender deception provided in chapter 1 (public gender presentation communicates genital status) in two ways. First, it deepens the account of deception by showing how this abusive representational relation is integral to the very constitution of men and women. I replace *genital status* with *intimate appearance*. Meanwhile, *public gender presentation* becomes *proper appearance* to accommodate the way in which the two appearances contrastively constitute what I call the "physical person."

Second, I provide an account of pretense and its relation to this sex-representational system. Specifically, I argue that the sex-representational character of the system is hidden in cases of misalignment through the replacement of one intimate meaning with another—a replacement that constitutes the phenomenon of gender make-believe. (Let me note, however, that this account is still not fully complete and won't be until I discuss the folk system's situation within the colonial/modern system. As it stands, the discussion in this chapter veers toward what María Lugones calls "the light side" of gender.)[1]

As we proceed, let me forewarn that my investigation into the folk system is an extensive debunking project that exposes the system's various ruses. In my view, as in the view of social constructionists, what seems to be natural is often not. More generally, I will argue, the everyday world is simply not what it appears to be. Because of this, the chapter might be regarded as a "red pill."[2]

The most important phenomenon—the one that is central to my account—is that of **nakedness**: a state assumed to be natural and free from cultural intervention.[3] On the contrary, I argue, nakedness is a sociomoral phenomenon. And in claiming this, to be clear, I don't merely mean that a **naked body** can have different cultural meanings assigned to its nakedness. Rather, nakedness itself is a cultural-moral phenomenon.[4] Without the concept of clothedness, there could be no concept of nakedness. Without the social phenomenon of being clothed, there could be no corresponding social phenomenon of being naked. Crucially, this, in turn, leads us to another insight: namely, that folk people—men and women, boys and girls—are not merely biological organisms subsumed within the folk system. They are what I shall call "**vestorgs**" on the analogy of the "cyborg." That is, they are not organisms but organism–artifact complexes, since even without them on, the artifacts are necessary to their constitution.[5]

The Physical Person

PROPER AND INTIMATE APPEARANCES

I call the sensory appearance of men and women within the folk system "the physical person." It's the person one *has* rather than *is*. Thus, one may say that one was carrying a knife "on one's person" or that "one's person" was searched. Consider, now, the following *Oxford English Dictionary* definition of *person*:

> The living body or physical appearance of a human being; *spec. (a)* the body *regarded as distinct* from the mind or soul, or *from its clothing*, etc.; *(b)* the body regarded *together with its clothes and adornments*.[6]

I will call "the body regarded together with its clothes and adornments" the "proper appearance" and "the body regarded as distinct from its clothing" the "intimate appearance," although we'll see in this chapter that the notion of "the body" itself is problematic here.[7]

More accurately, by *proper appearance* I mean the required appearance of objects in standard, nonintimate configurations, and by *intimate appearance* I mean an appearance allocated to intimacy and that stands in contrast to the former. While this differentiation is not a necessary distinction in all sensory appearances in all systems, it is also not necessarily restricted to the folk system either. The key point for us is that in the folk system, the difference between intimate and proper appearance principally concerns the social artifact we call "clothing."

Both phenomena are to be understood in terms of interpersonal spatiality and, more specifically, a strip in which clothedness and unclothedness are alike stages. This strip—call it the *"physical strip"*—is more complex than the ones I've discussed thus far as it doesn't merely involve the temporal-moral ordering of boundaries on sensory access; it implicates literal spatial arrangements with regard to bodies and culturally manufactured artifacts that are (or are not) placed upon them.

We can discriminate arrangements based on where the artifacts are placed and how many artifacts are placed on a body relative to other arrangements. The different spatial arrangements can then be set into different stages of boundary strip—where the boundaries primarily concern visual and secondarily tactile access. The initial stage is proper appearance, the last stage is intimate appearance, and there are stages that exist in between.

In the folk system, of course, there are two physical strips.[8] The female strip, unlike the male one, has two major moral stages—topless and complete—where the former is determined in terms of the exposure of breasts (specifically, nipples). That is, nipples are morally decisive with respect to toplessness in the way that genitalia are decisive with respect to bottomlessness, yielding a tiered female physical strip but not a male one. These different physical strips are further differentiated by the relative force of the boundaries.

We must be clear that the way in which the different arrangements are ordered in the strip need have no correlation to any ordering with respect to spatial arrangement. There's no reason an arrangement with artifacts on must count as proper, while the arrangement with artifacts off counts as intimate.

Imagine, for instance, a society in which people do not put artifacts on themselves at all in standard nonintimate configurations.

Suppose, instead, that every individual possesses certain unique manufactured items hidden away at an early age. Placing these items on themselves may be viewed as constituting a very important appearance such that in certain intimate contexts an individual may place these items on themselves for another as an act of intimacy. In this case, proper appearance involves the lack of the artifacts, while the intimate involves the presence—the opposite of the folk system.

This example further illuminates the phenomenon of nakedness. In this proposed society, nakedness wouldn't just not constitute an intimate appearance—it wouldn't exist at all. This is because the cultural phenomenon of nakedness does two things: it takes the arrangement in which the artifacts are off, and it allocates this arrangement to intimate appearance in a strip ordering arrangements from most to none. While this imagined society does the former, it does not do the latter. On the contrary, in this society, the arrangement with artifacts on is the intimate appearance, while the arrangement with them off is the proper one. (Such considerations are by no means hypothetical. When I eventually turn to examine the colonial/modern gender system in chapter 7, we will see that not all interpersonal systems need include the phenomenon of nakedness.)

A few final remarks about proper appearance: in the folk system, proper appearance serves as the cue-providing appearance of the object for initial subsumption. It therefore indicates *that* interpersonal boundaries are at play and *which* boundaries are at play—female or male—where it is precisely through the boundaries that one is enabled to be present to others at all as an agent. Clothing, in this respect, can be regarded as the uniform of personhood. Without it, one would be entirely "out of uniform" insofar as "nakedness," as Thomas Nagel puts it, "is disqualifying."[9] And as proper appearances are differentiated in terms of moral sex, we can likewise speak of female and male clothing as the uniform of womanhood and manhood, respectively.

When we think of people in the folk system, we think of them with their clothes on, since thinking about a person as naked is an **intimate cognition.** More correctly, we don't even think of people as having clothes on. We simply presuppose clothed appearance without ado. Expressly thinking about a person as having clothes on is likewise intimate as it brings into view the possibility of them not having them on. This underscores the centrality of proper appearance as crucial to the way we think of people as people. One way to put this is to say that the maintenance of proper appearance indicates participation within the system. Because of this, proper appearance ought to be understood as a basic ground for legitimacy as a folk person at all.[10]

Since intimate appearance, by contrast, is marked against the taken-for-grantedness of proper appearance, proper appearance admits not only of movement toward intimate appearance but also of movement from implicit to explicit. We can say that proper appearance itself operates in **singular mode** and **contrastive mode**. In the former, there's no intimate thought about boundaries at all. In the latter, proper appearance is explicitly contrasted with intimate appearance by way of an intimate cognition.

THE NATURALIZATION OF NAKEDNESS

Just how these artifacts are understood cannot be taken as given. That is, the content of the relevant intimate cognition cannot be taken for granted. After all, these artifacts might be understood as technologies by which one connects with the spiritual realm. They could be understood as mere costumes. They could be understood as part of one's outer layer. They could even be understood as detachable parts of oneself. But they aren't in the folk system. They're taken as technologies of concealment—or, more commonly, clothing. This, then, is the intimate meaning of proper appearance. And it creates an extraordinary illusion.

Specifically, the intimate appearance is wrongly imagined to be the most true and accurate presentation of "the body itself," where "the body" is imagined to be a culturally independent being that is also somehow magically saturated with moral boundaries—a "naked body" that demands concealment. Proper appearance is taken as the effect of concealing the body itself with clothes, and intimate appearance is taken as the exposure of the body previously concealed.

In this construal, the body itself is taken as some sort of morally saturated being forbidding visual access and demanding this covering. Even though it's the body-artifact complex that is subject to the boundary on access, the alleged "naked body" is then cited as the reason for clothedness. This conflation of *boundaried arrangement* with *boundaried thing* is promoted through two other related moves. First, this naked body is imagined somehow to be there present underneath the clothing. Second, intimate appearance itself is viewed precisely in terms of exposure of this naked body.

This is all false. Nakedness isn't an entity but a culturally marked mode of appearance. And as such, that appearance cannot be there under something else. Contrary to the popular saying, we're not naked under our clothes. One is either present in that mode of appearance or not. To be sure, there's a physical entity that cannot be seen because other physical entities surround it or that can be seen because they do not. But what's not there, in all cases, is the naked body itself, either concealed or revealed.[11]

Taken quite literally, this analysis yields the shocking conclusion that no clothing exists at all—a conclusion only mitigated by the equally outrageous but oddly consoling conclusion that neither does nakedness. These claims, while humorous, are virtually paradoxical—in effect, a philosopher's delight—and must surely be treated with, at the very least, some delicacy. In the view I prefer, both clothing and nakedness do exist. Recalling chapter 2, I view clothing, nakedness, physical persons, and, indeed, men and women as on par with religious practices, artifacts, and monuments. They all exist, but not in the way consistent with their internal logic. That is, they're simply constituted through social practices that perpetuate false views about their nature.[12]

That said, it is not crucial that one commit to the existence of clothes and the like. I only propose that approach to mitigate the shock to supposed common sense. What is crucial is only that we clearly distinguish between the content of the intimate meaning— the mythological representation—and an analysis of the interpersonal practices in which those mythological representations inhere. Since it may be difficult to resist the temptation to regard clothing as concealing a naked body, it may be worth constantly reminding oneself why this is false. There isn't a naked body underneath the clothing. Rather, there's just a contingent intimate meaning assigned to proper appearance that becomes explicit in cases of intimate cognition.

This allows us to understand how complex illusions can be generated through an interplay of the practices and the mythological content. I'll give two examples now, although we shall encounter several others as we proceed. First, what is in fact merely the final stage of a strip governing visual access to ordered arrangements of organism-artifact is, under the illusion of concealment, treated as the thing itself—the naked body. As such, it seems to possess a kind of moral structure subjecting naked body parts to boundaries. For instance, while there are no boundaries on face and hands, there are boundaries of increasing strength on buttocks, female nipples, and genitalia. And as the physical strips are differentiated by moral sex, we end up with a sexed distinction in *forms of nakedness*. In truth, both female and male intimate appearance are alike in simply being the final artifactless arrangements, differentiated only insofar as they are part of different strips. Through this ruse, however, the entire differential strips are now, as it were, projected onto the final stages of the strip as a kind of structure so that we may speak of female and male forms of nakedness.

Second, when proper appearance is in singular mode, clothing is just as integral to a person's proper appearance as are their face and hands. There's no significant difference, as all elements that appear are blended together on par to create this presupposed way that any individual is given and thought about. While we may be expressly aware that people can wear different clothes, the alleged function of clothes as concealing the naked body isn't explicit. Once proper appearance shifts to contrastive mode, the effect of concealing "it" is no longer given as blended but, rather, as composite. Head and hands are no longer on par with clothing. Clothing as a form of concealment pops into relief, and the head and hands become part of the hidden, naked body, major regions of which are concealed. In this way, the very movement from blended to composite can effect the illusion of concealment.

THE HETERORELATIONAL COMPLEX

Before I conclude this overview of the system, I want to get more specific about the sort of intimacy to which intimate appearances are allocated. (This is necessary for my account of playing along and the *calamities of intimacy* and, ultimately, the colonial/modern gender system.) Strips are immanent in pathways, and the pathway in which male and female nakedness strips find meaning is one called "sexuality." More correctly, for reasons that will soon become clear, the strips are immanent in the *heterorelational complex* of which the sexual pathways are one aspect (I'll consider sexuality first, expanding to the larger complex in due course). To examine this complex, I first examine an expansion of the false mythology of nakedness introduced earlier. Then, I examine the practices that are obscured by this mythology.

Consider the content of the intimate meaning of proper appearance. As I've already noted, it posits a mythological naked body that is concealed by clothing. Further, even though the naked body is imagined to be governed by moral boundaries, it is also thought to be natural in contrast to clothing, which is, in turn, imagined to be thoroughly cultural. Focusing on the intimate meaning of female proper appearance alone, let me expand the mythology as follows.

1. The female naked body is imagined to be the source of male sexual desire.
2. Sexual desire is conceived of as something like a powerful force that, once set into motion, can hardly be stopped.
3. The female naked body is regarded as inherently subject to violation unless some mitigating cultural intervention occurs.
4. The preceding three are natural features of sexuality.

Obviously, these beliefs help constitute folk personhood in a sexist way.

One might object that I have presented a rather outmoded picture of sexuality that no longer has much play—certainly not in the mainstream United States. So let me clarify that I mean not necessarily expressly articulated views but, rather, those that are frequently implicit in actual practice, only becoming explicit on occasion. These views notably do become explicit in cases of blaming the rape victim, making acquaintance rape difficult to expose, and more generally leaving women vulnerable to absurd heterosexual manipulations.

Given the preceding, the intimate meaning of male proper appearance is easily dealt with since the same mythological content can function for both—the difference, rather, merely consists in positioning with regard to the intimate meaning. In effect, this display of the male body to a female gaze would simply reflect the sexual desire of the male toward the female, constituting an offending sexual move.

Let me note the relation between this proposed mythology and well-known racist mythology—particularly that of the "Black male rapist" and "oversexualized Black female." As I mentioned in chapter 1, I hope to show reality enforcement not only as a participant in a racist, sexist, and heterosexist system but as itself already inherently racialized. A deeper focus on the underlying mythology is one of the keys to accomplishing this.

Having elaborated the expanded mythology, my next step is to take a preliminary look at the practices themselves—the practices that actually constitute the heterorelational complex. I'd like to expose what's really going on underneath the four false views about sexuality outlined above. Let me begin by noting that the fact that eroticism and intimacy are connected is already a contingent aspect of the system. They are connected in two arbitrary ways. First, erotic experience (and certainly the acting on it) is allocated to intimacy—that is, it is subject to boundaries and arranged in a pathway. Second, the content of eroticism is provided for by the pathway—that is, intimate movement down the pathway is itself eroticized.

Let's consider the latter first. Movement down the female physical strip from proper to intimate appearance is obviously part of the content of canonical straight male eroticism. That is, the form of eroticism in this case is one that concerns a particular increase in sensory access. So, what is in fact the mere eroticization of movement down a strip is falsely construed as the attractive force of the naked body itself, as if the naked body were the target and sensory access thereof the aim. That is, the mythological claim that (1) "The female moral body is imagined to be the source of male sexual desire" is promoted through a false construal of the eroticism involved.

Let's now consider the former: the contingent fact that eroticism is allocated to intimacy. To say that some interpersonal configuration is allocated to sexuality is to say that this configuration is a stage in a pathway that is denominated "sexuality," where erotic experiences are to be expected. For instance, should a man see a woman barebreasted, all things being equal, this will constitute a stage in the heterosexual pathway, regardless of whether anybody experiences any eroticism or even intends to. The point is that the mythological posit of (2) "an unstoppable male sexual desire" is promoted through a false construal of the way configurations are denominated "sexual" regardless of whether they are experienced that way and that, further, these configurations are arranged on pathways involving increasing intimacy.

To understand the practices implicated in (3)—the notion that the mythological naked body is capable of moral violation—I now expand my study to the heteroromantic complex that I mentioned at the outset. While I've said that (hetero)sexuality is a dialogical pathway, it is more correct to regard it as part of a larger complex integrating sex with emotional-romantic intimacy in a socially recognized relationship. This complex involves the differential distribution of intimate self-revelation.

Specifically, while the baring of deep feelings is made integral to male intimate self-revelation, sexuality—both desire and behavior—is made integral to female self-revelation. One thinks here, perhaps, of the blushing bride or, more likely, the woman who has been forced to conceal her own tremendously powerful libido. The crucial upshot, at any rate, is that the sexual pathway, taken by itself, leads to increased and unreciprocated female vulnerability. As such, the sexual side of the complex is constituted to inflict intimate disregard on the female without some sort of broader "relational containment," if you will. Underneath the illusion that some naked moral body can be violated, we find, instead, the infliction of dialogical abuse.[13]

This flows easily into (4). Although sexuality and the development of an emotional relationship toward a relational status are alike sociomoral phenomena—features of the folk system of interpersonal spatiality—the former is falsely regarded as precultural (natural) while the latter is regarded as a sort of cultural intervention with regard to it. In this way, sexuality becomes naturally abusive to females. The same can also be said of any mitigating circumstances preventing sensory access from constituting sexual intimacy that are represented as a kind of social intervention, whereas the sexual intimacy is itself viewed as natural—somehow prior to any cultural workup. Both, however, are equally cultural-moral in character. Both are configurations in a contingent system of interpersonal spatiality. Indeed, this so-called natural sexuality is naught more than a highly specific and well-organized dialogical pathway. The consequence is that as intimate appearances are falsely regarded as natural, so too is the intimate pathway to which they are allocated.

With this analysis in place, I conclude this section by exposing two additional ruses of the system. First, heterosexuality is written right onto (principally female) nakedness as a sort of teleology. Previously, we saw how a structure is projected onto the naked body. We can further add now that as the physical strips are, in fact, immanent in the naturalized heterosexual pathway, the various body parts of the naked body that are subject to structure are also allocated to a natural sexuality with its own built-in erotic course. Any eroticization of body parts and any use of body parts into eroticized activities that do not conform to the pathways written into male and female nakedness will go against the natural sexual functionality of these body parts.

Second, as the sex-differentiated appearances impute sex-differentiated interpersonal identities, the relationship of the "who" to the physical person is likewise distinct. While the male "who" will seem to have an internal depth, a vast wealth of unshared feelings and thoughts, the female "who" will seem to have a modesty that holds back the potential for a relentless sexual self-expression.

REALITY ENFORCEMENT AND THE PHYSICAL PERSON

We arrive now at my account of reality enforcement. In the folk system, there are two proper appearances; each proper appearance has a specific intimate meaning assigned to it and each specific meaning picks out a specific intimate appearance. (We might understand this as analogous to a Fregean account of reference according to which a term has a meaning assigned, which in turns picks out a referent.)[14] This is to say that each proper appearance, through its intimate meaning, represents the respective intimate appearance. The system is sex representational.

The system needs to be sex representational because the false belief in the naked body establishes the priority of intimate over proper appearance. Intimate appearance, rather than proper appearance, now takes the priority in determinations of moral sex. This, in turn, yields something of a conundrum. On the one hand, morphological information is concealed, and the express discussion of an individual's genitalia is constituted as boundary violating. On the other hand, this morally saturated morphology grounds further information that is ever socially salient since we need to know which boundaries to observe and how to observe them and which boundaries to traverse and how to traverse them. Jumping ahead now seems required, and the consequence is a system that facilitates the communication of such information in violation of the very boundaries it lays down. To put it differently, the intimate meaning of proper appearance both requires that information be hidden while simultaneously serving as the vehicle by which that information is provided.

The sex-representational character of this system is hidden. It is hidden, in the first instance, through mass compliance. As proper appearance is taken as the effect of concealing a naked body and intimate appearance is taken as the effect of revealing one, the alignment between the two allows smooth movement from proper to intimate—from concealed to revealed—as if the naked body were there the whole time, thereby hiding the fact that there is no such naked body and that the smooth movement from one to the other is the effect of compliant truth-telling. In this way, the very characterization of men and women as possessing naked bodies is predicated on abuse and the mystification of that abuse. Indeed, the very coherence of one's interpersonal identity—and therefore one's self-identity—depends upon a hidden abuse through compliant truth-telling.

Of course, since misalignment remains a social possibility, total compliance is never guaranteed. And in case even one individual misaligns proper and intimate appearance, the illusion of the concealed/revealed naked body will be shattered since the naked body concealed is now not the naked body revealed and, so, the unity of the naked body is broken. There needs to be a further mechanism that obscures this possibility. And that mechanism is the social phenomenon of gender make-believe.

Gender Make-Believe

I begin by noting that when practices are social, the line between the practice itself and the ersatz engagement in the practice is likewise social. For instance, there's a difference between playing chess and pretending to play chess, even though both are social endeavors. In these cases, the line between social reality and social make-believe is socially determined and, as such, is contingent and subject to alteration. There are also social phenomena that pass themselves off as natural. As we've seen, for instance, the social phenomenon of nakedness is falsely taken as precultural. In this case, the character of the pretense may likewise be hidden.

The specific claim I want to pursue is that the naturalization of nakedness obfuscates the true character of gender make-believe and that the phenomenon of gender make-believe itself participates in this naturalization—another ruse of the system. Because of this, the purpose of the true character is obscured. The true character, as I said, is to provide a mechanism by which the illusion of the naked body is maintained even in cases of failed compliance with the communicative mandate.

To understand how gender make-believe operates in detail, we need to understand how pretense is constituted in the folk system, as well as how it is falsely represented. Let's start with the latter. As women and men are taken to possess naked bodies that exist prior to culture—naked bodies that can either exist underneath clothing or without—to pretend to be a man or a woman is to pretend that one has this naked body either underneath clothing or without. In this way, the use of clothing allows one to imitate the supposed other sex. Under this illusion, the pretense appears analogous to that of the person who dresses up like a gorilla. One copies the natural appearance of a gorilla and, through this, generates the misleading impression that one is a gorilla. The gorilla, by contrast, can't be likewise said to do anything at all. He just *is*.

As we know, however, this analogy rests on an illusion. First, while the gorilla might be said to have some natural appearance, this is untrue with respect to people. Neither appearance is natural. Furthermore, naked bodies can have neither proper nor intimate appearances since naked bodies don't exist.

What really happens is this: insofar as women and men are interpersonal objects, playing along involves behaving in boundary-regulated ways (e.g., boundary observation). Since boundaries are reflexively instituted through gestures, there's a sense in which both real and pretend boundaries involve "acting as if." What makes the former real, however, is their integration within a system of pathways within which they're holistically determined. By contrast, what makes a boundary mere make-believe is that any stretch of gestures within which it is immanent are disconnected from the full system of pathways. That is, playing along involves acting as if certain boundaries existed where these boundaries are disconnected from the usual pathways of the network.

The disconnection is accomplished through the following mechanism: one intimate meaning is replaced by another. The female proper appearance, say, is now understood as the effect of concealing a male moral body rather than a female one. Through this change in intimate meaning, clothing becomes a disguise. Of course, a male moral body is no more "under the female clothes" than a female moral body is. Such entities do not exist.

Because the standard intimate meaning must be replaced with an alternative one, it becomes imperative to signal and thereby effect this replacement. One must therefore disclose the pretense at the outset. This disclosure needn't be overt or explicit. There simply needs to be a communication (or foreknowledge) enabling rerouting to a different intimate meaning. This effectively requires the disclosure of intimate appearance, either implicitly or explicitly, in a way that is highlighted rather than hidden in the system. It yields a structural asymmetry in vulnerability from which the trans person has no redress. For even if they refuse the question (e.g., "Have you had the surgery or not?"), their intimate appearance remains asymmetrically—inappropriately—ideationally salient to all in that social situation.

In light of this, the possibility of misalignment—deception— with which we began is now eliminated. Instead, deception merely involves the failure to disclose that one is engaged in make-believe. That is, it consists in failing to disclose private information in advance. This is a mystification of what deception involves, however. What enables the deception is the fact that female proper appearance has a specific intimate meaning allocated to it—a specific intimate meaning that picks out a specific intimate appearance in just the way that a term has a meaning that picks out a referent. The fact that the trans individual has not declared intimate appearance to facilitate a change of intimate meaning matters only subsequently in case of exposure. That is, the trans person is retroactively regarded as failing to disclose the pretense—one intimate meaning replaced by the other and the previously integrated intimacies disconnected from the system—to preserve the illusion of the naked body and to hide the sex-representational character of the system.

Intimate Meaning

Let me conclude the account by turning to the calamities of intimacy. To do so, let's discuss the alternative intimate meaning. While the alternative meaning is used to disconnect trans people from the networks of intimacy, it also simultaneously provides mythological justifications for the system's boundaries. That is, it perpetuates the mythology already found in the original intimate meaning. For instance, in the calamity of trans women entering into intimate spaces designated for moral females, the new intimate meaning is used to justify the exclusion of trans women (male body underneath the clothes), thereby disconnecting any initially observed boundaries from the usual pathways, while at the same time justifying the sex segregation in the first place (females vulnerable to males in intimate contexts).

This gives us a clear picture of how the disconnection works. As pretense operates in the standard domain, there's no reason at all for the intimate meanings to surface. Consequently, it might appear that boundaries are being observed in keeping with the proper appearance at play. At first, proper appearance is in singular mode, blended. However, in taking the pretense too far—using a certain restroom, say—the alternative intimate meaning will invariably emerge as a sort of warning via intimate cognition, so that in composite mode what pops into relief isn't the usual female body under female clothes but, rather, a male body under female clothes.

Crucially, the point of citing the calamity isn't to protect females at all. Rather, it is to constitute females as ever in need of protection. In this case, the constitution of females as ever in need of protection is accomplished precisely through the relegation of trans women to make-believe—a relegation necessary to the preservation of the system (i.e., making sure that the representational character of the system remains hidden).

That the appeal to protecting females has nothing to do with actually protecting females is made plain by the way defenders of policies and bathroom laws seem to forget about the logistic consequences that would arise from counting trans men as female and requiring them to use female-designated spaces.[15] One can only imagine the chaos created by the presence of these men in women's public restrooms, change rooms, and housing facilities—men whose material intimate appearances will have been significantly informed by androgenization and possibly surgical alteration. Add to this the real possibility that some may decide to protest institutionalized reality enforcement within the space itself.[16] One wonders how it would work.[17] This is never considered, of course. Or if it is, it's considered dismissively and unrealistically. What it shows is that the justification for excluding trans women has nothing to do with actually protecting (nontrans) women. It has, rather, to do with simultaneously constituting moral females as vulnerable and preserving the system through the phenomenon of make-believe.

Consider, further, the lengths to which the trans-excluders will go—the shocking claims that these justifications include. For instance, in my experience working to change the Los Angeles Police Department's policies to ensure better treatment of trans people, breathtaking scenarios came into play. With respect to housing, for instance, constituents voiced concerns that trans woman—viewed as "really men"—would attempt to gain intimate visual access to (nontrans) women (i.e., "peek") and even the bizarre fear that trans women would commit indecency offenses against nontrans women by exposing themselves by waving their penises at them.[18]

There were even more ridiculous concerns about our proposed procedure in invasive searches. We wanted to let the individual trans person determine the sex of the officer doing the searching, since how trans people understand our intimate appearances is so complex. Fantasies of trans women overpowering (nontrans) women police officers and raping them grew in the telling. Sudden concerns about how women officers would feel about searching trans women eclipsed any notion that they might be trained professionals. Meanwhile, that monster called "litigation" lurked in the background.

The point is this: while the empirically verifiable falsity of such allegations against trans women has been noted, not enough attention has been paid to the extreme hyperbole involved. In light of the fact that these claims have nothing to do with protecting (nontrans) women, we have to recognize that these claims about supposed biological sex and the allegedly likely egregious behavior of trans women (a.k.a. "men") actually have nothing to do with biological sex and everything to do with moral sex—indeed, everything to do with constituting moral sex.

Unsurprisingly, investigation into the calamity of having sex with "the wrong sex" yields similar results. Specifically, the cited justification is used to rationalize the disconnection of previous boundaries from the rest of the network while perpetuating the mythological content of the system. In this case, the mythological content is the capacity of the female "naked body" to incite sexual desire.

Just as before, in nonintimate contexts, the trans woman's proper appearance will remain blended—this time, until suggestions of sexual intimacy arise. Once that happens, the intimate cognition will bring the alternative meaning to the fore, and the trans woman will, in this composite presentation, be cognized as a male disguised as a woman. She will then be rendered ineligible for prospects of sexual intimacy, disconnected from the usual pathways. Of course, in case somebody wants to maintain their sense of self as a good person, this new intimate meaning may never come to the surface precisely through avoiding any circumstances in which an intimate cognition might become socially salient. Even here, however, the make-believe has been instituted. After all, the foreclosure of any intimate cognition isn't due to a vigilant boundary observation. The impossibility of there ever being movement—the foreclosure of intimacy altogether—belies the so-called acceptance of the trans person.

At any rate, whereas the exclusion of trans women from sex-segregated spaces in the previous case has nothing to do with actually protecting nontrans women from violation, the exclusion of trans women from straight sexuality in this case has nothing to do with eroticism. After all, many trans women are indistinguishable from nontrans women, in which case it's unsurprising a straight nontrans man might be attracted to her (and, in any event, a blow job is a blow job). This is just to say that the erotic phenomenologies involved in having sex with a trans woman and a nontrans woman will be similar, if not identical (as is well elucidated by my theoretical understanding of straight, nontrans male sexual desire as the eroticization of movement down a particular strip).

The point is brought into plain relief by the phenomenon of trans women as dirty little secrets. First, that a trans woman can function as a supposed replacement in the first place makes the case about straight male (nontrans) eroticism. Second, his keeping her a secret has everything to do with what others will think and nothing to do with the eroticism itself. The secret that is kept—that he is supposedly bi or even gay—does nothing more than perpetuate the myth of the naked body as the source of sexual desire in the first place. It does so, of course, by simultaneously disconnecting the trans woman from the full network of pathways—in this case, the heterorelational complex—thereby relegating her to make-believe.

Here, the relegation to make-believe is more dramatic, because far more has occurred than the simple boundary observation one finds in the public realm. To put it differently, in the cases we've examined thus far, the justifications have been used to prevent movement from standard configurations to intimate ones. In this case, we begin in intimate configurations while the justifications prevent movement into the public, and, of course, in the intimate realm, plenty occurs besides boundary observation. Intimate gestures—attention, self-display—and therefore boundary traversals abound. By disconnecting these intimate negotiations from the heterorelational complex, the intimate movements are relegated to a form of deviant sexual role-play in which the trans person is merely pretending to be female. That is, the gestures are relegated to "as-if" behavior in contrast to the real thing. Through the ruse of the system, of course, the trans person is represented as imitating a woman. But in reality, nothing more has occurred than the disconnection of the intimate movement from the usual pathways.

Foreclosure

Let me conclude by pointing out that, in truth, reduction to make-believe through disconnection from the rest of the pathways occurs before the actual exclusion itself has occurred. That is, once the new intimate meaning has surfaced as an intimate cognition or a public recognition, it is already too late precisely since there's already been an alternative movement of intimacy.

The fact that trans disconnection occurs not because the cited justification is heeded but, rather, through the very emergence of the justification in the first place brings to the surface the way in which infraintimate attempts at recoding are both enabled and foreclosed. Let me explain.

As C. Jacob Hale and Julia Serano both discuss, for at least some trans people, specific body parts are open to reinterpretation in the erotic arena, and these **intimate recoding practices** can alleviate or even

eliminate negative phoria and can also yield positive phoria.[19] There
are many ways this can be accomplished, and I'll just mention a few.
First, through straightforward resignification, a penis can become a
clit and an anus can become a vagina. As Hale points out, in some
communities (e.g., leather), what's called a vagina in mainstream
culture can be reconfigured as a "boyhole" or "fuckhole." Second,
through incorporation, an inanimate thing (e.g., a dildo) can "take
on some of the phenomenological characteristics of erogenous body
parts."[20] Third, through elimination, a body part can be "written out"
of existence through excluding certain forms of sexual interaction
from the repertoire or through variant forms of the sexual interaction.

It is important to understand that the intimate activities facilitating the recoding are not role-play. Rather, they are generative in
character. They are forms of the complex intimacy (introduced in
chapter 3) whereby new pathways and boundaries are created. What
allows for this possibility is the existence of the infraintimate (also
introduced in chapter 3). Acts of intimacy are themselves subject to
boundaries on access—that is, they are intimate in ways that exceed
individual privacy. What occurs in an intimate context, for example,
is itself subject to boundaries. And in this case, intimate content can
be cocreated by interactive partners where this content itself can be
subject to infraintimate boundaries on access by any others. That is,
the intimate meaning by which the intimate intelligibility of these
activities is foreclosed is precisely that which provides the intimate
cover under which the gestures can become binding and therefore
generative.

Beyond the Beyond-the-Binary Paradigm

Having developed my account of the phenomena of gender make-
believe in terms of the physical person, I want to show the inadequacy
of the beyond-the-binary paradigm in explaining reality enforcement
by considering the theories of Harold Garfinkel and Judith Butler. I'll
also show, by contrast, how my own account can elucidate oppression
through the binary in new and informative ways.

While I've spoken of the beyond-the-binary account as if it were
one view, the truth is there are many variations of this basic idea.
There are two important ones that I characterize now, and both these

theorists—Garfinkel and Butler—capture the spirit of one of them in arguably the deepest, most insightful of ways. The first focuses on the strict regulations of sex (or gender) whereby those in the middle are forced out and movement from one gender to another is ruled out by appeal to the normative notion of the "natural." The second says that there are more than two sexes or genders and that the delegitimization of these other genders is an effect of the way in which the two are set up as "natural" and "original."

HAROLD GARFINKEL

We begin with the groundbreaking work of ethnomethodologist Harold Garfinkel and, in particular, his notion of sex as a culturally conferred status. His theories played an important role in that of other ethnomethodologists, such as Suzanne J. Kessler, Wendy McKenna, Candace West, and Don H. Zimmerman, and, further, this entire ethnomethodological approach to sex and gender has played an important role in trans theory.[21] As such, Garfinkel's notion of the natural attitude about sex is particularly useful in formulating the strict binary attitude that is supposed to inform trans oppression. By showing how my account can capture Garfinkel's basic notion of the natural attitude, while also pointing to some of the difficulties with Garfinkel's own account of it, I hope to show the inadequacy of an appeal to the binary in accommodating reality enforcement.

The ethnomethodological approach was pioneered in Garfinkel's case study of "Agnes," a transsexual woman who, in 1958, presented herself to the Department of Psychiatry at UCLA as a (nontrans) woman with intersex traits.[22] Garfinkel highlights the work that Agnes did, with the help of others, in positing herself as "naturally female." He uses this "breaching" (disruption of the social order) to answer the guiding ethnomethodological question, succinctly formulated by Kessler and McKenna:

> What are the methodological ways by which members of a group produce, in each particular situation, this sense of external, constant, objective facts which have their own independent existences, not contingent on any concrete interaction?[23]

Garfinkel draws on the ideas of the phenomenologist Edmund Husserl, according to whom there exists a pretheoretical, common-sense view that posits a natural world existing independently of our minds ("the natural attitude").[24] Like Husserl's phenomenology, Garfinkel's ethnomethodology proceeds by "bracketing" this attitude. In his study, he brackets what he dubs "the natural attitude *about sex*"—an attitude maintained by "normals" who "are able to take their own normally sexed status for granted."[25]

For Garfinkel, the natural attitude about sex is distinctively moral in a broad sense. From the perspective of these "normals," "the population of normal persons is a *morally* dichotomized population." That is, they see it as "populated with natural males, natural females, and persons who stand in *moral* contrast with them, i.e., incompetent, criminal, sick, and sinful."[26] In identifying this attitude as moral, Garfinkel means to capture several things: namely, cultural mores, morality as an ethical notion of right and wrong (the criminals and the sinners), and *natural* as a normative/evaluative expression, roughly synonymous with *proper* or *meant to be that way*.

According to this attitude, every person is either male or female (sex status is exhaustive), no person is both male and female (sex statuses are mutually exclusive), changes in sex cannot occur (sex status is invariant), and, since all of the above is "natural," any exceptions to these rules are to be dismissed as aberrant.[27] These beliefs—the commitment to natural exhaustiveness, exclusivity, and invariance of sex—characterize what trans politics will come to recognize as "the binary" (or at least a version of it). So, as Garfinkel is interested in exposing it as a sociomoral, rather than natural, affair, his project is congenial to that of trans politics.

Crucially, Garfinkel also appears to recognize something like the phenomenon of gender make-believe. Specifically, he recognizes transfers that are "ceremonially permitted" in the natural attitude. He notes such transfers are "accompanied by the well-known controls":

> Our society prohibits willful or random movements from one sex status to the other. It insists that such transfers be accompanied by the well-known controls that accompany masquerading, play-acting, party behavior, convention behavior, spying and the like. Such changes are treated both by those making the changes as well as those observing them in others as

limited both by the clock as well as by occasions and practical circumstances. The person is expected "after the play" to "stop acting." On the way home from the party the person may be reminded that the party "is over," and that he should conduct himself like the person he "really is."[28]

Obviously, an appeal to either exhaustiveness or exclusiveness (or both) cannot do any work in explaining the phenomenon of the ceremonial transfer.[29] Instead, for Garfinkel, the ceremonial character of these "transfers" is a consequence of the invariance of sex. Notably, he places considerable stress on invariance in his account. He writes: "The dichotomy provides for persons who are 'naturally,' 'originally,' 'in the first place,' 'in the beginning,' 'all along,' and 'forever' one or the other."[30] They "are essentially, originally, in the first place, always have been, and always will be, once and for all, in the final analysis, either 'male' or 'female.'"[31] Further, Garfinkel is fairly clear that much, for him, depends upon the time-limited character of these transfers. These limitations "mark" the social context as exceptional and disconnect it from the normal course of daily life. As "ceremonial," such situations are "special occasions."

However, Garfinkel's appeal to time limitation simply misses the mark in explaining the phenomenon of gender pretense. First, it's not as though one is allowed, during this time-limited transfer, to actually change one's sex status, as he appears to suggest. We can imagine cultures in which genuine transfers are countenanced for limited occasions. Even within the ceremonial context, however, it's well recognized that what's occurring is nothing more than pretense. So how is it—indeed, what is it—for the transfer to be constituted as "mere pretense" given that the time limitation is itself insufficient? Second, as trans people perpetually presented as make-believers know all too well, one can live an entire life relegated to pretense. That is, regardless of whether one "abides by the clock," one is constituted as pretense—the time limitation seems inert.

Further, there's an oddity in how Garfinkel regards the ceremonial transfer in the first place. For Garfinkel, genitalia are, in the natural attitude, the essential insignia of sex status. They are, Garfinkel says, "essential in their identifying function."[32] They are what usually qualify a person as possessing one sex status or the other. One wonders, then, how this ceremonial transfer is brought about. Or, rather, we know it occurs through a change in public gender presentation (proper appearance). But we are left wondering what lipstick and heels have to do with vaginas.

In my account, the answer is plain. Because proper appearance means intimate appearance (where genitalia are the telos of the latter), a change in the former can signify a change in the latter. And, of course, as I've shown, gender make-believe is made possible through the disconnection of certain as-if behavior and appearance from the pathways of the network. That is, gender pretense is constituted not through time limitation but through a form of disconnection in interpersonal space.

While Garfinkel's notion of the natural attitude cannot account for gender make-believe, my notion of the physical person can account for the natural attitude. In my view, the natural attitude about sex is an effect of—or, perhaps more correctly, a part of—the organized practices of interpersonal spatiality in the folk system. Rather than regard sex as a status that is conferred upon the person, in this view, folk personhood is already differentiated into males and females. There is no "sex-neutral" person upon which we confer a status. Rather, our access to folk people (interpersonal objects) is already bifurcated by a difference in cues, boundaries, strips, and gestures. Both the exhaustiveness and the exclusiveness of sex are accounted for by the naturalization of nakedness. One ends up with two structures of nakedness falsely projected onto bodies—where these structures are taken to exist independently of the cultural. Anybody that does not conform, by having no structure, a different structure, or an in-between structure, will be regarded as aberrant—as failing to conform to "nature."

The invariance of sex can be explained similarly, although it requires a bit more discussion. Garfinkel distinguishes the possession of a penis or a vagina as a cultural-moral event from the biological one: it's with respect to the former that genitalia function as essential insignia.[33] One of the things this means, for Garfinkel, is that should a male person lose his physical genitals in an accident, a "normal" would still speak of the penis "to which he was entitled" (i.e., meant to have).

While Garfinkel doesn't use it, the expression *moral genitalia* captures what he has in mind. In the natural attitude, what's taken as invariant isn't actually one's **material genitalia** but one's moral genitalia. Typically, moral and material genitalia coincide. The latter instantiates the former; material genitalia are material-genitalia-in-the-moral-order. But the two can also come apart. For example, a (nontrans) man may have his material genitals amputated due to a war injury. And sometimes, through surgery, new physical genitals may be constructed that instantiates the moral ones. Garfinkel writes, "The legitimately possessed vagina is the object of interest. *It is the vagina the person is entitled to.* Although 'nature' is a preferred and *bona-fide* source of entitlement, surgeons are as well if they repair a natural error, i.e., if they serve as nature's agents to provide 'what was meant to be there.'"[34]

The projection of structured nakedness onto bodies is again illuminating. Sex-differentiated forms of nakedness outstrip genitalia: A person's moral genitalia are given by the more comprehensive intimate appearance attributed to them. This marked cultural appearance is then treated as the true presentation of the precultural moral body, the body that is naked under the clothes, the body that is nothing but the alignment between projected intimate appearance and disclosed intimate appearance. As intimate appearance is taken as prior to culture as the moral body, the structurally determined genitalia of the attributed intimate appearance becomes the genitalia that were meant to be there, "intended by nature" insofar as this culturally constituted appearance is posited outside of culture, as some natural state. That is, a certain genital is a structural feature of that form of intimate appearance that is then "naturalized." While the man who has lost his penis lacks the material genitalia, he still has a moral penis insofar as a male *form of nakedness* is attributed to him that includes a penis, as a structural feature, within that form of nakedness. This explains why, even when it's publicly recognized that one has had reconstructive surgery on their appearance (i.e., one's material genitalia), one can still be subject to reality enforcement—namely, proper appearance represents moral genitalia, not material genitalia, although they typically align.[35]

An additional beneficial feature of my account is that we can recognize how the naturalization of moral genitalia is bound up with a sense of *moral* oddly not discussed by Garfinkel at all: genitals are "private parts." After all, how can we seriously consider the role of penises and vaginas within a moral order without considering their status as private, one wonders? The essence of my account is precisely that conferred sex is determined through this moral dimension. Additionally, the constitution of genitalia (as well as other parts of the body) as private affords the possibility of specific privacy and decency violations committed by normals themselves—a possibility that Garfinkel himself does not recognize.

This helps shed light on phenomena that, while distinct from reality enforcement, share important similarities. First, consider, nonconsensual surgeries performed on intersex infants. Genital surgeries, in my view, bring material sex into alignment with moral sex. To put it differently, individuals whose bodies do not conform to the two nakedness structures of the system will be made to fit that system. Crucially, given the nonconsensual nature of surgery on intersex infants, one could argue that this is not only a violation but a kind of *sexual* violation, or at least a violation of the intimate appearance. This underwrites claims from some intersex people themselves.[36] For instance, Sharon E. Preves cites one woman as saying, "I was forced to be surgically mutilated and medically raped at the age of fourteen."[37] And it highlights the degree to which intersex children may find themselves subject to abusive genital scrutiny. Cheryl Chase writes: "Intersex patients have frequently been subjected to repeated genital examinations, which create a feeling of freakishness and unacceptableness."[38] And the infamous Money protocols can be viewed as securing the alignment between proper and intimate appearance, thereby ensuring that genitals are ever communicated through public gender presentation.[39] Why else would genital surgery be necessary? Moving through the social world—particularly as a child—requires only proper appearance.

Second, consider somebody who presents in ways that may be construed as "inconsistent," "androgynous," "gender-blended," or "incomprehensible." In such cases, it may not be clear from the presentation just what the person is, and we can easily imagine such a person being abusively called an "it"—a form of misgendering and, in this case, also an explicit denial of folk personhood. Unsurprisingly, this relegation to "it" coincides with a disconnection from the pathways of intimacy and with the constitution as utterly asexual. Meanwhile, they'll still be subject to scrutiny to determine "what's between their legs." However, rather than being regarded as a deceiver or make-believer, they'll be regarded as failing to disclose any genital status at all.

The point is this: while an appeal to the gender binary (exhaustiveness, exclusiveness, invariance) does not explain the relegation of trans people to make-believe, the underlying theory that I've used to explain this relegation can also explain cases in which individuals have indeed been harmed by the binary. More than that, it illuminates the way in which this harm can be sexually abusive and, further, how it is related to the harm of reality enforcement. That is, it allows for a comprehensive account that can show the differences, similarities, and underlying causes of various forms of oppression and abuse.

JUDITH BUTLER

I conclude by considering Butler's groundbreaking work on gender in the early nineties—work that set the foundations for nascent queer theory and, with that, served as a touchstone for much of early trans studies (although the relationship between the two was complicated).[40]

Part of Butler's brilliance is to afford a broader view of gender oppression and resistance that exceeds a traditional feminist purview. Drag, says Butler, needn't involve gay men mocking women (as a lesbian separatist might have it) but, rather, may constitute a way of making fun of heterosexuality.[41] Butch–femme relationships, says Butler, needn't be replications of patriarchal arrangements but, rather, may constitute forms of relationality that subvert heteronormativity.[42] What gets left out by fusing lesbianism with feminism, shows Butler, is the fact that there are forms of gender oppression that do not reduce to sexism.[43] By looking at gender through a "queer eye," Butler brings this fact into focus.

Imitation, for Butler, is the central concept. Butler claims that imitation is at the heart of all gender behavior—straight, queer, or otherwise.[44] While straight gender behavior is imitative behavior that conceals this fact, setting itself as the original, queer gender behavior can expose this fiction of originality by deliberately enacting an enactment. (Here, the early films of John Waters, such as *Female Trouble,* are excellent examples of what Butler has in mind.) In this way, queerness can expose and therefore subvert the imitative character of the heterosexual project.

One crucial consequence of this is that there can be a multiplicity of gendered behavior—most of which deviates from the norm. Rather than two forms of gendered behavior that arise from two gendered beings, argues Butler, there's a plethora of gendered behaviors that don't involve the traditional alignment of desire, behavior, and sex, yielding a proliferation of genders.[45] The source of the problem in this view, then, is that some genders create the fiction of their own originality, setting themselves apart from the others. To participate in that fiction is to perpetuate, rather than subvert, hegemonic forms of gender.

Alas, this account leads to unhappy consequences for those trans folks who take themselves to be "real." There's a difference, after all, between the campiness of drag, its capacity to pillory the delusions of heterosexual enactments of gender, and the earnestness of a trans woman in her being born a woman. The latter, in this view, must be regarded as delusional in just the way that heterosexuality is. What does one say to the trans person who takes their gender so seriously? They seem like a reactionary dupe.

Something has gone wrong, since any account in which it turns out that a trans person trying to affirm their self-identity in a world that denies it to them is somehow reactionary or self-deluded cannot be accepted as an adequate representation of trans oppression and resistance. We need a different account that illuminates the resistance. And to do that, we need an account that illuminates the oppression. So, while I understand why Francisco J. Galarte writes of Gwen Araujo, "Performing racialized trans femininity and Latina excess in the pursuit of 'realness' does not yield forms of being and action that are easily incorporable to narratives of 'subversion and reinscription of norms,' yet her death enabled the work of LGBTQ activists to become valuable," I feel compelled to add that we *need* different narratives—narratives that illuminate trans resistance in all its forms.[46]

Unsurprisingly, at the time of Butler's ascendance, there were several trans theoretical critiques of Butler's account—most of which involved rejecting their heavily social-constructionist position.[47] None of these, however, did what really needed to be done—namely,

broaden our view of gender yet again so that it encompassed, in this
case, *trans* oppression.[48] That is, what was needed was to look at gender through a *trans* eye. Let's do so now. We begin with the following
quote from Butler:

> Here is something like a confession which is meant merely to
> thematize the impossibility of confession: As a young person,
> I suffered for a long time, and I suspect many people have,
> from being told, explicitly or implicitly, that what I "am" is a
> copy, an imitation, a derivative example, a shadow of the real.[49]

Butler responds to the charge that gays and lesbians are viewed as
"copying" heterosexuality, which sets itself as the original. A butch–
femme relationship, for example, might be viewed as aping heterosexuality. For Butler, then, relegation to copy is very much at the
heart of queer oppression.

However, there's a difference between the charge of imitation and
the charge of deception or pretense. While butch masculinity may be
taken as a copy of the supposedly natural masculinity of men, it's not
necessarily taken as pretending to be "the real thing." Butches aren't
necessarily viewed as trying to fool anybody or as playing dress-up.
They're judged, rather, as *like* men—as secondary, perhaps pathological, duplications of an original.

To be sure, one can use imitation to deceive or pretend. But it
needn't be used that way. The account that Butler provides focuses
on imitation but does not concern itself with or even notice the other.
Yet it's just this relegation to make-believe, rather than to copy, that
reveals the resistance of a trans individual in their claims to be real.

To understand the relegation of trans people to deceivers and
make-believers, we need different tools—tools I have provided in this
essay. Instead of the notion of imitation, we need the notions of representation and disconnection. The former allows us to understand
the charge of deception—deception that occurs against the backdrop
of an abusive truth-telling that perpetuates the fiction of the naked
body. The latter allows us to understand trans relegation to pretense
through the disconnection of as-if behavior from the networks of
intimacy.

This latter is particularly important as an intervention in Butler's
view. Specifically, to effectively say, as Butler does, that all gender is

as-if behavior (i.e., performative) is to miss the fact that some as-if behavior lacks integration within the networks of interpersonal spatiality—a lack that cannot be removed through mere repetition or imitation.[50] While the nonintegrated as-if behavior certainly has the capacity to create a social pretense, it cannot contribute to the constitution of social reality without this integration. In light of this, we can see how Butler's response to the charge of queer imitation—namely, it's all imitation—obscures what's going on in the case of reality enforcement. Recall, after all, that trans pretense is, in the folk system, likewise regarded as an attempt to imitate, and this move obscures the true character of gender make-believe.

To press my examination of Butler's queer theory through a "trans eye," let's turn to the film *Paris Is Burning* and the theoretical and political discussions that emerged shortly after its release. Partially in response to bell hooks's critique of both New York's Ballroom scene of the eighties and Jennie Livingston's directorial choices, Butler reads the film through a queer lens, drawing on and developing their own theory.[51] Here, Butler is keen to acknowledge that not all drag is subversive. Indeed, some serves the purposes of heterosexuality itself. The practices of the Ballroom scene, argues Butler, exemplify what they call "ambivalent drag."[52] They write, "In these senses, then, *Paris Is Burning* documents neither an efficacious insurrection nor a painful resubordination, but an unstable coexistence of both."[53]

One of the key people who is taken to exemplify this ambivalence is Venus Xtravaganza—a transsexual woman who is ultimately killed, presumably by a client. It becomes immediately clear (to any trans person) that, unfortunately, Butler lacks the resources for elucidating the oppression that Xtravaganza faced. Indeed, Butler offers two different accounts—neither are adequate. The first is an appeal to homophobia.[54] The second is the claim that Xtravaganza was treated "in the ways in which women of color are treated."[55] Let's discuss both in order.

On the surface, the first seems right. The client, upon subsequently discovering Xtravaganza's "little secret," would have regarded her as a man and then experienced horror and anger because he had, unbeknownst to him, engaged in homosexual sex. That's homophobia. Or, contrariwise, we might suppose that he knew about her "little secret" and, upon finishing the erotic experience, came to face the fact that "she was really a man" and, again, experienced these intense feelings of horror and rage.

What isn't explained, however, is the basis for her misgendering and, of course, the reality enforcement that sustains it. My account explains this. Not only have I already provided a rich account of trans sex work and reality enforcement in chapter 1, in light of my account of gender pretense in this current chapter, more details emerge. First, we now know that this misgendering and simultaneous reduction to pretense are made possible through the replacement of one intimate meaning with another so as to maintain the myth of the naked body by obscuring the sex-representational character of the system. Second, this misgendering is specifically crucial to maintaining the myth that the precultural naked body is the source of sexual desire. This means that when the client fears that he experienced homosexual desire, the fear arises not only as a consequence of the misgendering but also via the myth of the naked body as the attractive source.

Note, also, that the same can be said of the other calamity. Venus Xtravaganza, if arrested, would have been excluded from female-segregated space and subject to an abuse specific to trans women, and, furthermore, no programs and shelters for women would have enabled her right of exit. The replacement of the one intimate meaning with another to secure the illusion of nakedness under clothes would have served the important antifeminist function of perpetuating the view that (nontrans) women are—even without culture—perpetually vulnerable to violation.

Let's turn now quickly (as it has been discussed by others) to Butler's other claim that Xtravaganza was ultimately treated in the way that women of color are treated.[56] Obviously, this ignores the fact that the conditions for her murder involved her being regarded as a man (of color) pretending to be a woman. However, I also suspect that this, for Butler, is more of a metaphoric claim operating in tandem with their earlier claim that Xtravaganza seeks transcendence from the conditions of race and class *through* gender.[57] The point of their claim about Xtravaganza being treated like women is to illustrate how the system prevents precisely that transcendence.

Of course, Butler's claim that, for Xtravaganza, gender merely served as a vehicle of transcendence involves eliminating what were for Venus Xtravaganza gender phoric experiences. And this is largely why other critiques accuse Butler of using Venus Xtravaganza as a discursive lever in their theoretical project—in this case, to show not only that race and class are interblended with gender but also that the former are the primary forces for Xtravaganza.[58]

What I shall add is that obviously Xtravaganza's experiences of phoria were interblended with racial experiences—as they are for all of us, whether we're conscious of it or not—and, further, obviously the conditions for her homicide were likewise a function of the integration. As I've said, I'll soon be expanding the mythology of nakedness to reveal its inherently racialized character. Specifically, we will see how both the myth of precultural female violation (violation of the naked body) and the myth of the naked body as attractive are actually part of a larger racist mythology.

At present the crucial point is simply this: Butler wrongly conflates the "realness" sought by Xtravaganza with the "realness" that rules the Ballroom scene. Realness, according to Butler, is achieved through a project of imitation in approximation of the ideal in which a "read" is not possible.[59] And in their view, while the Ballroom participants seek to *do realness,* Venus Xtravaganza seeks to *be real.* So, while the former involves exposing the imitative character of the ideal itself, the latter takes realness "too seriously" and "can culminate only in disappointment and disidentification."[60]

However, once we see the situation through a trans eye, we see that Xtravaganza is not even pursuing Butler's realness in the first place—seriously or otherwise. We understand that Xtravaganza is pursuing an escape from the relegation to fiction, as many of us trans people do. She is seeking integration within the networks of interpersonal spatiality. She is thereby engaged in a resistant project in opposition to the abusive sex-representational folk system. To be sure, her project is also politically problematic in many ways. But so are many resistant projects, as white feminism repeatedly demonstrates. (I'll return to this theme of resistance in chapter 6.)

At present, I want to state the moral of the story: the proliferation of genders is utterly unhelpful so long as it fails to contribute to the real possibility of intimacy and distance. To put it differently, by itself, the project of the proliferation is doomed to fail because it ignores the way in which both social make-believe and social reality can be created performatively. The mechanisms by which the distinction between gender make-believe and gender reality is determined involve more than as-if behavior. And the appeal to the way heteronormative genders posit themselves as the original cannot elucidate how this distinction is determined socially. Consequently, if the beyond-the-binary account is predicated on that appeal, it is inadequate as an account of trans oppression—in this case, the relegation of trans people to gender make-believe. Furthermore, if our conception of trans resistance is predicated on this idea of mere gender proliferation, it is inadequate as a form of resistance. What we need, instead, are new forms of intimacy and distance that are not hostile to our existence.[61]

Chapter 5
The Phenomenology of Illusion

IN THE PREVIOUS CHAPTER, I explained the relegation of trans people to make-believe through my account of nakedness and physical personhood in the folk system. We turn now to the second goal—namely, to provide an account of trans gender phoria. In the first part, I argue in favor of my own account of gender phoria—the *interpersonal account*—and against what I call the "*incongruence account*," an account that serves as the basis of the wrong-body model. In the second part, I take up the phenomenon of pretransition self-recognition, and I use the interpersonal account to explain it. Here, I place my account into affective dialogue with Gloria Anzaldúa's characterization of mirror experiences in *Borderlands/La Frontera*.

Crucially, to accomplish my account of self-recognition, I draw on my account of gender make-believe provided in chapter 4. This allows me to show how the phenomenon of self-recognition arises in resistant tension with trans oppression—specifically, reality enforcement. To put it differently, while self-recognition arises in a liminal, apparitional state, reality enforcement aims to reduce this state to the mere structural form of make-believe provided for the system. In this way, trans people—apparitionals—can find themselves somewhere between appearance and reality.

Preliminaries

The two main questions that shall concern us in this chapter are the following: First, how should we describe gender phoria in a theoretically illuminating way? (The phenomenological question.) Second, what causes it? (The explanatory question.) Not enough attention has been paid to the first question, in my view, and how one answers it has a significant bearing on what one will be able to say about the second question. One ought not jump to the latter without having something to say about the former. Indeed, there are clear problems with the second question—at least as commonly posed—that I shall turn to later in this chapter. Suffice it to say, at present, that answers to the latter typically involve appeals to innate features of the brain ("born that way"), socially learned behavior ("socially constructed that way"), or both.

A good answer to the phenomenological question depends upon descriptive accuracy and thoroughness in theoretically elucidating trans phoria through phenomenological and other philosophical concepts. Consider for example, Jay Prosser, who takes "the image of wrong embodiment" as the correct way to characterize the phenomenology of trans gender phoria. He contends:

> That transsexuals continue to deploy the image of wrong embodiment because being trapped in the wrong body is simply what transsexuality feels like. . . . The image of wrong embodiment describes most effectively the experience of pre-transition (dis) embodiment: the feeling of a sexed body dysphoria profoundly subjectively experienced.[1]

Whether this exact experience is had by all transsexuals and whether this experience is the only characteristic experience of transsexuality can be put to the side for now (as it does matter). What I want to draw attention to instead is the theoretical apparatus that Prosser puts into play to elucidate that experience—one that posits a misalignment between one's supposedly internal gendered sense of self and the external body. Prosser explains:

> For the transsexual the mirror initially reflects not-me: it distorts who I know myself to be.[2]

And:

> The difference between gender and sex is conveyed in the difference between body image (projected self) and the image of the body (reflected self).[3]

This is endorsed by other theorists as well. Gayle Salamon, while departing from Prosser in key respects, certainly agrees that the appeal to the psychoanalytic notion of a body ego is useful because it "shows the body of which one supposedly has a 'felt sense' is not necessarily contiguous with the physical body as it is perceived from the outside."⁴ She further writes, "Proprioception offers us as a way of reading and understanding the body beyond the visible surface of its exterior."⁵ Similarly, Henry S. Rubin writes: "The body image is more than just a map of the corporeal body as it is materially; it is a psychical representation of the body as it is for the subject. The body image need not correspond directly with the physical body."⁶

This account can be captured in terms of the following classic "before" and "after" transsexual mirror experience:

> Before: One looks into the mirror and experiences an incongruence between the visual body reflected in the mirror and one's own internal experience of the body (i.e., body-scheme, proprioceptive awareness, etc.).

> After: One looks into the mirror and there's no longer any incongruence. One's internal experience of oneself is reflected in the visual representation of oneself. As the incongruence between the two now gives way to a congruence, the gender discontent is alleviated. Behold, one is whole!

We may ask, however, whether the phenomenology has been adequately described theoretically by what I will call the "incongruence account."

Consider two other possibilities. First, what I'll call the *"aspirational account"* posits a sheer desire to become a woman or man. In this view, a trans woman doesn't believe or experience herself to be a woman prior to transition. Rather, she *wants* to be one, and transition satisfies that desire.⁷ In such a view, the experience of wrong embodiment would be described as the desire to have a different body.

Second, in what I'll call the *"affective account,"* for a trans woman to feel gender dysphoria is simply for her to "feel bad" as a man, and for her to feel gender euphoria is simply for her to "feel good" as a woman. The bad feeling isn't to be explained by appeal to the psychological experience of an incongruence or an unsatisfied desire, and the good feeling isn't to be explained by appeal to achieved congruence or satisfied desire. The bad and good feelings, rather, aren't explained in terms of a further phenomenological state at all. To be sure, more details about the exact nature of these feelings are required in such an account, but that is not the point for now. The point for now is that, in this view, wrong embodiment is described in terms of positive and negative valences of phoria without any appeal to an incongruence or primary desire.

In all three cases, we find the deployment of a theoretical model to elucidate the experiences of wrong embodiment. The issue then turns on which model, if any, captures these experiences. Aside from the adequacy of the theoretical resources in describing the experience itself, there is the question of how a theory illuminates different sorts of experiences and their relation to each other. To be sure, since trans people have different experiences, it's questionable to propose a monolithic account based on only one sort or set of experiences. However, a theory that provides resources for explaining different sorts of experiences and their relations to each other is a better theory than one that does not or that outright requires a different apparatus to explain different experiences.

In this chapter, then, I provide new theoretical resources for understanding trans phoria in a way that better enables the inclusion of all (or at least more) trans experiences. Methodologically, I draw on my own experiences and those of others with whom I have had deep discussions about gender phoria. I presume that while my experiences may be different from those of others, there are also important similarities.

My aim is to defend a very specific version of the affective account —one that involves interpersonal sentiments—modalities of awareness of oneself as an object. Further, my opposition to the incongruence account is a sustained one, crucial in understanding how my appeal to interpersonal spatiality contests key assumptions underlying the deployment of the modern concepts of *person, self,* and *subject* (as shall be developed in chapter 9). Because the aspirational account is of less importance to the overall aims of this essay, I submerge my treatment of it into the notes.

Against the Incongruence Account

CONSCIOUS GENDER IDENTITY AND EMBODIMENT

Let's begin with the most superficial rendition of the incongruence account that posits an incongruence between conscious gender identity and the sexed body. (I borrow the expression from Julia Serano.)[8]

As I shall define it, conscious gender identity is an aspect of what I introduced in chapter 2 as a self-conception. In this sort of view, to have a conscious gender identity is to conceive of oneself as a man or woman (or boy or girl) in the world. This, in turn, involves a conception of what both men and women are and, therefore, a conception of others as men and women. It is likewise to recognize a difference in the meaning and shape of a life course and the events within it (e.g., the importance of marriage, parenthood and its relationship to one's career or job) and, therefore, to understand one's own temporality as reflected in that life course.[9]

Now this appeal to conscious gender identity as a way of anchoring the incongruence account simply can't work, as it conflicts with trans experiences. For many of us, our experiences of phoria, at first, failed to show up in conscious identity at all. Instead, they existed at the periphery of our current life projects, future goals, and remembrances in ways that are roughly similar to the experience of gay or lesbian self-closeting.[10]

Thus, for many of us, our conscious gender identities had to change over time. "I did not have the quintessential trans experience of always feeling that I should have been female," says Julia Serano. "For me, this recognition came about more gradually."[11] And as Janet Mock explains, "I grew to be certain about who I was, but that doesn't mean there wasn't a time when I was learning the world, unsure, unstable, wobbly, living somewhere between confusion, discovery, and conviction."[12] We did not always know who and what we were—this was something we had to discover through struggle. Often this experience was a painful one.

It involved undoing one conscious gender identity and developing another. We were raised as boys or girls, told that we were either boys or girls. And we came to believe it. But it didn't work, and over a long and sometimes difficult process we had come to undo these beliefs, come to adopt new ones. Coming to adopt a new conscious gender identity helped alleviate gender unhappiness. Once we came to regard ourselves in a new way, we recognized that the conscious gender identity we'd held onto for so long had been keeping us down, making us unhappy. By embracing a new conscious gender identity, we came to feel better about ourselves.

If this is so, conscious gender identity can't be the anchor of transition since it's one of the things that was itself changed—a change that itself alleviated gender unhappiness. Of course, once a new self-conception is fully formed, external realities that invalidate that identity will be experienced with great discontent as they threaten one's very sense of who and what one is. But this is beside the point. If it turns out that conscious gender identity can be one of the things that we change to become happier, we need something else to serve as the "internal" incongruent of the incongruence account.[13] (One upshot is that the process of developing a new conscious self-identity then emerges as an important topic of analysis in its own right. Another upshot is that identity itself can be a locus of phoria, both positive and negative.)

A better version of the incongruence account—the one that principally concerns us—appeals to, rather than a conscious gender identity, a deep internal experience of one's body. We all have an internal sense of our body from the inside out. We know that we're standing without looking. We can experience our limbs and the rest of our bodies without looking. And sometimes this experience of body can disagree with the material facts of the matter. People have phantom limb experiences after losing those limbs; they experience the limbs as being there when they're not. People also fail to experience limbs as part of their body when they are; they can have bodily agnosia. If our internal maps of our bodies are maps that include the sex of our bodies, then these maps can be incongruent with our physical bodies.

In such a view, dysphoria arises due to the conflict between that internal representation of one's body and the external representation thereof. Alternatively, the internal representation is at odds with the material reality of the situation. Happily, this accommodates transition for both those who know right away and those who don't. Since what is at stake is an internal sense of embodiment, this may or may not show up in one's conscious self-identity right away. There may need to be transformations in one's conception of the world and oneself in order for one's experiences to find articulation. In order to explain gender phoria, therefore, something else is posited that is taken to exist prior to conscious identity. Serano, for example, calls it "subconscious sex."[14]

With this in mind, I now offer a preliminary argument against this incongruence account. (I will offer another in the last half of this chapter, and I will take up the incongruence account again in chapter 9.) This first argument consists in two premises: the internal sense of one's body cannot be innate, but the incongruence account can only work on the condition that the internal sense of one's body is innate. Note that this argument not only concludes against the incongruence account but also concludes against the innatist claim, and therefore concludes against two of the key claims of the wrong-body account. In the following section, I'll focus on establishing the first premise; in the section after that, I'll focus on the second. This will enable me to introduce my own account in the third section.

AN ARGUMENT AGAINST THE INCONGRUENCE ACCOUNT: PREMISE ONE

The born-this-way answer to the explanatory questions requires something that doesn't depend upon culture, doesn't vary across cultures. And the only thing that fits that bill is, of course, this sense of having either a male or female body—this sense of sexed embodiment. However, if we take seriously those trans people who transition without altering their physical bodies and who achieve gender happiness doing so, then this innatist appeal is out of the running. To be sure, we could draw a sharp theoretical line between "true transsexuals" (those who change their physical bodies) and the "merely transgender" (those who do not). But I've known too many trans people who had to think long and hard about whether they wanted to change their bodies and, if so, how. Some, for example, went on hormone replacement therapy only to find that it wasn't what they wanted, for whatever reason, and then went off. I haven't noticed any glaring differences between those trans people who have "the surgery" and those who don't, those who go on hormones and those who don't. I've known too many trans women who strongly identified as women, lived their lives as women, and died as women but did not feel the need to change their bodies. They didn't identify as women any less. It's not as if they were less committed.

Besides, this proposal isn't even phenomenologically adequate for those trans people who do seek bodily alteration by making it seem that gender "dysphoria" ultimately concerns the body alone. I would venture that probably in all cases, trans people experience various forms of dysphoria that do not concern the body at all. Certainly, one may feel dysphoria about one's public gender presentation, just as those who don't seek bodily alteration do. And while one might propose that this additional phoria is merely the effect of primary experiences with one's body, this proposal can't get off the ground if we've already included the trans folk discussed above. Indeed, the fact that it occurs in both cases strongly suggests that there isn't a sharp divide. And if it's primary in the first case, why would it be merely secondary in this second case?

Finally, the incongruence account doesn't even accurately describe its own focus—namely, body dysphoria. As I pointed to in chapter 4, some trans people can avail themselves of recoding practices. The very possibility of such recoding—the sensitivity of phoria to interpretation and the fact that often multiple workable interpretations are possible—suggests that an internal representation of one's body cannot be innate. Indeed, it also advances a further argument against the incongruence account by suggesting that trans gender phoria is about interpretation. In a hostile context, a trans man who has not had phalloplasty may be viewed by others as unequivocally female. In a friendly context, that same trans man may be viewed by others as unequivocally male. Depending upon his own idiosyncrasies, it may be that in the first case there is engendered a dysphoric state, while in the second case there is engendered a euphoric one. (To be clear, these needn't be the case. Often our experiences of phoria are recalcitrant, despite efforts at recoding.)

The point is that it's risky to assume that a trans man will have discomfort with having a vagina (assuming he does not call it something else) just because he sees himself as male. On the contrary, it may be that while he experienced or experiences dysphoria around having breasts, he feels quite content with the rest. He may self-identify as centrally, paradigmatically, unequivocally male. Indeed, it may be that his vagina—or whatever he calls it and however he uses it—far from undermining his manhood, serves to reinforce it. Such claims may make complete sense in trans-friendly subcultural contexts where he is accorded authority in his explanations and self-identifications.

Crucially, this is not, in fact, a clash between the external and the internal. Rather, it's a clash of competing interpretations—interpretations that can be publicly shared.[15] In order to frame phoria in terms of a clash between inside and outside, we need to lock down the internal sense of body as male, say, and the external body as female. In doing so, we need to fix the interpretation of sex category and body parts at the outset. That is, we need to say, *this* particular bodily configuration is male and *that* particular configuration is female.

AN ARGUMENT AGAINST THE INCONGRUENCE ACCOUNT: PREMISE TWO

Having argued that the gendered sense of one's body cannot be innate, I now want to show that unless this sense is innate, the incongruence account cannot be correct. Let's open with the following claim by Serano:

> My female subconscious sex was most certainly not the result of socialization or social gender constructs, as it defied everything I had been taught was true about gender, as well as the constant encouragement I received to think of myself as a boy and to act masculine.[16]

This argument is extremely compelling for many of us who have transitioned. Our feelings of dysphoria didn't seem to come from our cultural environments; rather, they seemed to directly contest them. This seems to run in the face of constructionism about the body and gender.

Now Salamon correctly points out that constructionism isn't merely some claim about how we're forced into social roles. The "cultural" is far broader than notions of "social constriction, or social role, or social control, or cultural expectations." The "cultural shaping" of a body "happens at the conceptual level, in that what we are able to imagine about what our bodies are or may become—even to decide what 'counts' as a body and what does not—is structured by the history of how bodies have been socially understood, by what bodies have been. But that imagining is not only a conceptual act, not 'merely' a theoretical undertaking; the same social forces that constitute a body as legible or illegible also shape the very feelings of embodiment that would seem to be most personal, most individual, and most immune to regulatory injunction."[17] And if constructionism is right about the body and gender, then it is hard to see how one's embodied sense of belonging to this or that sex can be innate.

Unfortunately, while a broad social constructionist approach obviously undermines a born-this-way answer to the explanatory question, such an approach, by itself, actually hasn't really provided a viable answer of its own. In this respect, born-this-way and constructionist accounts may be operating at different theoretical levels. While the born-this-way account purports to provide an attractive answer to the explanatory question, it appears to fall prey to general constructionist insights. By contrast, while the broad sweep of the constructionist argument appears convincing enough, it provides insufficient detail in explaining how gender dysphoria could possibly arise. Salamon's own apparent answer to the explanatory question, for instance, only ends up sharpening Serano's point.

While Salamon draws from many psychoanalytic thinkers, Paul Schilder's account of body image plays an important role in her understanding.[18] In this view, the postural body image, rather than arising innately, is built up over time through experiential contact with the world (including interactions with other people).[19] Crucially, this body image is much dependent upon one's history of experience—unintelligible without memory. That is, the body image is historically layered and encrusted as an accumulation over time.

The result is that the body image may well be at odds with one's actual body at the moment, allowing for a lack of complete fit between body image and the material body. It's unsurprising, then, that Schilder works to depathologize phantom limb experiences, pointing to the normality of a disjunction between internal body image and the material body. After all, this experience isn't that uncommon. Those of us who've grown older, for example, may have an internal sense of our bodies as youthful while the reality belies that. This is important for Salamon, who wishes to argue that since an incongruence between body image and body is an ordinary affair, trans people who experience this incongruence cannot be viewed as aberrant. This is a nice consequence: the marking of trans people as exceptional is thereby undermined. Moreover, because the body image concerns the positioned and moving body within culture, the account is not nearly as exclusionary as the born-this-way version.

This environmental engagement account fails quite dramatically, however. Consider, a trans person who's raised to see themself as male and to follow supposedly proper gender norms. This person should, in the environmental account, develop a postural body image that would be described as roughly "male." While the body image may be layered, saturated, and encrusted through historical accumulation, it is hard to see why there would be a significant gendered incongruence between body image and the material body in this account. What are the worldly experiences that this trans woman might have had that ever could have given her the body image of a woman, given her constant subjection to the norms of male gender? On this hypothesis, she's never had any such female-embodiment experiences that could be incorporated into her body image.

This difficulty for Salamon's account underscores the strength of the pressure toward the born-this-way account. Given that we move against everything culture has tried to impose on us, how on earth could the basis for our gender unhappiness also be cultural? How could it not be innate? Recall Serano's claim that her "female subconscious sex was most certainly not the result of socialization."[20] Or, as Prosser puts it: "The material flesh may resist its cultural inscription, because it goes against the flow of theory's insistence on the cultural constructedness of the body."[21] Since we become who we are in the face of what everybody tells us, how could whatever it is that accounts for our transition be anything but inborn?

To be fair to Salamon, I have deliberately ignored a key component of Schilder's notion of body image—the "libidinous" level.[22] By *libidinous*, Schilder means affective and erogenous investments in the body. And, undeniably, we take an interest in our bodies, have strong emotions about them. Salamon writes, "Without that investment, our relationship to our bodies is one of depersonalized estrangement: my sense of the 'mine-ness' of my own body—and, crucially, even my sense of its coherence—depends on this narcissistic investment."[23]

This appeal to libidinous investment provides a way to move beyond the limitations of (socially regulated) environmental experience: such affective attitudes aren't subject to the same type of worldly constraint—there's less of a tethering. And in light of what we've learned about the environmental account, it appears that if there's to be a substantial gendered incongruence between felt sense of body and material body, it must be largely with respect to libidinal invest-ment that it develops.

I've put this portion of the theory aside because—funnily enough, as it turns out—it isn't a variant of the incongruence account in the first place. Rather than positing that negative phoria arises due to the incongruence, we can now simply speak of the negative and positive affective investments in one's sexed body and leave it at that. That's just a variant of the affective account! So, let's simply ask: How well does this version of the affective account work?

Taken literally, not very well. For notions such as *libidinous* and *ero-togenic* suggest sexual motivations. On the face of it, therefore, the ac-count appears to reduce trans motivations to sexual ones. To be sure, there's been a long transphobic history of reducing supposed cross-gender identification to a kind of sexual fetish, to elide trans gender (dis)content as a discrete phenomenon. But no account can endorse such a view on the grounds of its phenomenological inadequacy.

One might say that in psychoanalytic discourse there's actually an ambiguity in terms such as *libidinal* between the literally sexual and broader understandings that include almost any affective investment at all. The danger in using expressions such as *libidinal investment* to accommodate this internal felt sense, however, is that either the impetus to transition is being reduced to sexual desire or else there's a coy flirtation with such a reduction, which at least invites serious confusion. The deeper problem is that no account of any nonsexual affective investments in the body is forthcoming.

What are these feelings, exactly? To the extent that nothing of substance is said, it becomes immediately clear that rather than an account of phoria, we have the complete absence of one. Indeed, the ambiguous use of *libidinal* may well serve as a convenient way of pa-pering over the lacuna—metaphorically suggesting the sexual with-out saying anything informative. One remains mystified. This ver-sion of the affective account, I claim, cannot be accepted.

INTERPERSONAL SENTIMENTS AS GENDER PHORIA

Given our abandonment of the incongruence account, and the inad-equacy of this initial libidinal version of the affective account, I pro-pose that rather than one's body, phoria concerns oneself as an inter-personal object determined within the folk system of interpersonal spatiality. As such, it principally concerns awareness of oneself as an object for others.

In the folk system, interpersonal objects are distinguished into two sorts: male and female. The difference, recall, is not merely in the presented differences between the two objects but in the structured modality of interpersonal awareness as a whole. Gender dysphoria, in this context, is grounded in dispositions to experience irregular and typically unpleasant modes of awareness of oneself as an object—interpersonal sentiments—in various interpersonal and solitary contexts and situations. And since, as I shall argue in chapter 7, moral sex is inherently bound up with race, experiences of gender phoria will likely be so.

In light of this, we must shift from the notion of embodiment to that of empersonment. In such an approach, we reject the notion of the precultural naked body. This means that intimate appearance isn't to be taken as more fundamental than proper appearance. Rather, the two are dialectically bound together, and both are morally saturated, constituted within a specific system of interpersonal spatiality. This shift rules out privileging trans people who alter their bodies physically over those who do not and instead centralizes the various ways in which trans people can alter their physical persons.

The incongruence account's emphasis on the body can be viewed as falling prey to the illusory naturalization of nakedness. It falsely believes in the existence of the "naked body," thereby prioritizing intimate appearance at the expense of proper. Consider that in Prosser's view, the transsexual change in embodiment is deep, while a mere change in public gender presentation—a mere change in clothing—is superficial. "In the cultural imagination," Prosser writes, "that figure of the body as costume is surely welded most firmly to the transsexual. The transsexual changes sexed parts like a set of clothes, treats the body as tractable, provisional, immaterial."[24] This is a view, recall, he strongly rejects.

In my view, by contrast, public gender presentation—proper appearance—gets a serious upgrade. As the uniform of personhood, for example, clothing turns out to be something of considerable consequence both insofar as it's essential to one's proper appearance and insofar as its presupposition lays the conditions for the very possibility of nakedness. Indeed, insofar as clothing is crucial in helping constitute our proper appearances—and therefore our intimate appearances—it's the most basic and essential technology of person-hood we've ever had.

The "body" gets something of a downgrade. Rather than the thing itself, it becomes an intimate appearance on par with and dialectically related to proper appearance. Specifically, it's an appearance allocated to intimacy. That said, the appearance in question isn't "mere." Rather, it's through both proper and intimate appearances that we self-manifest to others as people. Consequently, we speak of affective investments not in the body but rather in the physical person.

Any mystery concerning what these feelings are is dispelled immediately. The feelings, as I said, are largely irregular modalities of one's awareness of oneself as an object for others—vulnerability, self-collection, shame, and dignity—that arise in ways inappropriate to the folk system. (And we might also include negative feelings concerning the disposition to experience such feelings—that is, unhappiness over the very tendency of these feelings to emerge in inappropriate contexts.) Insofar as all forms of oppression in the folk system concern *being* a folk person and *possessing* a physical person, we can recognize how phoria will involve idiosyncratic experiences that are an integrated affective response to one's location in the social order.

The resonance of recoding practices can then be explained in terms of interpersonal spatiality. As boundaries, strips, and pathways are immanent in our practices of intimacy, recodings can be understood as different practices of intimacy that impute different boundaries. This includes replacing one boundary with another, changing the force, changing the order, changing an intelligibility step and thereby the boundary's significance. For instance, the overall structure/strip of nakedness can be rewritten to include body parts not normally included. Thus, a female intimate appearance can be rewritten so as to include a penis, while a male intimate appearance can be rewritten to include a vagina. Further, nonorganic artifacts, such as dildos, can likewise be incorporated. After all, the physical person is already partially constituted by such artifacts. The only difference here is that the artifacts become part of intimate rather than proper appearance and, therefore, the intimate meaning determines it is as a private part, capable of exposure along the strip, rather than a device deployed for purposes of concealment.

We can also explain the very phenomena that the incongruence account purports to accommodate. Before: One looks into the mirror to see one's intimate appearance and feels bad. One feels bad owing to various forms of awareness of oneself as an object for others. For instance, one might feel shame. One might feel intimately dead. And so forth. After: One looks into the mirror to see one's intimate appearance and feels good. One no longer feels shame or one no longer feels intimately dead. Rather, one feels capable of vulnerability to another in the context of intrinsic intimacy.

Indeed, this approach can also suggest some ways in which one's conscious identity can itself be subject to phoria. Consider, for instance, that at least some of the content of a self-conception is subject to boundaries on access, owing to the cosmological backdrop. Further, how to share about oneself—when, where, with whom, and how much—is subject to ordered boundaries. As the boundaries are sex-differentiated, different content and modalities of self-sharing are subject to differential boundaries as well. Already, then, given that we've understood phoria as irregular experiences of vulnerability in given interpersonal configurations, we can see how one's self-conception can be the subject of phoria, attended by various sentiments such as intimate hemorrhaging, intimate deadening, and shame.

Finally, we can even make some gentle moves regarding the explanatory question by positing the *affective makeup*—one's idiosyncratic constitution to experience or not experience affective sentiments under various conditions. It's certainly not implausible to imagine that one's idiosyncratic affective makeup develops over time in interaction with others. How else could it be developed? And, given that, it's also not implausible to imagine that irregular patterns of interaction may lead to the development of irregular makeups. For instance, repeated subjections to contempt or forced *ideational intimization* may yield the experience of intimate hemorrhaging when interacting with others and an overall sense of defectiveness. One imagines, further, that these affective makeups can begin to develop when one is very young—almost as soon as one is put into clothes. Already, one is being trained into boundaries, after all, whether one knows it or not. And with those approving or disapproving looks, one is on one's way, surely even before one is toilet trained.

There's also no reason to deny that one's material constitution at birth and as it develops over time may likewise contribute to the makeup. Indeed, one would expect that it plays some sort of causal role not only in the capacity to experience various interpersonal sentiments but also in one's preference for certain sentiments over others (say, self-containment over vulnerability). However, if it is true that moral sex is merely a feature of one particular system of interpersonal spatiality rather than something inherent in interpersonal spatiality per se, then it simply won't make any sense that one can possess an innate sense of one's moral sex. And this is all to the good for reasons that have hopefully already been made plain.

To be clear, however, while I make some gentle moves with regard to the explanatory question, I do not regard these as deeply explanatory. Nor do I think that a philosophical work of this sort needs to provide details so specific. The companion move is just to obviate the question altogether as commonly posed. The starting assumption there is that trans people require some explanation that nontrans people do not. We don't ask why nontrans people don't transition, after all. There's something already unacceptable, then, that lies behind certain ways of posing the question.

Instead, I see the question as part of the existential WTF. As a trans person, one may want to make sense of one's life, and seeking an answer to this question may be part of that. Once one is raising questions about virtually everything, however, the explanatory question needn't position oneself as the problem. The question isn't "What's wrong with me?" The question, rather, is part of a more general "What the hell is going on here?" When posed in this way, an account of trans oppression becomes an essential companion to any take on the explanatory question. Indeed, it has crucial consequences for it.

If the folk system is regarded as multiply oppressive—sexistly, racistly, heterosexistly, and so forth—then the allegedly dysfunctional or even pathological character of irregular dispositions is placed in a different light. Disruptions of a harmful system can be good. In this way, the explanatory question itself is shifted. Given the oppressive character of the folk system, it's little surprise that irregular responses to the system should arise. Insofar as trans gender phoria opposes this system, it's perhaps less of a pressing question why trans gender phoria arises. Why wouldn't it? A better question is why it doesn't arise for others.

On Recognizing Oneself

THE PHENOMENON OF SELF-RECOGNITION

Thus far, my account is highly general and does, I suspect, apply to a great many people—trans, nonbinary, gay, lesbian, bi, discontented, and otherwise. The folk system affords plenty of opportunities for unhappiness. So, while this account provides a bedrock for understanding trans gender phoria, it also doesn't provide enough detail. I'd like, then, to turn to the experience of "already being" prior to transition. To be clear, I don't attribute the experience of already being to all trans folks. However, I do think it is a crucial experience for many. And while my hope is that other sorts of experiences can likewise be accommodated by appeal to interpersonal spatiality theory, this experience is particularly important for the purposes of this essay. Specifically, in my view, the experience of already being is formed in opposition to the phenomenon of reality enforcement. In this way, my account enables a move from a more-or-less pathologizing model to one that reframes this experience as existing in resistant tension with the forces of an oppressive system.[25]

In this section, I'll also continue opposing the incongruence account. While the argument I provided in the first part of this chapter is useful, it does not point to some of the deeper issues I want to pursue. Specifically, while the incongruence account posits a conflict between one's internal representation of one's body and the external manifestation of one's body to others, I posit a conflict between a positive awareness of oneself and the state of gender make-believe in which this awareness arises. In the former, the pretransition sense of self is an internal representation. In the latter, it is a pretransition experience of oneself in a liminal social state of make-believe that I shall call the *"blank open."* Of critical import, while the former involves an awareness of oneself as subject, the latter involves an awareness of oneself as an object for others. This shall be further pursued in chapter 9.

To set the stage for my critique of the incongruence account in this section, I want to place my disagreement in a larger context of recent critiques. Specifically, the efforts of Andrea Long Chu, Cameron Awkward-Rich, and Hil Malatino call into question the notion of a fairy-tale ending posttransition and, in particular, the classic "incongruence" appeal to an unhappy "before transition" and a satisfied, if not triumphant, "after transition."[26]

Becoming socially recognized as a woman, for instance, brings all sorts of disappointments and pain. It also doesn't alleviate racial, class-based, or disability-based oppression or undermine corresponding privileges. Transitioning may merely alter gendered modalities of that oppression and privilege. Finally, in direct opposition to the incongruence account, many of us continue to experience bouts of dysphoria, often tied to experiences of invalidation as well as internalized transphobia long after transition. Chu writes:

> Like many of my trans friends, I've watched my dysphoria balloon since I began transition. I now feel very strongly about the length of my index fingers—enough that I will sometimes shyly unthread my hand from my girlfriend's as we walk down the street. When she tells me I'm beautiful, I resent it. I've been outside. I know what beautiful looks like. Don't patronize me.[27]

And:

> Nothing, not even surgery, will grant me the mute simplicity of having always been a woman. I will live with this, or I won't. That's fine. The negative passions—grief, self-loathing, shame, regret—are as much a human right as universal health care. . . . There are no good outcomes in transition. There are only people, begging to be taken seriously.[28]

Malatino likewise writes:

> Even these moments of affirmation are mediated by the deeply bifurcated affective discourse that governs tropes of trans representation. . . . This isn't to say it wasn't genuine; rather, it's to point out that when we see, over and again, such single-note representations, something deeply significant falls out of the picture: the durability of negativity, the bad feelings that persist before, during, and after such moments of euphoria,

the bad feelings that aren't ameliorated by such euphoria, the bad feelings that transition doesn't, can't possibly, eliminate.[29] There are plenty of negative experiences of phoria after transition. And this fact runs directly in the face of the idea that transition yields satisfaction by resolving an incongruence. That is, it refutes the "before" and "after" mirror story.

I would suggest that for many trans people, the relationship to the mirror is highly complex. There are many mirror stories.[30] A common one involves looking in the mirror after transition and experiencing nothing but invalidation and dismay. A trans woman, say, looks in the mirror only to see "a man in a dress." She sees only a make-believer. Perhaps she even starts to feel that her entire life is a sham and, as a consequence, falls into abject despair. Since there's no longer any actual incongruence between internal sense of the body and external body itself, however, it's hard to see why there might still be negative dysphoria in that account. Here, crucially, the experience of this dysphoria is bound closely with reality enforcement.

What I want to discuss mostly, however, is a second experience, self-recognition, that likewise disrupts this before-after pattern, but in the opposite way, by allowing for a positive experience that occurs prior to transition. This experience typically concerns public gender presentation—that is, proper appearance. It's Halloween. Perhaps one puts on their mother's dress. The point is that one engages in a form of make-believe via proper appearance. Yet even though this is a socially recognized state of make-believe, there comes a profound and visceral experience of self-recognition. One *sees* oneself—perhaps for the first time.

Such experiences are ephemeral. They can be easily extinguished, yielding a stunningly profound sense of loss and yearning for reactivation. Thus, self-recognition defines, in turn, a specific dysphoric state—namely, the loss of the experience and thereby the loss of she who one has just experienced oneself to be. This loss can happen once the pretense has terminated—Halloween is over, the contest is finished. But it can also happen when one becomes expressly aware that this is make-believe and the spell is broken. Note, then, that the posttransition dysphoria mentioned above just seems to be a variant of this—namely, the loss, the failure to achieve that post experience of self-recognition. Somehow, *she* is gone. If she ever existed at all.

How can the phenomena of self-recognition and loss be explained? Certainly, the incongruence account has failed us. And I would further propose that the very underlying conception of the mirror has failed us too. Happily, it is not the only conception of mirrors. And it is for this reason that I look elsewhere. While I shall explore this further in chapter 9, at present I would like to turn to what Anzaldúa has to say in *Borderlands/La Frontera*. She writes:

> In ancient times the Mexican Indians made mirrors of volcanic glass known as obsidian. Seers would gaze into a mirror until they fell into a trance. Within the glossy surface, they saw clouds of smoke which would part to reveal a vision concerning the future of the tribe and the will of the gods.[31]

And:

> During the dark side of the moon something in the mirror catches my gaze, I seem all eyes and nose. Inside my skull something shifts. I "see" my face. Gloria, the everyday face; Prieta and Prietita, my childhood faces; Gaudi, the face my mother and sisters and brothers know. And there in the black obsidian mirror of Nahuas is yet another face, a stranger's face. *Simultaneamente me miraba la cara dede distintos angulos. Y mi cara, como la realidad, tenia un character multiplice.*[32]

These passages—and others I shall turn to at the end of the chapter —speak to me far more powerfully than any other articulations of trans mirror experience. Perhaps this is not as surprising as it might seem. As AnaLouise Keating writes of Anzaldúa:

> I am struck by the profound ways that her words resonate with so many different types of people . . . including many who do not self-identity as Chicana, Latina, feminist, lesbian, and/or queer. They are shocked by the intimacy of Anzaldúa's insights; they feel like she's speaking directly to them.[33]

Of course, in appealing to Anzaldúa I want to be cautious not to appropriate experience and struggle that is not mine. Nor do I wish to impose on Anzaldúa an experience and struggle that is not hers. I also recognize the reality of her own appropriations of Indigenous iconography and, for my part, have no need to appeal to this iconography.³⁴ However, there are affinities in the affect behind these passages that cannot be denied—resonances that exceed the iconography which Anzaldúa articulates for herself.

To be clear, I can't say that my own account will accord with her views. As her ruminations are of a poetic sort, any attempt to dissect them would drain them of resonance. I can say, however, that she captures feelings that aren't present in the standard incongruence account's use of the mirror. And I can also say that my account is in affective dialogue with hers as the remainder of the chapter proceeds.

THE BLANK OPEN

Two questions confront us. First, the phenomenological question made specific: What is this experience of self-recognition? How can it be described theoretically? Second, how, exactly, is it even possible to experience genuine self-recognition in mere make-believe contexts? My answer to the first is effectively the same idea that I've already been defending—namely, phoric experiences are various irregular modalities of object self-awareness, affective sentiments. In the case of self-recognition, the modality (or set of modalities) is obviously positive. And the chief affective modality—the affective sentiment—by which one recognizes oneself in the mirror, I propose, is a sense of rightful self-collection, "togetherness," dignity, poise.

When one looks into the mirror and "sees" oneself, one experiences this sense of collection that stands in contrast to any other sentiments that one may have had of oneself in the mirror. It's not an experience one is supposed to have. What one is supposed to see is merely the effect of dressing up. But what one experiences is the very condition of one's presence to others. What one experiences is one's very sensory appearance, the very condition for one's comportment to others. And it is through this experience of self-collection that one experiences this gender presentation as one's proper appearance. To put it differently, it's through the experience of self-collection that one appropriates it to oneself as one's own.

We're well prepared for the second question as well. As we've seen in the previous chapter, gender make-believe is not what it appears. While it is viewed as a form of imitation within the system, this is, in fact, an impossibility. There are no morally saturated naked bodies that exist magically beyond the social. Rather, make-believe consists in the disconnection of boundary observations and crossings from the rest of the system.

Far from deluded, I say, self-recognition is a profoundly perceptive apprehension. What is grasped, in part, is that the intimate significance of a proper appearance is not inevitable. It is, rather, entirely socially contingent. We grasp the possibility that the make-believe needn't be make-believe. We grasp the possibility of social transformation. We grasp the fragile state of this (un)reality. And we understand that whether this moment ends, is relegated to mere pretense, depends only on how we are received, how we are recognized, and that this is a contingent matter of the social.

In this respect, the recognition might be regarded as a deployment of what Anzaldúa calls "*la facultad.*" We see "in surface phenomena the meaning of deeper realities, . . . see the deep structure below the surface." Obviously, I don't mean that we understand through my theory. It is, rather, "a quick perception arrived at without conscious reasoning."[35] Nonetheless, this intuition is sufficient to open a small aperture in social reality, allowing room for a new awareness of oneself as an object. Or, rather, the emergence of this affective awareness just is that intuition.

What makes this possible, I claim, is the phenomenon of infraintimacy coupled with the contingency of the intimate meaning. In grasping the contingency of the intimate meaning, one grasps the possibility of multiple ones. Since two have already been put into play (the original and the alternate, recall), one could imagine a host of others. And as this variability is recognized, the indeterminacy of the meaning of one's proper appearance is recognized. This indeterminacy is tantamount to an unintelligibility—so many intimate meanings could be in play, after all. I call this state of indeterminacy the "blank open." And here, the possibility of an infraintimate experience of self-containment can emerge. For it's precisely this unintelligibility—this lack of determinate intimate meaning—that affords a sort of infraintimate containment not possible in the folk system.

The positive experience of infracontainment likely alleviates other, more negative, irregular sentiments. While I don't wish to get so specific about what might be going on, an obvious candidate is certainly that of intimate hemorrhaging. In this case, the sentiment of self-containment, for its required contrast, draws on the painful feelings of perpetual leakage in the dominant world. It's in experiencing this block to the bleeding that one experiences a particular proper appearance as one's own.

Indeed, the structural characteristics of the folk system themselves already provide for this. Consider that, as I have established, the folk system involves a sort of structural leakage built right into it, whereby the private is communicated publicly. Once one has experienced feelings of self-containment that don't derive from that system, the abusiveness may be more easily perceptible and, consequently, a further basis for contrast may be put into play.

As it stands, however, the experience is only one of self-containment in the blank open, and this is insufficient for the experience of self-collection—dignity, poise, and the like. The latter must include a sense of capacity for self-display, of willful, communicative vulnerability to another. Alas, the suspension of all intimate meanings would appear to make sharing with another quite impossible. Rather, one would be locked within a solitude of unintelligibility.

To complete the account, then, we need to leave behind the solitude of the mirror to consider gender make-believe in intimate interactive contexts. To be clear, I don't just mean interacting with those at a Halloween party, say, who merrily play along. I mean, rather, genuinely creative interactions with a resistant quality that can occur in subcultural contexts or simply among those who find themselves willing and able—the sort that may involve the recoding practices discussed earlier.

In this case, it is the very suspension of the intimate meanings, the unintelligibility effected by that suspension, that makes this infraintimacy possible. What relegates intimate negotiations to mere role-play is precisely their lack of integration in the projected strip (or lack of coherence with the feigned nakedness structure). As these steps are suspended, there are no preset guidelines for intimacy, no preexisting structure with which to conform.

Here, there is a genuine experience of intrinsic intimacy whereby one lays down boundaries through traversing them—that is, through acting as if they existed. It's an exploratory, creative activity that does not require the existence of boundaries beforehand. While, in a system, communicative gestures of self-display and of attention (observation/traversal) are correlated in advance, here they are co-constituted on the fly through what Lugones characterizes as "*tantear.*"[36]

At issue is not one's having had these experiences but the anticipation, the capacity to have them. It is here that an individual's affective makeup would be given the opportunity to resonate with and find expression in the new forms of intimacy provided—ones that aren't possible in the folk system. That is, the irregular dispositions introduced in my more general account can now be viewed as the affective bed from which more distinctive trans affective investments flower.

I propose that what affords the experience of self-collection in self-recognition is just this sense or anticipation of blossoming, of new forms of connection and self-display. Beyond recognizing the contingency of the intimate meaning, one also apprehends the productive power of intimate interactions. One anticipates the possibility of an unprecedented vulnerability. To be sure, no actual experiences of vulnerability can be experienced except under circumstances of actual interaction with another. Yet this does not mean that the possibilities aren't registered in the experience of a similarly anticipatory sense of self-collection.

In light of this, we can speak of a certain class of irregular dispositions wedded to a particular sort of social state—namely, the liminal state of gender make-believe. What defines these dispositions is their phoric relation to social states of make-believe in which the experience of self-recognition is prone to arise. This means we can speak of such dispositions even prior to any actual experience of self-recognition—dispositions that may yield, from time to time, an ineffable sense, in advance of self-recognition, that might appear in brief imaginings thereof, glimpses, fits and starts, abortive anticipations.

APPARITIONAL LIMINALITY

The being—the apparition—that exists in the liminal state is multiple insofar as it is open to various possibilities that resonate in various ways in varying degrees.[37] There needn't be any one set of negotiated intimacies and distances predetermined. In this respect, it is more accurate to speak of the being that is revealed in the blank open not as a complete object but, rather, as an almost-object or proto-object—

something in between the object in the folk system and a slew of possible objects that one might become. One is not reduced to the folk system, but one has not yet been integrated in new forms of interpersonal spatiality. This state can be viewed as a space in between, a threshold, or, better, a preliminary or preparatory state and a portal to other worlds. It's something like a way station—on the one hand, beyond the limits of "normal" self-awareness and yet, on the other, prior to the establishment of any alternative social reality.

There is also a tension. On the one hand, this liminal state is well characterized by what Lugones calls a "germinative stasis." Drawing on the fecund discussion of the *Coatlicue* state in Anzaldúa's *Borderlands/La Frontera*, Lugones speaks of "isolating the self from harmful sense to make germination of a resistant self possible," introducing "a more contained, more inward sense of activity of the self in metamorphosis. Like in a cocoon, the changes are not directed outward."[38] Here the infraintimate protection is critical, for it is what makes partial departure from the folk system possible. Yet, on the other hand, there is here a yearning that is constitutive of self-recognition as an anticipatory state. This can be experienced as something like a summons—almost as if one were visited by oneself from an otherworldly future. And what the call demands is realization—the process by which one becomes an interpersonal object in networks of interpersonal spatiality.

Although the exact character of this realization is undetermined—it is possible to find various forms of realization in different worlds—two features are key: First, there must be a deep resonance, grounded in one's affective makeup. Second, the proper appearance that in the folk system had been reduced to a disguise must constitute a genuine proper appearance. That is, it must serve as the condition for subsumption and the enablement of comportment to others. The yearning to find realization is, at its very inception, activated through self-recognition in a state constituted "make-believe."[39]

In its very existence, then, self-recognition must be regarded as pressing against relegation to mere make-believe, as genuine feelings do not typically arise in scenarios regarded as mere fiction. Meanwhile, relegation to mere make-believe presses against self-recognition in three respects: First, given the content of the intimate meaning, the possibility for interpersonal relations with others in the folk system is undermined. Second, given the fact that a single intimate meaning is attached to proper appearances, the multiplicity inherent in the self-recognition—the possibilities of complex vulnerability—are foreclosed. Finally, the self-collection that was made possible by the elimination of all intimate meaning is undermined, inducing a form of intimate hemorrhaging.

In the loss of self-recognition, however, there is also hope for its retrieval, the impetus to transcend the limits of this single-worldly make-believe. In its most developed form, self-recognition/loss can outright motivate a project of realization whereby one attempts to transform this alleged make-believe into a social reality. In all respects, then, self-recognition is in contestation with the phenomenon of reality enforcement that constitutes trans people as "make-believers." I call this liminality "apparitional" and those who are formed through it "apparitions."[40]

With this in mind, let's conclude by turning to the resonant words of Anzaldúa—words that convey the intensity of interpersonal sentiments.

> I would look into the mirror, afraid of *mi secreto terrible,* the
> secret sin I tried to conceal—*la seña,* the mark of the Beast. I
> was afraid it was in plain sight for all to see. The secret I tried
> to conceal was that I was not normal, that I was not like the
> others. I felt alien. I knew I was alien. I was the mutant stoned
> out of the herd, something deformed with evil inside. . . .
>
> She felt shame for being abnormal. The bleeding distanced
> her from others. . . .
>
> Her soft belly exposed to the sharp eyes of everyone; they
> see, they see. Their eyes penetrate her; they slit her from head
> to belly. *Rajada.* She is at their mercy, she can do nothing
> to defend herself. And she is ashamed that they see her so
> exposed, so vulnerable. She has to still her eyes from looking
> at the feelings—feelings that can catch her in their gaze, bind
> her to others.[41]

Cut open, she closes up.

> *Voy cagándome de miedo, buscando lugares acuevados.* I
> don't want to know, I don't want to be seen. My resistance

to know some truth about myself brings on that paralysis,
depression—brings on the *Coatlicue* state. At first I feel
exposed and opened to the depth of my dissatisfaction. Then
I feel myself closing, hiding, holding myself together rather
than allowing myself to fall apart.[42]

But Anzaldúa descends into the underworld—the unconscious—to
protect herself. Something forces her to return to the mirror, to look.
Yet she fights it.

I don't want to see what's behind *Coatlicue*'s eyes, her hollow
sockets. I can't confront her face to face; I must take small sips
of her face through the corners of my eyes. . . .
    Behind the ice mask I see my own eyes. They will not
look at me. *Miro que estoy encabronada, miro la resistencia*—
resistance to knowing, to letting go, to that deep ocean where
once I dived into death. I am afraid of drowning. Resistance
to sex, intimate touching, opening myself to the alien other
where I am out of control, not on patrol.[43]

The solitude—the recognition of oneself—provides a protection,
sealing off the possibility of intimate bleeding through the stripping
away of the intimate meanings. And, yet, without connection to others, there can never be any realization of this self-recognition at all.

It is her reluctance to cross over . . . that forces her into the
fecund cave of her imagination where she is cradled in the
arms of *Coatlicue,* who will never let her go. If she doesn't
change her ways, she will remain a stone forever. *No hay más
que cambiar.*[44]

To face oneself is to take heed of the call, to open up to others, to seek
the relational sustenance on which any reality depends.[45]

Chapter 6

The Operations of Theory

IN THE TWO PREVIOUS CHAPTERS, I provided an account of trans oppression and resistance, arguing against the beyond-the-binary account (BTBA) and the wrong-body account (WBA), respectively. In this chapter, I conclude my discussion of these theories by considering the work they perform. This will serve as a conclusion to "Part II: The Main Idea" and a segue into "Part III: The Buried Lede." In the first section, I show how both the BTBA and the WBA operate to secure trans identity claims. In the second section, I discuss the work of my own account in providing illumination in the face of the existential WTF.

Preliminaries

As ground-bound philosophers, it's our business to examine not only what a theory *says* but also what that theory *does*. Consider, for instance, a transphobic account that typically frames itself as a neutral examination of the issues. Part of the work of the theory is to marginalize the views of trans people as nonobjective, and therefore irrelevant, while at the same time masking its own agenda. Often, these theories are put to this work cynically, although it does sometimes happen that theories perform work in ways that do not fully show up on the conscious radar (we'll meet some).

In this chapter, I'm interested in theories that are trans friendly, as are all three theories—the WBA, the BTBA, and mine. And I want to consider the work that they do for us. I want to suggest that some tasks to which the WBA and the BTBA are set are problematic, and I want to show that the deployment of my theory in this essay deliberately avoids these tasks while accomplishing others.

As this project is metaphilosophical in character, it's important to acknowledge that, because significant aspects of my metaphilosophy derive from my philosophy, things will get a little self-referential toward the end. For the most part, I don't think this should be a problem—after all, this would hardly be the first time that a philosopher's metaphilosophy flowed from their philosophy. But I suppose that's for others to judge.

In considering the work of theory, I take the perspective of one who is typically theorized *about*. I look at theory from the other side. Sometimes these theories are like flying objects hovering on high and occasionally taking shots. Other times, these theories operate like clothes or sticky webs in which we get tangled. And yet at other times, these theories simply eat into our brains, leaving us incapable of doing anything. The point is that theories about us are often intimate, woven into flesh and blood. And these experiences are obviously quite different from the experience of a theorist working on a problem or issue they merely find intriguing but are not personally affected by. In this chapter, I want to consider the role that such theories can play with regard to the real-life trans experiences of coming into identity, transition, and self-revelation.[1]

The Work of the WBA

The wrong-body account, recall, consists of three ideas: an appeal to the incongruence model, innateness of gender identity, and the view that gender identity can be used to vouchsafe a trans person's claims to be a man or woman. The idea here is that because a person's innate gender identity is that of a man, they count as one. Often, the way it operates from the first-person is like this: "I've always been a man. I'm just trapped in the wrong body."

I reject this claim. My own view is that the determinations of gender membership do not necessarily hinge on gender identity. As an ontological pluralist, rather, I regard the deployment of terms such as *man* and *woman* as given by worldly discursive and extradiscursive practices. So, gender identity would determine gender membership just in case those practices operate that way.[2] Alas, in the overworld, that is typically not the case.

I am, however, interested in this appeal to the WBA to validate one's identity. Specifically, I'm interested in the always-already claim as a reply to reality enforcement and the work that the WBA does in helping to accomplish this reply. What I want to show is that the WBA—somewhat ironically—is used to contest reality enforcement by inverting the appearance–reality contrast. I begin with Jay Prosser's discussion of the always-already claim within the context of narrative self-identity. Then I'll show how the WBA is used to invert the appearance–reality contrast. I'll then provide a political critique of the work of the WBA, as well as the BTBA. Finally, I'll move on to discuss the work of my own theory and show how it contrasts with the work of the other two.

PROSSER AND NARRATIVE SELF-IDENTITY

Although Prosser adopts a narrative conception of self in general—"narrative composes the self," he writes—he's particularly interested in what he regards as the tight relation between narrative self-conception and transsexuality.[3] The subtitle of the book is "The Body Narratives of Transsexuality." And he calls them "*body* narratives" in part because they point to the continuing importance of the "materiality of the body."[4] More importantly, he does this because "transsexuality is always narrative work, a transformation of the body that requires the remolding of the life into a particular narrative shape."[5] Again, "the resexing of the transsexual body," he says, "is made possible through narrativization, the transitions of sex enabled by those of narrative."[6] "Narrative is also a kind of second skin: the story the transsexual must weave around the body in order that this body may be 'read.'"[7]

While Prosser's specific focus is WBA "transsexuality" grounded in the medical-psychiatric apparatus, he affirms the process of "coming into identity."

> For the transsexual even to discover the possibility of trans-
> sexuality—to transform it from private fantasy to realizable
> identity plot—takes place "in" narrative. To learn of trans-
> sexuality is to uncover transsexuality as a story and to refigure
> one's own life within the frame of that story.[8]

One of the key features of the incongruence account endorsed by Prosser is that it serves as the basis for a plot. We have a beginning—

the incongruence. We have a middle—the journey, transition. We have the end—the achievement of congruence and integration. Prosser therefore sees trans dysphoria à la incongruence and the narrative plot as profoundly linked, inextricably bound up together in the phenomenon of transsexuality.

While the autobiographical character of one's self-conception is always at work in transsexuality, Prosser identifies two key moments in which it plays a pivotal role: at the beginning of the journey in the clinician's office and at the end of the journey in the form of what he calls "the published return"—that is, the written autobiography.[9] The latter, of course, is not a necessary juncture in the life course of all transsexuals. But it is particularly useful to Prosser as it reveals in greater depth just how to understand the operations of the narrative self in the first place. It will also prove useful for me, so please keep it in mind.

The autobiography, claims Prosser, heals the split in gendered plots: "I was a woman, I write as a man. How to join this split? How to create a coherent subject?"[10] The transsexual journey provides an accounting of this and thereby provides a sort of intelligibility. Indeed, the autobiographical form mimics the split and the healing. As the story opens, the narrator and the protagonist are separated by a temporal distance and by the changes that the protagonist will undergo in their journey toward the person the narrator is. In the case of transsexuality, this distance is a gendered one. The protagonist begins as one sex, while the narrator is another. By the end, the protagonist has become the narrator, has changed sex.

Not only does the transsexual narrative possess a progression—a plot culminating in unification. There's also a form of retroaction by which transsexuality insinuates itself as already there. As Prosser notes, in autobiography, the past is given a retrospective rereading in light of the present by the narrator. The account of the past, as it progresses toward the present, is given a trajectory of culmination, of teleological unfolding that is, no doubt, a distortion of what had actually been the case. Prosser writes:

> The transsexual autobiography that we read is therefore the life as remembered by the envisioning, knowing "I." The entire life is filtered through the present moment of remembering. . . . The "epiphany" in Morris's *Conundrum* illustrates

this textualization of autobiographical narrative time. Morris claims to be able to fix her recognition of a transsexual self to a very precise instance when, as three- or four-year-old James, she (as he) is "under the piano" his (her) mother is playing; it was then, Morris writes, that he (she) grasps "that [she/he] had been born into the wrong body, and should really be a girl" (3). But when does this moment really acquire this significance of absolute marker beginning the transsexual plot? While Morris may well have been aware of a deep-rooted sense of difference at the time of the experience, this difference does not become schematized as part of a transsexual narrative until that narrative is discovered and conceived—and this is surely not in the moment recounted, not by the young child.[11]

To properly understand the operations of transsexual self-identity, thinks Prosser, one must understand this tension between the progressive and retroactive character of the narrative as constitutive of the process.

It's in light of this that Prosser attempts to elucidate the always-already claim. The issue comes to the fore when Prosser aims to answer the charge (made by Bernice L. Hausman, an antitrans Foucauldian feminist who had caused quite a commotion at the time) that there is a contradiction in the claim to "always having been a woman or man" and the project of "sex-change."[12] Prosser explains that "transsexual autobiographies conform as narrative to a generic form: they conform above all as autobiography" and "the genre of autobiography operates precisely on a set of reconcilable and constitutive oppositions."[13] Thus, Prosser makes it seem that retroaction is central in explaining the always-already claim.

The move fails. Prosser conflates the phenomenon of retroaction with a particular narrative claim—namely, one in which there never really was a change in sex at all. Consider the following counternarrative: instead of saying that I was always a woman (or, rather, always female and, when I was young, a girl), I shall say that I was a boy who grew up to become a woman. (While the ostensible purpose of this story is to simply serve as an argumentative prop, I do like the story.) Crucially, this counternarrative is much like a conversion narrative. In such narratives, one does not start off as somehow already a Christian, say. Rather, the story posits a deep, radical change. To be sure, the current narrator is projected into the past, so a retroaction occurs, and the narrative is given its teleological trajectory, unfolding, as it does, with conversion. Nonetheless, there's no need to say that one was always-already Christian.[14]

Rather, a Christian-style framework may subtly be imposed on the account of the past. Christianity may lurk there, prior to conversion, as a kind of implied destiny. But this simply isn't the same thing as saying that one was always-already a Christian. My counternarrative is like that. While it can certainly admit of retroaction, it does not position me as having always been female. The problem with Prosser's account is that he conflates the general structure of autobiography with a specific autobiographical narrative. It is the latter, not the former, that implicates the always-already claim. And so, the question of how to explain the appeal to the always-already claim remains unanswered.

Of course, Prosser's narrative account does not, in general, appeal to me at all. And this matters as well. First, as I've already made clear, I reject the incongruence account, along with any happily-ever-after stories that attend to it. Indeed, in my view, not only are there other narratives besides the one Prosser provides, but narratives also needn't shape one's sense of self at all. On the contrary, one may merely lurch from one adventure to another, without any underlying heroic quest.[15]

What I do find crucial is the underlying conception of the world that frames one's sense of self and, in particular, what Sonny Nordmarken calls "gender conceptualizations and models."[16] I take these to include not only taken-for-granted presumptions about the world but express reformulations that may be brought into play when the former have been called into question. When I speak of "theories" such as the WBA and BTBA, I mean no more than this. So, "theories" include not only detailed philosophical accounts but also any individual attempt to conceptualize gender in accordance with their experience.

Second, Prosser ignores or at least underplays the important interpersonal dimension of sharing aspects of one's identity with others. Here, we must not think first of an internal conception by which one understands oneself but, rather, the external apparatus by which one makes public various details of one's identity that are presumably not known by the other. Further, we must recognize the boundaried character of such self-sharing. One takes something private and makes it public. This is so when one comes out to a clinician and to others as trans. And it is also so when one makes public an autobiography. In the following, I describe the external apparatus, and I show the role that the WBA plays with regard to the always-already claim and, more specifically, the use of it by trans people to overwrite one interpersonal identity with another toward the goal of realization.

REANIMATION AND THE ALWAYS-ALREADY CLAIM

Although the process of transition varies widely among trans people, it's fair to say that it can involve changes in proper appearance, intimate appearance (medically achieved or otherwise), name (legally achieved or otherwise), pronouns, and modes of relationships and relational interaction.[17] Further, as I've noted, it can involve conscious gender identity.

For some, achieving realization will likely be transition's guiding end. Because of this, while the changes made in transition may also reflect various forms of localized phoria, it is also likely that they are made as part of this resistant project of realization. Crucially, when the process of transition is one of realization, another change—recognizable or not—becomes central: a change in interpersonal identity. To put it otherwise, one must become a different "who."

This is why: Recall that the "who" is characterized in the folk system as possessing a precultural naked body that can appear both properly and intimately. Under this spell, the "who" is prior to the appearance. Consequently, the proper appearance one experiences as one's own in the blank open is, in the overworld, merely the effect of an action that the "who" has undertaken—namely, playing make-believe. This difference is critical. For the appearance one experiences in the blank open to be one's own, it cannot merely be the effect of some activity. It must be one's appearance simpliciter—the appearance under which the identity is imputed. This means that to have the proper appearance identified as one's own in the blank open become one's own, one would have to become an entirely new "who."

To (try to) become a new "who" in the overworld, what needs to happen is the following: the original interpersonal identity needs to be overwritten by a new identity in such a way that the overwriting process is not recognizable in the system. This is accomplished through the phenomenon of animation. Animation, recall, is the retroactive institution of the "who" as the source of self-display rather than the mere content of the interpersonal identity that is imputed in acts of attention, observation, and so forth. It is the process by which the interpersonal object enters the mythology of the system, comes to inhabit one of the characters within that mythology, through acts of self-display. In this case, one comes to animate "the transsexual"— framed, of course, in terms of the WBA. As the animation involves overwriting a previous identity, I'll speak more specifically of reanimation.

To animate this identity, the trans individual must engage in a process of intimate self-display. In sharing one's story, one bares one's soul, reveals who one "really is." One engages in a kind of intimate self-revelation. This includes not only self-narrativization but also the appropriate avowals ("I feel so miserable in this body") and appropriate physical and sensory dialogical comportment to others. In case one does this in a way that convinces the professionals, one will be identified as a transsexual—that is, come to have inhabited the identity in at least that context.

This much of the process is supported by the actions of the medical and psychiatric institutions facilitating transsexual transition. However, mirroring our discussion of autobiographical retroaction in the previous section, biographical retroaction likewise fails to explain the always-already claim. Specifically, while it is accepted that the individual has probably from the beginning been a transsexual, the claim that the individual was always, really, a man or woman need not be accepted.[18] Consider the following quote from Harry Benjamin's *The Transsexual Phenomenon*:

> Psychotherapy with the aim of curing transsexualism, so that the patient will accept himself as a man . . . is a useless undertaking with the present available methods. The mind of the transsexual cannot be changed in its false gender orientation.[19]

It's clear—at least as presented in this passage—that Benjamin does not really think that transexuals are who they think they are. He thinks they have "a false gender orientation."[20] So, while he appeals to an incongruence between mind and body, he also rejects the thought that this is sufficient to make the transsexual who they believe themselves to be. That is, he rejects the third claim of the WBA—namely, that having an innate gender identity as a so-and-so, makes one a so-and-so.

To understand the always-already claim, then, we must go beyond the retroactive apparatus by which one becomes a transsexual and look to a more ambitious project of reanimation involving the resistant inversion of the appearance–reality contrast.

Let's begin by noting that the previously mentioned self-revelation unfolds in a fascinating way. An *existential identity* is exposed that contradicts and overturns one's imputed identity. That is, the original biographical identity is revealed to be false and the facade of a deeper existential identity. This is a noteworthy departure from common disclosures that yield merely a more intimate access to the identity rather than the complete overturning of a surface identity. However, neither is it unique. Stories in which one intimately discloses that the life one has been living for the past twenty years isn't who "one really is" (or ever really was) are not that uncommon.

The point is that this form of self-revelation displaces the view that one is "really a woman disguised as a man" by disclosing a deeper truth: underlying this superficial view that one is a woman disguised as a man is the hidden truth that one is really a man.[21] Thus, we see the always-already claim playing its role in this inversion. "I might seem to be a woman pretending to be a man, but, in reality, I am a man who appears to be a woman."

Crucially, this inversion requires the positing of a moral sex at odds with the material one. This positing of moral sex is not an easy move to make. Recall our discussion of Garfinkel in chapter 4. There, we considered a (nontrans) man who had his penis amputated. In this case, there's a moral structure of naturalized nakedness that determines the moral genitalia he has and thereby the material genitalia "he is supposed to have." The original nakedness structure is provided for by the subsumption of this man via morphological cues into male moral sex. In the case at hand, by contrast, the morphological cues will subsume this trans man into female moral sex, thereby conferring a female nakedness structure. So he won't be able to appeal to a moral nakedness structure that determines the material genitalia that he is supposed to have.

He can, however, appeal to interpersonal identity (the one determined by the shared narrative, the narrative of depth). To be sure, one's interpersonal identity is typically imputed during the process of subsumption. And in such cases, the problem mentioned above would remain. In principle, however, there's nothing to prevent him from running it in the opposite direction. To assert that he has always been male is to avow a morally male identity that therefore lays claim to a male nakedness structure. Surgical transition, in this view, brings one's material sex—one's morphology—into alignment with the nakedness structure projected by one's avowed interpersonal identity.

In this view, one's intimate appearance (i.e., naked body) is a sort of superficial, misleading appearance that stands in contrast to the deep reality of the disclosed identity. Henry Rubin speaks, for example, of the common representations of bodies as betrayers.[22] Once relegated to a mere appearance, the body becomes "wrong" not only insofar as it was "not meant to be" but also insofar as it is nothing but a false appearance that misleads us about the true moral sex.

The reversal is plain in Prosser's work. In fact, it's remarkable how closely Prosser's account inverts the original terms of reality enforcement. Drawing on transsexual autobiographies, he sets out the analogy of the wrong body to clothing. The material body ends up being viewed as a kind of "second skin" (a garment) misrepresenting the "inner body."[23] Crucially, in drawing this analogy, he rejects what he sees as the postmodern representation of the body as nothing but a costume. Prosser writes, "That figure of the body as costume is surely welded most firmly to the transsexual. The transsexual changes sexed parts like a set of clothes, treats the body as tractable, provisional, immaterial."[24] He would reject a view that sees everyone in costume/clothes (i.e., postmodern bodies), with the transsexual merely changing bodies/clothes. Instead, he analogizes trans bodily transformation to stripping.

> Transsexual subjects frequently articulate their bodily alienation as discomfort with their skin or bodily encasing: being trapped in the wrong body is figured as being in the wrong, or an extra, or second skin, and transsexuality is expressed as the desire to shed or to step out of this skin.[25]

He cites Jan Morris, who "began to dream of ways in which I might throw off the hide of my body and reveal my pristine self within." He cites Leslie Feinberg, who thinks "how nice it would be to unzip my body from forehead to navel and go on vacation." He cites Raymond Thompson, who "needed to be out of my body, to be free" feeling as if his "'inner body' was forcing itself to the ends of my limbs."[26]

According to Prosser, "Surgery strips the body bare to what it should have been."[27] Prosser doesn't just analogize the wrong body with clothing, then. He also posits a hidden, inner body, beneath the clothing in the case of transsexuality. This inner body, for Prosser, is an internally felt sense of embodiment, a body ego or self. One experiences one's body as male or female through an internal body image or scheme. In this way, the material morphological sex misrepresents the internal moral sex via an inconsistency in nakedness structure.[28]

RESISTANCE AND PRIVILEGE

This inversion of the appearance–reality contrast to achieve realization is not a movement recognized *within* the WBA. It is enacted, rather, *by means of* the account. Rather than accepting the wrong-body account and then building a politic on the basis of it, the very appeal to it (at least as it operates in the external apparatus) is an oppositional response to reality enforcement—indeed, a reversal of it. Moreover, it's a very specific use of the WBA that is adopted by trans people alone.

Neither is this form of resistance recognized by the BTBA. On the presumption that "the oppressive binary" exhausts our understanding of trans oppression, any resistance work in the WBA is impossible to see. From that vantage, it will appear essentializing, reactionary, conservative, and so forth. Only by recognizing the possibility of other forms of trans oppression that do not concern the binary can we begin to alter the long-standing representation of appeals to the WBA as gender conservative and even reactionary. We can approach the position with more subtlety, looking for trans resistance where we can find it rather than foreclosing the possibility from the outset.

Let me tarry, then, with some thoughts about how this fact is occluded. Consider, for example, Garfinkel's description of Agnes. He notes her claims to "have always been a girl" as well as her "remarkably idealized biography in which evidences of her original femininity were exaggerated while evidences of a mixture of characteristics, let alone clear-cut evidences of a male upbringing, were rigorously suppressed."[29] He points to her representation of her penis as "an accidental appendage used for the sole purpose of passing urine. . . . It was never a source of pleasurable feelings; it had always been an accidental appendage stuck on by a cruel trick of fate."[30] And he cites her disidentification with "homosexuals and transvestites": "Just as normals frequently will be at a loss to understand 'why a person would do that,' . . . so did Agnes display the same lack of 'understanding' for such behavior."[31] Thus, Garfinkel refers to Agnes's discursive self-presentation as that of the "120 percent female."[32]

In these respects, Agnes does appear rather conservative in laying claim to the moral order of the normal. As Garfinkel shows, in order to successfully secure this moral status, one will have to position oneself as a normal—one will have to appeal to the natural attitude about sex. One was always and forever female. And, of course, one will have to maintain the central importance of genital surgery in order to maintain a "what nature intended" attitude. That is, genital surgery will have to be the telos of transition.

We need to be very careful here, however. First, it's not as if trans people are the only ones who endorse the natural attitude. A lot of people do. So, we need to raise serious questions about the transphobic selection of trans people for specialized scrutiny in this regard. Second, once we understand the natural attitude as deriving from the constitution of physical persons within the sex-representational system, we can also recognize Agnes's opposition to an oppressive system. Specifically, we see the way in which she contests the representation of "really a man in a dress" by reversing the terms ("really a woman, trapped in a misleading body"). Finally, we need to wonder how this *selective targeting* functions to erase the resistance of trans people.[33] It is one thing, after all, to endorse the natural attitude to maintain an identity in the face of perpetual invalidation and quite another to endorse it merely as an aspect of one's unquestioned position within the moral order.

Having said that—having defended this appeal to the WBA as a resistant gesture—let me be clear that the resistant deployment of the WBA is scarcely immune to criticism. There are obvious worries about its efficacy. First, as I've been pressing, it is very difficult to effect this sort of transformation in the overworld without being merely reduced to a make-believer. This strategy is even more difficult because one must have others accept the WBA in order for there to be a viable interpersonal identity to animate. That is, one's realization depends upon others' deep acceptance of a theory that challenges standard conceptions of gender.

Second, even if the theory is accepted, we find yet another iteration of the appearance-reality contrast—this time between "real" transsexuals and "pretend" ones. So, one's claim to be a woman trapped inside the body of a man can be overturned by another claiming that one is not really a transsexual but merely passing oneself off as one. Of course, if one is merely pretending to be a real transsexual, one is really a man disguised as a woman (or contrariwise). Finally, the very theory itself—the very WBA—can be subject to reversal. This is evident, certainly, in Bernice L. Hausman's work: the WBA as a mere cover story for the actual truth, the exposed truth—namely, the sheer desire for self-engineering.

The most serious worry, to my mind, is that this project marginalizes other ways of being trans. I regard such an appeal as a sort of resistance predicated on privilege—typically class- and race-based privilege. Certainly, the WBA is deeply connected to genital reconstruction technologies, outlining a standard telos, so that a failure to abide by that telos yields ineligibility—that is, it restricts access to womanhood or manhood itself. And it does so through hegemonic class-, race-, and culture-inflected modalities. Consider, after all, that technologies of bodily reconstruction cost a lot of money and, when not covered by a health-care system, are out of reach. More generally, desires are shaped by what is envisioned as possible and by what is valued within a given local subculture; some trans subcultures simply don't center genital reconstruction surgery at all. Other body modifications such as breast augmentation or facial reconstruction are more central.

The problem is this: the WBA ends up getting enshrined as *the way* to find realization, *the* conditions under which reality enforcement is reversed. That is, this form of resistance builds the theory into the background picture of the world against which the interpersonal identity is formulated. As such, it makes claims about the world that need to be built into the background picture of all identities in that world—since background conceptions of the world are shared. Because of this, it requires that this theory structure the background of one's own self-conception, leaving one's sense of self vulnerable to the success (or failure) of that theory. Should one's experience not conform to the WBA, one may retain lurking doubts about one's legitimacy as a transsexual.

Similar concerns, I would argue, in some cases, apply to the BTBA. In such cases, coming out as nonbinary or trans, say, can likewise serve the function of reanimation. That is, self-declaration and sharing serve the function of writing over an old interpersonal identity by animating a new one in the overworld. This is certainly so when one comes out as trans or nonbinary, revealing a different identity that was buried beneath the superficial one. (Note, however, that self-revelation isn't deployed to invert the appearance–reality contrast, unlike the WBA.) But it can also occur when there are no deep revelations to be made (say, one begins to self-identify as nonbinary due to political considerations about gender, as well as various phoric experiences.) The question is whether theory is deployed to secure one's location in the overworld. If it is, the same worries apply.

While we're here, note that there are ways in which the BTBA may also be deployed against the appearance–reality contrast that differ from the inversion attempted by the WBA. Consider, for instance, the view that gender is just socially constructed and there is no one gender that has any priority (sex is viewed as just another aspect of gender, in no way decisive). As the social is often taken to mean that gender is "not real," the strategy is to eliminate the "reality" part altogether. Another way to put it is to say that the reality of sex is simply excised, leaving only apparent (say, performative) gender. In this case, rather than inverting the appearance–reality contrast, the deployment of the BTBA knocks the legs out from under it.

There are other strategies, too. Consider these remarks by Kate Bornstein:

> Years earlier, when I went through my gender change from
> male to female, I glided through life under the commonly
> accepted assumption: I was finally a real woman! That worked
> for me until I ran into a group of politically smart lesbians
> who told me that I wasn't allowed to co-opt the word "woman."

Woman was not a family word that included me. My answer
to this exclusion was to call myself a gender outlaw: I wasn't a
man, I wasn't a woman.[34]

Note that Bornstein is explicit that her gender outlaw self-identification is about political positioning—presumably with regard to
the overworld. Rather than engage in direct contestation—"You say
I'm really a man, I say I'm really a woman"—Bornstein splits the difference, giving up womanhood in exchange for freedom from manhood. "You say I can't be a woman. Okay, at least I'm not a man."
Here the strategy might be described as "sidestepping."

The main point, in any event, is that when the BTBA is used to
construct an interpersonal identity in the overworld for reanimation, it has fallen prey to the same difficulties that beset the WBA.
Specifically, it rules out other ways of being trans, and it places
constraints on one's own self-conception, leaving one at risk of self-
invalidation should one's experience not conform to the theory.

The Work of This Essay

I now turn to the work of the theory developed in this essay. There
are no doubt things the theory does that are not now obvious to me.
My hope is that those things are not harmful. But the expressly stated
work is twofold. First, it is to provide illumination for myself, other
trans and nonbinary people, and our friends—illumination in the
face of the existential WTF. Here I also situate the essay with regard
to the appearance–reality contrast. Rather than invert it, cut the legs
from under it, sidestep it, this essay aims to expose it in graphic detail, casting a light on its most intimate features. Second, the work is
to (hopefully) develop new friendships—friendships with others who
are likewise subject to forms of oppression and who philosophize for
their lives. Crucially, one of the most important things this theory
does not do is to seek realization in the overworld through the exposé.
Instead, its work is to turn away from that project, endorsing, instead,
the second task stated above.

Recall that I began this work with a starting point—namely, the
presumptive validity of trans identity. This starting point depends
on no theory at all. Consequently, the presumption of validity doesn't

depend on the success or failure of my theory. To be sure, ontological pluralism is an aspect of my theory, but it isn't intended to validate trans identities in the overworld. The claim, rather, is simply that there are subcultures with discursive and extradiscursive practices in which trans people are who we say we are. That's not just a piece of my theory; it's simply an undeniable empirical fact.

One must imagine that this essay is written in a community of other trans thinkers and writers. It is addressed to members of this community (these communities), to friends, and to those who would become friends. For instance, one might consider trans philosophers attempting to find their way in a field that is often hostile to us. We can recognize and witness each other; we can draw sustenance from each other. Within this world, our identities are not in question. The philosophy we perform within such worlds is of a different order. To better elucidate how, I want to begin by discussing world-travel as a form of realization distinct from reanimation. Then, I'll discuss the work of the theory itself, in greater detail, contrasting it with the work of the WBA and the BTBA.

WORLD-TRAVEL

World-travel does not require the animation of a new identity in the overworld. Rather, by immersing oneself in a different world—a trans underworld, say—one finds oneself integrated into entirely different practices of interpersonal spatiality that, in turn, require different domains of intelligibility and that therefore secure different interpersonal identities.

Unlike animation, world-travel does not lead to the overwriting of a previous identity. The previous identity continues on in the overworlds one has left. (It may be the one secured through reanimation. It may not.) Should one find oneself in such a world again, it may even come to pass that one's old self-identity will likewise reactivate. (Indeed, one doesn't even need to be back in the old world for the older self-conception to reactivate. Sometimes one can experience both self-identities at once, the two, as it were, dueling with each other.) That said, it is precisely because transformation in the overworld is not the aim that realization is more likely to be successful.

While these trans worlds are far from perfect and are scarcely devoid of transphobia, I don't want to dwell upon their many shortcom-

ings right now (i.e., what I describe below is a bit of an idealization).³⁵
What I want to point to is simply how these worlds depart from the
dominant one with respect to the practices of interpersonal spatiality
in ways that allow for realization therein.

In the dominant world, the proper appearance a trans person
adopts is constituted as either a pretense or a deception and, consequently, can never count as the basis for subsumption and therefore comportment to another. In the resistant world, by contrast,
what had been a disguise or costume becomes proper appearance
simpliciter—that is, becomes one's sensory appearance, the condition
of subsumption and comportment. This is because the content of the
intimate meaning is different in that it does not cite any specific sex-
differentiated strip in advance or, indeed, any strip all. Instead, one
is simply subsumed into the system through boundary observation,
traversal, and self-display, where proper appearance is opaque with
regard to anything else.

In these worlds, proper appearance no longer communicates the
structure of intimate appearance, provides no information whatsoever about the nature of the person's genitalia or even their body and
its moral significance. First, it's never readily apparent what changes,
if any, a trans person may have made with regard to their bodily
morphology: given the wide spectrum of possibilities with regard to
medical interventions, the actual morphology implicated in intimate
appearance can never be read off in advance. Second, and more importantly, this is so because of the operations of intimate practices of
recoding I discussed in chapter 5. The existence of these practices—
their presupposed regularity—means that proper appearance can no
longer communicate a preset strip up front, and, therefore, the illusion of the precultural naked body with an intricate moralized structure written therein is abandoned. (This is not to say that the illusion
of the naked body is abandoned—just the preset strips.) In effect,
there's no way the negotiations of pathways can be announced up
front. Rather, learning about a person's intimate appearance becomes
part of the negotiation toward intimacy rather than something that's
disclosed as a condition of having a proper appearance at all.

These changes then have consequences concerning the very
meaning and reference of terms like *woman* and *man*. According to
the interpersonal spatiality hypothesis, in the overworld, the terms

man and *woman* name different kinds of interpersonal object. In trans underworlds, by contrast, there are no preset differentiated strips. Rather, movements of intimacy and limits on intimacy are communicated and negotiated in the moment. This means that in trans worlds, *man* and *woman* do not have different kinds of interpersonal objects to name. Furthermore, the very conception of what men and women are—those conceptions that were linked to intimate meanings in the dominant world—is dislodged. It now becomes a far more open question just what men and women are. Of course, even the function of communicating an intimate structure euphemistically through the terms (e.g., "discovered to be a woman") has no place.

This isn't to deny that the interpersonal identities have any content built into them. Necessarily, there must be some background conception that confers intelligibility upon the various organized practices of the underworld. And, further, there will be overlaps with the dominant and other worlds as well. So, for instance, the conception of a student may be stable across worlds.

It is to say, however, that while various—and sometimes competing—views about trans and nonbinary folks, theories about gender and so forth, circulate in the underworlds, nothing specific is built into the imputed interpersonal identity itself. Because of that, there's room for exploration and reflection on one's own.

Unsurprisingly, we find a change in the very deployment of the terms *man, woman,* and the like. Instead of merely broadening the application of the term in trans underworlds (as I considered in chapter 3), what we find is that utterances like "X is a woman" take on a different illocutionary force. Specifically, in the dominant world, there's no different force in such an utterance regarding first-, second-, or third-person. In trans subcultures, by contrast, when such utterances are made in the first-person, their function is akin to first-person performatives and first-personal avowals.[36]

In some cases, saying, "I am a man," or, "I am nonbinary," may function like a straightforward performative self-naming, as in "I do hereby self-identify as . . ." This may be used for various political purposes. For instance, one might claim transsexuality in a context that fails to recognize transsexuality just to make a point. Here, one is making an official self-naming pronouncement. And what follows, one hopes, is the attendant community respect for this self-identification. In other cases, however, saying, "I am a man," may be articulating something crucial about one's interpretation of one's life experience—an interpretation of who one is in an existential sense. When used as a gesture of intimacy, there may follow conversations of depth, as participants share what it means to say one is a so-and-so.[37]

In other contexts, however, the avowal may serve as a refusal to share intimately as when somebody asks, "How are you?" (disingenuously), and one replies (disingenuously), "I'm fine." What enables this refusal is the openness of meaning attending to gender terms, so that when somebody says, "I am a man," it is in some ways unclear just what is meant. In this respect, just as we found in our discussion of the blank open, the plethora of possible meanings attending to the gender terms serves as a form of opacity, securing infraintimate privacy. For a boundary to operate here (rather than a mere barrier), the addressee of the avowal must tacitly refrain from imposing their own interpretation of the gender term. That is, they must observe the infraintimate boundary.[38]

EXISTENTIAL IDENTITY AND ILLUMINATION IN THE WTF

In light of my discussion of trans discursive and extradiscursive practices, I now point to some differences in the operation of my own theory with that of the WBA and the BTBA—differences that hinge on the fact that my theory is not deployed to secure realization in the overworld. The first concerns coming into identity. The second concerns self-revelation to others. The third concerns new forms of realization in world-building. Let's take them in order. And let's begin the first with a brief discussion of the process of self-identity transformation.

Coming into Identity, Self-Conception, and Illumination in the WTF

Prior to coming into identity, one's underlying interpersonal affective dispositions may be in extreme tension with one's conscious identity. In this case, one's conscious gender identity will undercut and discredit the phenomenon of self-recognition and interfere with any movement toward realization. In such cases, *irregular interpersonal sentiments* and even interpersonal situations will be moved to the periphery of the self-conception or hidden away altogether. So there will be a psychic splitting between what is represented consciously and what one experiences under the radar.[39]

It's also true that these interpersonal sentiments that have been put to the side will continue to operate—seeking out realization when possible. More than that, they may attack one's self-conception by pressing against the internal coherence of the interpersonal identity. At some point, the egg begins to crack and one starts to come into identity, which, as we saw, is the process of coming to develop a conscious sense of oneself as a gendered being. Nordmarken says this can involve "self-reflection in relation to (1) exposure to new gender conceptualizations and models, (2) gender experimentation, (3) difficult experiences, and/or (4) conversations with others."[40]

While it's natural to think that coming into identity must be the earliest step in the process of transition, the rest of what follows being directed in terms of this self-conception, it's often more complicated. Sometimes one needs to explore first, and this exploration might lead to real changes. Indeed, one might begin to transition outright without having any clear sense of self or even having made a decision at all. In such cases, one's conscious gender identity will follow along behind the journey, constantly trying to make sense of things as they unfold.

That said, changes in one's original conscious gender identity open up possibilities that had not hitherto been recognized. And this, in turn, can allow one's interpersonal sentiments to come to the surface in ways that they hadn't before. Perversely, then the corrosion of an old conscious gender identity and the development of the new one can serve the additional purpose of increasingly allowing for these sentiments to show up more centrally on the conscious radar than they had before. This can, in turn, have the effect of an increase in desire to transition and, with that, a further corrosion of the old conscious gender identity.

Crucially, as this process unfolds, one will find oneself confronting the existential WTF. To make sense of what is happening, the underlying conceptions of the world will need to be jettisoned and, because of this, things would cease to make sense—if they ever did. Here gender conceptualizations and models become particularly relevant, as they can serve the function of addressing the WTF. This can happen in two ways, however, depending upon whether the conceptualization is also serving the function of realization.

Since both the WBA and the BTBA seek realization in the overworld through the process of reanimation, they supply an underlying conception of the world that forms the basis for self-identity. This means that in case the theories are not used strategically or cynically, they close over the existential WTF—that is to say, eliminate it—by replacing the original conceptions of gender that have been undone. In such cases, the theory so thoroughly shapes one's self-identity that it is scarcely identifiable as a theory at all. This, in turn, can effect a new psychic split comparable to the one with which we began. Specifically, the role the theory plays within the larger apparatus of self-revelation toward the end of realization—the reversal of the appearance–reality contrast—is entirely hidden. One's resistance to the overworld is thereby hidden, as one loses touch with what is going on.

The theory I share here, by contrast, does not provide the basic underlying conception of the world(s) by which one might make sense of oneself. Rather, to the extent that I myself have such a conception at all, it is derived from the presupposed background in the constitution of my interpersonal identity in resistant worlds—it is the one acquired when I transitioned through world-travel, and it's one that includes recognition of the existential WTF. The ideas developed within this essay, by contrast, are idiosyncratic reflections that are designed to cast light on the existential WTF without presuming to eliminate it altogether. My essay therefore merely serves an explicit function of providing some orientation rather than the grounding of self-identity.

SELF-REVELATION

While the WBA and the BTBA are presumed in the sharing of one's identity, the theories are not themselves shared (rather, the theory must be endorsed across the board in order to ground the identity). In my case, the theory is precisely what I am sharing. However, as the theory is an important part of my interpersonal identity, to share it is to share something deeply intimate of my existential identity, is to engage in an intimate gesture.

These reflections, after all, are deeply personal. They're based on my own struggles and experiences in interactions with others over the course of my life, and they are therefore invested with deep feeling. And because being a philosopher is a fundamental component of my sense of self, any work of any significance that I undertake under those auspices marks my life. In answer to the question "Who is Talia, really?" the ideas shared here would have place of prominence—at least in some worlds.

To make the point, let me confess that earlier versions of this essay included narrative passages that were autobiographical in character. I shared stories about my transition, about experiences with transphobia, and so forth. I discovered, however, that I felt no vulnerability with regard to these experiences. I had become intimately dead—so inured I had become due to the customary trans requirements of self-revelation. It turned out that I had instead been using these narratives to hold back, to obscure, my ideas themselves. I realized that what truly terrified me was sharing the theory fully, spelling it out in all of its idiosyncratic detail. So, I stripped away the autobiographical segments, leaving the theory—and myself—exposed.

In this respect, the essay may be viewed as a theoretical return to the early days of my transition and my coming into identity many years ago—a return that is analogous to Prosser's autobiographical return that I discussed earlier. Ironically, while Prosser speaks of his own work on autobiography as an "oblique" way of articulating his own—an autobiographical return, of sorts—it might instead be viewed as a theoretical return and a sharing of his own existential identity.[41]

On this point, we might contrast the uses of avowal. In the traditional deployment of the WBA, one avows in accordance with the WBA in order to inhabit a particular identity and animate a particular "who" in the overworld. This self-revelation takes the form of overturning one identity in place of another identity concealed underneath. In the second, however, one does not need to inhabit a new identity, overwrite an old one, since one already has one (or more). Rather, one's avowal is expressly, strictly, connected to one's sense of who and what one is—one's existential identity that one shares in a gesture of intimacy.

In a very real sense, one might understand this theory as, in part, my intimate elaboration of my self-identification as a woman—a sharing made possible through trans community. Of course, as this sharing occurs out in the open, those with ill-intent might overhear the conversation. That is always a risk. I hope that they at least experience themselves as unwelcome interlopers. And I take consolation that they will not truly understand what is being said anyway.

On this point, let me add that I see no reason the WBA and the BTBA can't likewise be shared as an expression of how one makes sense in the WTF. Here, however, neither theory would do any work attempting to secure realization in the overworld. Both, rather, would be shared via the discursive and extradiscursive practices of the trans underworld.

To be sure, one would have to be careful, lest the line between underworld and overworld becomes blurred, leading to an attempt to find realization in the overworld through underworld practices. For instance, in case one comes to self-identify as nonbinary while presenting as readable as either a man or a woman, it would be a mistake to suppose one's erasure in the overworld—one's self-identifications are not taken seriously there—is due to an oppressive binary. The erasure, rather, is due to the fact that the oppressive practices of the overworld do not allow for self-identification in the way that trans underworlds do. The supposition that the erasure was specifically due to the oppressive force of the binary evidences the use of the BTBA as a background account of the overworld in order to achieve realization there.

Transition and Realization

While I stated that I do not seek realization in the overworld, this does not mean I don't seek realization at all. This is, after all, precisely the task of making new friends—friends who likewise struggle against forms of oppression, attempting to find some illumination in the WTF. Further, this might be understood to apply to trans communities themselves, which are heterogeneous. Once we drop the convenient idealizations above, we recognize that, of course, rather than a single underworld, there are multiple ones intersecting in both tension and coalition, subject to the interblending of oppression/resistance and privilege.

This means that I cannot rely on the practices I identified in my trans worlds. Rather, to the extent that interpersonal spatiality is possible across worlds, the pathways must be made from scratch. And the content of interpersonal identity cannot be presumed—not even the rather open ones provided in my trans communities. On the contrary, if any new story and background conception is to unfold, it will be precisely about the generation of new networks of interpersonal spatiality.

On this front, I turn to María Lugones's notion of complex communication—particularly among those who are positioned in entirely different ways "within the limen." Lugones is interested in the possibility of coalition across multiple liminal sites. She regards it as a project because she rejects the presumption of communicative transparency—that is, the idea that just because we are both oppressed, we will be able to understand each other without effort in liminal space.[42] In this rejection, however, Lugones recognizes a creative possibility. As she writes of third-order anger:

> [It] does not depend solely or mainly on recognition of cognitive content, but it calls for an emotional noncognitive response, and it further asks that the emotional response, the echo, acquire cognitive content, that is, that it become fully anger. This acquisition of cognitive content requires that we "listen to its rhythms," that we "learn with it, to move beyond the manner of presentation to the substance."[43]

And of complex communication:

> Complex communication is creative. In complex communication we create and cement relational identities, meanings that did not precede the encounter, ways of life that transcend nationalisms, root identities, and other simplifications of our imaginations.[44]

For Lugones, one must begin by recognizing that a resister is multiple and that they occupy a liminal space, even if this multiplicity is opaque to oneself. This means that what they seem to be doing or meaning may not actually be what they're doing or meaning. One needs to anticipate the polyglossia. While the content of address may be opaque, the form of the address need not be. Precisely through the polyglossia, it says, "We live among colonizers, let's disrupt the monologism by extending the intercultural polyglossia toward a far more subversive conversation."[45]

I would like to further suggest the structural invisibility of another's liminality—precisely their unintelligibility—provides for their infraintimate privacy and protection, their sense of containment. Like the state of the blank open, so central in pretransition self-recognition, a pause in recognition of a hidden depth holds the anticipation of intimate gestures—gestures not predetermined but, perhaps, resonant, formed in the crucible of the infraintimate.

Here, we must start with the presumption of unfathomable existential depth—a capacity for intimate vulnerability far beyond one's ken. It is precisely through this recognition that a permeable boundary can be recognized—not a block but an observation, a deep breath necessary for self-display and therefore intimacy. The content of self-display—say, of one's existential identity—will itself be opaque. But the form can be recognized as conveying a complex vulnerability, as an attempt at comportment. Perhaps it says, "We live among colonizers; let's disrupt the abusive folk system of interpersonal spatiality by extending the intercultural forms of complex intimacy toward far more subversive forms of connection—both distant and close."

Of course, for those of us who have not experienced the effects of colonization, who have benefited immensely from the brutality of our forebears, this will require significant transformative work. Yet this third-order intimacy is suggestive. It can return those of us who came from the blank open back to the blank open, reminding us that before integration into any world, we were proto-objects, open to multiple possibilities. That we became *those* interpersonal objects in *those* worlds was not a given. Neither are the interpersonal objects we might become.

Part III

The Buried Lede

The Liminalities among Us

Chapter 7

The Coloniality of Intimacy

IN "PART II: THE MAIN IDEA," I provided an account of trans oppression and of trans phoria by appealing to interpersonal spatiality theory. My task now is to situate this account within a larger theory of oppression. In this chapter, I argue that the folk system of interpersonal spatiality is a crucial feature of what María Lugones calls the "colonial/modern gender system."[1] Then, in chapters 8 and 9, I examine the transformative emergence of the philosophical concepts *person, self,* and *subject* from within that system during the Enlightenment. I show how interpersonal spatiality theory undermines the false and abusive assumptions underlying their deployment. In all chapters, the question "Who and what are we?" looms large. In this chapter, I begin by introducing Lugones's account of the colonial/modern gender system and some of the challenges it poses. Then, I elaborate my own account of the coloniality of the folk system of interpersonal spatiality. Finally, I return to show how my account helps address some of the challenges mentioned above.

Preliminaries

In his account of "global Euro-centric capitalism," Aníbal Quijano posits two axes of power: the coloniality of power and modernity. The coloniality of power, for Quijano, involves the Eurocentric imposition of racial categories on the world's population in a way that informs and infuses "the areas of social existence"—namely, labor, sex, collective authority, and subjectivity/intersubjectivity.[2] Modernity, according to Quijano, involves the production and centralization of a way of knowing (i.e., rationality) that naturalizes the experiences and cognitive needs of those with power in the colonial capitalist system.[3] Modernity consolidates a view of populations and history according to which Europeans are "culturally advanced" and non-Europeans are "primitive." This effectively positions the latter earlier in time relative to the conceived progress of the human species instantiated in the imagined cultural advancement of the European world.

Seeking to unearth what the concept of intersectionality points to but does not spell out, Lugones introduces "the coloniality of gender" by transforming Quijano's account of the colonial/modern system. According to Lugones, Quijano presumes a Eurocentric account of naturalized gender relations.[4] Specifically, she says he assumes that sex as an area of social existence merely concerns male heterosexual access to females. This assumption involves taking the following three things for granted: heterosexuality, sexual dimorphism, and the inferiority of anatomical females. Lugones, by contrast, understands these three beliefs as contingent, part of the coloniality of power.

In her own account, gender is a feature of the colonial/modern system and is then imposed upon Europeans and non-Europeans alike. Rather than one of Quijano's basic areas, it saturates them all. (One presumes reproduction will remain one of the basic areas of human existence—divested of those assumptions.) Racialized, however, the system possesses both a light and a dark side. On the light (white, European) side, heterosexuality, sexual dimorphism, and feminine weakness are taken for the universal configuration of gender relations.[5] Meanwhile, on the dark side, non-Europeans are positioned outside of and prior to this arrangement. Those who are colonized and enslaved are viewed as deficient—possessing aberrant sexualities, being less sexually dimorphic, and having greater equality in strength, energy, and sexual aggressiveness.

Already this helps reveal the limitations of common formulations of oppression—sexism, heterosexism, and what we might call binarism—as operating exclusively on the light side of gender. A focus on heterosexism as the taken-for-granted form of sexuality—in queer theory and politics, say—risks ignoring the dark side in which those who are enslaved and colonized are characterized as sexually deviant precisely in hyperheterosexuality.[6] A focus on sexism as the construction of women as weak, passive, and subject to violation—perhaps in feminist theory and politics—risks ignoring the dark side in which enslaved and colonized women are characterized as sexually wild and

animalistically powerful. Finally, a focus on the oppressive character of enforced binarism—in trans or intersex theory and politics, for
instance—risks ignoring the dark side in which those who are enslaved and colonized are already represented as aberrantly less sexually dimorphic.

While in her initial introduction of the coloniality of gender,
Lugones speaks of the multiplicity of genders where race and gender
are ever fused, she subsequently begins to use *gender* in more complex ways that turn out to present challenges for transgender theory
and politics. First, she argues that, on the dark side, colonized and
enslaved non-Europeans are, in a sense, not taken to have genders at
all; they have only sex. In this respect, they're effectively constituted
as not women or men and, because of this, she says, not humans but
beasts. This means that gender taken as the correlate of sex cannot
be taken for granted. In some cases, "sex stands alone." She writes:

> Beginning with the colonization of the Americas and the
> Caribbean, a hierarchical, dichotomous distinction between
> human and non-human was imposed on the colonized in the
> service of Western man. It was accompanied by other dichoto-
> mous hierarchical distinctions, among them that between
> men and women. This distinction became a mark of the
> human and a mark of civilization. Only the civilized are men
> or women. Indigenous peoples of the Americas and enslaved
> Africans were classified as not human in species—as ani-
> mals, uncontrollably sexual and wild.[7]

Second, she rejects the view that gender is universal. She takes it
as a mistake—and, indeed, colonial imposition—to assume that all
cultures have gender systems. This is a challenge for trans and queer
theory, which, she rightfully claims, takes gender as universal, welcoming the proliferation of genders as a strategy of resistance.

> New thinking about gender has accompanied the critique of
> the binary provoked by focusing on intersexuality, transgen-
> der, transsexuality, and the introduction of "queer" as a non-
> binary understanding of gender. Yet, the critique of the binary
> has not been accompanied by an unveiling of the relation
> between colonization, race, and gender, nor by an analysis of

gender as a colonial introduction of control of the humanity of the colonized, nor by an understanding that gender obscures rather than uncovers the organization of life among the colonized. The critique has favored thinking of more sexes and genders than two, yet it has not abandoned the universality of gender arrangements.[8]

Finally, Lugones raises serious worries about the possibility of reclaiming womanhood, even in resistance to the dominant meanings. Since gender per se is simply a creation of the modern/colonial system, any resistance to it that still took the form of gender would remain part of that system. To put it differently, allegedly resistant reclamations of womanhood would obscure "the colonial difference." They would hide the way in which gender in its entirety was imposed on cultures that had no such analogue.

In this chapter, I put my account of interpersonal spatiality into dialogue with Lugones's account of the coloniality of gender. In doing so, I believe that I can put trans theory and politics on a new footing while enriching Lugones's decolonial approach.

"Presently, There Appeared Naked People"

The "nakedness" of those indigenous to the land was the first feature mentioned by Christopher Columbus in his journals.[9] And he continues to remark on their nakedness throughout his discussion of their initial encounters.[10] The association of non-Europeans with nakedness and the use of nakedness to signify savagery, primitivity, and animality is so obvious, so ubiquitous, so central to European colonialism that it scarcely requires a comment. It does, however, require an analysis.[11]

This alleged nakedness was, in truth, a complex affair. While in some cases the nakedness involved a complete lack of artifacts of concealment, in others it involved some degree of undress, and in others specifically concerned the exposure of female breasts. However, insofar as the proper appearance of Europeans was taken for granted, those who lacked this presumed appearance were invariably taken to be out of uniform. In effect, in failing to wear European clothing, they were taken to not be wearing clothing at all. Or, rather, because of how their own proper appearances—if they even had proper appearances, in my sense—were constituted, they were not regarded as such in the folk system and instead counted as marked intimate appearances.

Unsurprisingly, spreading the Gospel, converting non-Europeans to Christianity, and the saving of souls was bound up with clothing the naked. As the book of Matthew says: "For I was an hungred, and ye gave me meat: I was thirsty, and ye gave me drink: I was a stranger, and ye took me in: Naked, and ye clothed me: I was sick, and ye visited me: I was in prison, and ye came unto me."[12] William N. Brewster writes:

> The savage races know nothing of the use of clothing from a
> sense of modesty. But the moment these savages accept Jesus
> Christ as their Savior, the sense of shame is developt, and as
> the demoniac was soon clothed and in his right mind, sitting
> at the feet of the Master, so the savages of the South Seas, and
> of Africa have been clothed and transformed by the power of
> Christ.[13]

And, again, unsurprisingly, the relevance of this to commerce was lost on no one. New consumer markets were always in the making, while new labor resources became ready to hand, as Thomas Laurie explains:[14]

> Missions, by bringing the Gospel into connection with mind
> and heart, developed man in his earthly relations. He woke
> up to see that he was naked and needed clothing. The supply
> of this want necessitated commerce, and the need of buying
> clothing stimulated production at home in order to procure
> the wherewith to purchase the commodities of other lands.[15]

However, the spreading of the Gospel was, as Lugones puts it, "the euphemistic mask of . . . sexual violation, control of reproduction, and systematic terror."[16] While those who were colonized and enslaved had their own systems of interpersonal spatiality, the folk system was imposed on them. "Clothing the naked" (forcing them into European clothes) was, in fact, forcing them into an entirely different system—a destructive and abusive program of the highest order.

Aboriginal scholar Irene Watson writes:

> The coloniser—the bringer of cloth to Australia—through the use of force, rape, and violence dragged us into their world of dress and the covering of the naked body. By forcing the ancestors to be other than who they were, the colonisers did not apply law; instead they imposed theft and tyranny upon the indigenous law, its lands and peoples. As we were forced out of nakedness we moved away from living raw in the law.[17]

In being provided with clothing from within the folk system, those who were colonized and enslaved were also provided with nakedness itself. Or if they already had their own nakedness, they were provided with a new kind of nakedness—a folk nakedness.[18] Watson writes:

> In bringing the cloth the colonist also brought to us a reflection of our naked self. We came to know nakedness through the clothed body, and since that time, we have covered our raw and lawful being.[19]

And:

> There are no words that I have come across in our indigenous languages to describe nakedness. Prior to the colonists' invasion of our territories there was no reflection of our nakedness. The reflection of nakedness came with the other, the clothed colonising peoples. Now there are few who physically walk the land naked.[20]

As I read Watson, the social phenomenon of nakedness itself as a marked intimate appearance was brought in through colonization. To be sure, one can describe as naked the members of a culture without this phenomenon because they didn't deploy the same sort of concealment. But, in my sense, nakedness is a well-defined, socially constituted appearance allocated to intimacy, so, in this sense, there was no such thing in this culture prior to the arrival of the clothed colonizing peoples.

This sort of transformation likewise applied to those systems that did involve artifacts. The very meaning of those artifacts placed on the body was changed so that the artifacts *became* clothing, devices of concealment, when they had not already been. Or, even if they had

already been devices of concealment, the significance of the concealment was altered and the location of clothedness in the organized
pathways was changed. This, in turn, had the effect of erasing the
traditional functions of these artifacts—functions that may have
had nothing to do with concealment in the first place, such as sig-
nifying customary distinctions of rank, religion, age, and so forth—
sometimes preventing those who were colonized from engaging in
their traditional forms of labor.[21]

The point is that other systems of interpersonal spatiality were
transformed and forced into hiding. Meanwhile, those who were colonized and enslaved were forced to become different interpersonal
objects altogether—non-European vestorgs, of sorts. The entire sensory appearance of the interpersonal object was transformed, and so
too was the very cosmological background conception sustaining interpersonal identity itself. All the strips and pathways altered—the
gestures enabling intimacy altered. They found themselves in an entirely different interpersonal space.

Indeed, they found that their relation to literal space—the land—
transformed under their feet into property. Recall that systems of interpersonal spatiality implicate literal space and land. For instance,
in the folk system, the contrast between inside and outside is closely
connected to boundaries governing nakedness. We can see, then,
that what Watson is discussing is not merely a transformation in
proper appearance but a transformation in the relationship between
an interpersonal object's sensory appearance and literal space. That
is, "clothing the naked" was closely related to intimate land theft
through the transformation of the colonized into a certain type of
vestorg.

Clothing the Naked, Stripping the Clothed

Despite this catastrophic imposition of the folk system on colonized
and enslaved communities, they were still, ironically, considered
naked regardless of whether they wore clothes.[22] The notion of modesty (and the lack thereof) enabled this attribution. Part of this denial
of modesty no doubt derived from Europeans' initial failure to com-
prehend the existence of different systems of interpersonal spatiality
at play among Americans and Africans and to infer from their lack

of awareness of the folk system ("the only system") that they failed to possess modesty at all. After all, to be conscious of oneself as naked requires some conception of what nakedness is and how it is related to clothing. And Americans and Africans would not have been originally aware of the internal workings of this system—or at least the specifics of the European folk system(s).

However, it wouldn't have taken long to figure it out. Forced into a system, threatened with violence, one learns quickly what nakedness means both within that system and without. Nonetheless, the charges of immodesty proved recalcitrant. That is, despite being inculcated into the European system of interpersonal spatiality, these non-Europeans were thought to be ever incapable of mastering the system. There was something wrong with them. Of course, what really lay at the bottom of this constitution of non-Europeans as immodest (besides resistance) were the interpersonal practices that put them there. That is, the lack of modesty attributed to those who were colonized and enslaved was a consequence of how they were constituted as naked within the system, rather than the other way around. This is evidenced early by Michele de Cuneo's infamous 1492 letter:

> While I was in the boat, I captured a very beautiful Carib woman, whom the aforesaid Lord Admiral gave to me, and with whom, having brought her into my cabin, and she being naked as is their custom, I conceived the desire to take my pleasure. I wanted to put my desire to execution, but she was unwilling for me to do so, and treated me with her nails in such wise that I would have preferred never to have begun. But seeing this (in order to tell you the whole even to the end), I took a rope-end and thrashed her well, following which she produced such screaming and wailing as would cause you not to believe your ears. Finally, we reach an agreement such that, I can tell you, she seemed to have been raised in a veritable school of harlots (October 12, 1492).[23]

As Todorov comments, "These effects also permit, in a striking example, the identification of the Indian woman with a whore: striking, for the woman who violently rejected sexual solicitation finds herself identified with the woman who makes this solicitation her profession."[24] To put it differently, this woman was raped into whoredom.

As those who were colonized and enslaved were assimilated into the folk system, they were not simply funneled into the ordinary positions of man, woman, boy, and girl via standard cue-based subsumptions. They were cued differentially within it. They were fitted with a differential physical person and illusory naked body. They were vestorgs, but not the same sort. For instance, those who were colonized and enslaved were often given distinctive clothing to mark their position; wearing the wrong kind of clothing would lead to being literally stripped and chastised.[25]

To be sure, the general structure of the vestorg remained the same: moving from artifacts on to artifacts off, naked to clothed. However, their position with regard to mythological content of the intimate meaning was different, and so too were the practices in which the mythology inhered. In chapter 4, recall, I said that the intimate meaning effectively represents clothing as a technology designed for females to protect themselves from being raped. I also said that my account was only partial—preparing the way for one that expressly includes race. To complete the account, I now situate that intimate interpretation within a broader mythology—an origin account of feminine modesty.

Robert Michels writes in his 1914 *Sexual Ethics*, "The presumptive origin of the feminine sense of modesty may be regarded as known to the reader. It is most intimately connected with the fact that in primitive times, woman was a form of booty."[26] He then continues:

> Thus a dread of the male, that is to say, a dread of men in general, has come to dominate her life. Hence it has become instinctive in woman to conceal from the masculine gaze those parts of her body which are capable of stimulating man's sexual desires and of exposing woman to sexual aggression. On this view, the sentiment of modesty is a consequence of fear.[27]

In this origin story, the woman of present times contrasts with the woman of "primitive times." We find the "naked primitive" temporally prior to any civilization, behaving in sexual ways that are unchecked by social regulation. This allows for multiple differential positionings with regard to the intimate interpretation of proper appearance: primitive man and primitive woman, civilized man and civilized woman, the contrast between the unrestrained sexuality between men and women in primitive times and the restrained sexuality between men and women of present times—all fused together into a sexually explicit background mythology about the origin of clothedness.

Meanwhile, the actual practices of interpersonal spatiality created the reality of the situation. What really happened was that the physical strips of those who were colonized and enslaved were restricted to the sexual side of the heterorelational complex through differential practices of interpersonal spatiality. This is nowhere more graphic than in the institutionalized interpersonal treatment of enslaved Africans by the English-speaking colonizers. The enslaved Africans were kept naked in slave ships, forced to live in pens naked for purposes of breeding, forced to work with scant clothing.[28] C. Riley Snorton speaks more generally of "the unrelenting scopic availability that defined blackness within the visual economy of racial slavery."[29] And after emancipation, differential positioning continued. Under Jim Crow laws, while restrooms for white people were segregated according to sex, restrooms for "colored" people were not similarly segregated.[30] Rather, they were marked by racial segregation only. Thus, sex segregation was effectively a white segregation. Similarly, the historical inclusion of females in prisons relied on a sex segregation that was simultaneously racialized.[31]

Of crucial note, under the English version of slavery, unlike the Spanish version, those who were enslaved were not permitted to marry. Further, Kimberlé Crenshaw notes that "historically, there has been absolutely no institutional effort to regulate Black female chastity."[32] Indeed, as Saidiya V. Hartman shows, the rape of enslaved Black women was legally unrecognizable:

> In nineteenth-century common law, rape was defined as the forcible carnal knowledge of a female against her will and without her consent. Yet the actual or attempted rape of an enslaved woman was an offense neither recognized nor punished by law. Not only was rape simply unimaginable because of purported black lasciviousness, but also its repression was essential to the displacement of white culpability.[33]

The failure to provide practices of sex segregation, allocation to marriage, and legal or moral recognition of rape precisely exemplifies the differential constitution in nakedness through differential practices of sex segregation and sexual containment. One of the consequences of these practices was yet another ruse of the system. As we saw, the physical strip projects a moral structure onto the naked female body, informing body parts with a teleology provided for by the (hetero)sexual pathway. More than this, as this pathway is part of the larger (hetero)romantic complex in which female engagement in sexuality partakes in an intimate revelation, a limited emotional depth—modesty—is imputed to the female "who." By restricting so-called primitive females to the sexual side only, however, no such analogous depth is imputed. Lacking the self-awareness implied by modesty, she is reduced to surface, no depth whatsoever, no self-awareness. That is to say, by subjecting these enslaved females to the aforementioned strategies of abuse, an illusion of cognitive lack is also effected, and with that, too, a myth of unrapeability.

The consequence of this was a multiplication of forms of nakedness—the cues for subsumption now also sensitive to skin color and other morphological differences—giving us both present-day nakedness and primitive nakedness. Rather than four forms of nakedness, however, it was closer to three. Present-day nakedness imputed the capacity for self-revelation, where the character of self-revelation was differential. By contrast, primitive nakedness, while allowing for a difference in male and female structures, imputed no depth at all and hence no difference in this regard. I'll expand on this point in "The Coloniality of Gender," below.

A Transformation

It's important to recognize that this racialized origin account of nakedness superseded an earlier one.[34] The first was grounded in the book of Genesis—the tale of Adam and Eve. In this story, Adam and Eve sin by eating from the tree of knowledge of good and evil. In so doing, they become aware of their nakedness—aware of their sin—and, for this reason, conceal themselves. Here, nakedness bears the mark of sin, becoming an object of religious shame. As Father Jacques Boileau explains:

> *God* hates nakedness, because it is a sign of our defeat and
> overthrow; and the *Devil* loves it, because it is a mark of his
> Triumph: *God* hates nakedness, because it is the cause of
> sin; and the *Devil* loves it, because it is a proof of our mis-
> ery, and at the same time discovers our indigency, and our
> Crime. . . . *God* hates nakedness of Body, because it is a Figure
> of that of the Soul, and it represents to him continually our
> inward poverty; and the Devil loves nakedness of Body,
> because it makes him remember, that by his address and
> subtilty we have been dispoyled of all the Graces which did
> adorn our Soul.[35]

More than this, the mythology explicitly positions Eve as a temptress
who convinces Adam to eat of the fruit. This conception of the temptress is then written into a motivation for concealment—namely, "to
glorify God by the flesh the woman has to offer a body pure and
chaste, and ought not to expose it to the view and the desires of all
men . . . but to cover it with modesty. . . . She ought to avoid the
evil there is in tempting them by her nakedness."[36] Father Boileau
complaining of women in décolletage makes the link between Eve's
temptation and the temptation of female flesh clear:

> They applaud the victory that the *Devil* obtained over *Eve,* and
> in some sort renew her crime in conforming themselves to
> the estate in which she lived, as soon as ever she became a
> Criminal.[37]

The differences in the two mythologies are notable. In the secular conception, rather than a contrast between a state of innocence
and a state of sin, we find a contrast between a state of nature and a
state of civilization. Rather than indicating righteousness, clothing is
an indication of progress. Rather than women being viewed as more
wicked and sexual than men, active in techniques of temptation,
women are viewed as less sexual than men, passive and, indeed, victims. Rather than viewing the occurrence of sex as the consequence
of succumbing to temptation, it is viewed as the consequence of un-
leashing something like a powerful, natural force. Rather than being
viewed as a sin, sex is viewed as rape. Rather than indicating a deficiency in moral character, the origin account indicates a cognitive

or developmental deficiency. And, finally, most notably, unlike the older, the newer was racial—indeed, racist—in its very content.

Now, to be clear, the new, more secular account did not entirely eclipse or supplant this older one during European expansion. Rather, the two were operative at once, even interacting with each other. Certainly, the older one was in play during colonization—clearly evidenced in the discourse focusing on efforts to spread the Gospel. That said, the nakedness of a people ought to have jarred the Christian conception. If those Indigenous to the land were not clothed, were they somehow not "fallen"? Was this a sort of Garden of Eden? The preferred view—the one that justified colonization—was, of course, that these people were a degenerate form of humankind, a people fallen deeply into sin. Hence, the necessity of spreading the Word.

In this view, dark skin, particularly, Black skin, comes to indicate degeneration into the wicked, the depraved, the demonic (rather than "the earlier than civilization" of the secular account). In line with this, the enslavement of Africans was often justified by the English by appeal to the Curse of Ham—a curse, it should be noted in passing, that befell Ham and his descendants for his seeing his father, Noah, naked, instead of covering him up, as his brothers, Shem and Japheth, would later do (Genesis 9:20–27).

However, it is also clear that the secular mythology was better suited to the needs of coloniality. After all, the Spanish had to justify colonization by classifying their victims as "Enemies of Christ," and this inconveniently required them to introduce the inhabitants to Christ's love before stealing their land and enslaving them. So, it is unsurprising that the secular was of better use.

More than this, however, the new origin account had the benefit of not being a mere tale from days gone by. Instead, the past was made present through constituting those who were colonized and enslaved as "primitives" within that story. That is, mythological figures of the past were made present in a way that they were not in the older mythology. While Adam and Eve were nowhere to be found, naked savages were everywhere to be murdered or exploited. To put it differently, not only was a new mythology deployed in the operations of the European vestorgs—entirely new vestorgs were created so that the mythology could be instantiated in real time.

This shift can be situated within the context of Sylvia Wynter's remarkable "Unsettling the Coloniality of Being/Power/Truth/ Freedom."[38] Centralizing the question "Who and what are we?" Wynter investigates the colonial answer ("Man"). According to Wynter, the European answer shifted toward a thoroughly racialized one, in part, to help facilitate colonial expansion. The prior, medieval answer was, of course, solidly Christian, placing God at the center of the universe, relegating people's status to that of sinner. The new one—the one that emerged during the Renaissance—was humanist in character, placed man at the center, the universe waiting to be known. In the latter, the notions of culture and primitivity become central, supplanting "Enemies of Christ" and the sinner/righteous contrast.[39]

What I am adding now is the importance of sexually—or at least intimately—explicit accounts of the clothedness in answer to the question of what we are within the folk system. Further, I am suggesting that any answer to the question of what we are is shaped by the way in which interpersonal objects are constituted within a given system. It is only because we are constituted as vestorgs in the folk system that the question of clothedness becomes part of the question. And, of course, the answer plays a crucial role in the very constitution of the vestorgs.

Let me add that an understanding of the various localized ways in which vestorgs have been constituted ought to focus on the mythology of both sexuality and clothedness, as well as the practices of interpersonal spatiality. To return to Francisco J. Galarte's suggestion that deception is strongly associated with female sexuality in Mexican, Mexican American, and Chicano worlds, the questions that seem pertinent are how this mythology figures into female proper appearance through rationales of clothedness, as well as the relationship of this mythology to either the Christian or the secular mythologies (i.e., to seduction and rape).[40] I do not pursue this analysis here.

The Coloniality of Gender

My account articulates some of Lugones's most basic ideas while addressing some of her more challenging claims. The very content of the intimate meaning reflects the light and dark sides of sexism, heterosexism, and dimorphism. On the light side, woman is represented as vulnerable, sexuality is represented as socially contained, and, as

I shall develop shortly, because of this, there exists a dignity/vulnerability contrast between men and women. On the dark side, there are none of these things in the intimate interpretation of proper appearance. Further, the actual practices of interpersonal spatiality themselves were deployed to enact that content. Through rape, colonized and enslaved women became anything but vulnerable. Through lack of access to socially recognized relationships, those who were enslaved became hyperheterosexual. Through absence of moral sex segregation and enforced optic availability, those who were enslaved became less dimorphic.

My account may also be useful with regard to Lugones's more contentious claims. Recall that Lugones says that (1) those who were colonized and enslaved were not men and women; (2) those who were colonized and enslaved were not regarded as "human in species"; and (3) it is because those who were colonized and enslaved were not men and women that they were not regarded as "human in species."[41]

On the face of it, both (1) and (3) are exaggerations. As evidenced by some of the quotes in this chapter, those who were colonized and enslaved were most certainly called "men" and "women." And "human in species" belies considerable complexity. The fact is that under colonization the question "What are we?" was under considerable generative pressures. First, there was hardly one uniform view held by all, nor were those who were colonized and enslaved always categorized in the same fashion. Second, it is one thing to say that a certain class of human beings are animal*like* and another to say that they are not part of the human species at all. One might be using *animal* as a put-down rather than as a literal claim. Or, even when the claim is literal, this contrast may matter. For instance, Aristotelianism allows for natural slaves that, while animallike, are nonetheless human. Third, what is meant by *human* shifts depending upon scientific or religious approach and paradigm—Aristotelian or mechanistic. (Such subtleties matter, at least insofar as the very concept of a soul and its relevance to the question is concerned.) Finally, new concepts were being introduced, such as Lockean personhood, as we shall begin investigating in the next few chapters. This allowed for the possibility of humans who were not persons. (This is consistent with the bestialization that Lugones has in mind, but it does not have anything to do with exclusion from the human species.) Clearly, the claim that those who were colonized were re-garded as "not human in species," while sufficient for Lugones's pur-poses, is also a simplification.

Lugones does explain what she means when she denies that those who were colonized and enslaved were constituted as men and women within the system:

> If I am right about the coloniality of gender, in the distinction between the human and the non-human, sex had to stand alone. Gender and sex could not be both inseparably tied and racialized. . . . One may well be interested in arguing that the sex that stood alone in the bestialization of the colonized, was, after all, gendered. What is important to me here is that sex was made to stand alone in the characterization of the colo-nized.[42]

As I read her, Lugones means that while sex and "gender" were both socially constituted, they were constituted as distinct and separable from each other. In other words, she means that the sex–gender distinction was a socially constituted feature of the racialized system. To be sure, the word *gender* as it is used now was not used then. However, those who were colonized and enslaved were taken to lack what we now call "gender"—the civilized aspects that overlay sex. She means that something tantamount to the sex–gender dis-tinction, something that hinged on the nature–culture distinction, was necessary to the bestialization of those who were colonized and enslaved. Finally, she means that insofar as colonized males and fe-males lacked gender in this sense, they weren't men and women.

If we understand *man* and *woman* as requiring cultural aspects, then her point is clear. And in my account, the point can be made starkly: in the secular version of folk personhood, the contrast be-tween nakedness and clothedness is precisely one between nature and culture, primitivity and civilization (as opposed to sin and righ-teousness). For those who were colonized and enslaved, "sex was made to stand alone" in the stark sense that they were constituted as always already naked. Stated in this way, the abusiveness of the con-stitution becomes apparent.

Let's turn to Lugones's claim that those who were colonized and enslaved were regarded as "not human in species." Certainly, to treat somebody as an animal, regardless of categorization, is to dehumanize—that is, to deny them a value that humans are supposed to have. However, dehumanization isn't equivalent to the rather particular express denial of species membership.

What I think can be said is that those who were colonized and enslaved were, in a very plain sense, not *people* with respect to the underlying interpersonal structure of their physical persons and identities. If we recognize the existence of men and women prior to colonization, then it becomes plain that during colonization, new vestorgs were introduced. Meanwhile, the folk people who had already been in existence became expressly white. Whatever the enslaved and colonized vestorgs were, they were certainly not folk people (i.e., men, women, boys, and girls), whether marked white or not.

This idea can be further developed by returning to Lugones's own account:

> I propose to interpret the colonized, non-human males from the civilizing perspective as judged from the normative understanding of "man," the human being par excellence. Females were judged from the normative understanding of "women," the human inversion of men. From this point of view, colonized people became males and females. Males became not-human-as-not-men, and colonized females became not-human-as-not-women.[43]

What she has in mind is the fact that *men* has been used to stand for men, women, boys, and girls alike. For instance, when one says, "man began to roam to the earth," "the race of men," "all men are rational," one presumably means to speak of *all* people. She also means that the marked contrast is judged against the paradigm and found wanting. Aristotelianism captures this perfectly. According to Aristotle, "While the body is from the female, it is the soul that is from the male, for the soul is the reality of a particular body."[44] That is, "the female always provides the material, the male that which fashions it." Thus, for him, "the female is a mutilated male."[45] Or, as Saint Thomas Aquinas explains, a woman is a "defective and misbegotten male" (*deficiens et occasionatus*).[46]

Of course, it did not take Aristotle to make people sexist. And what I want to suggest specifically is that the paradigmicity of man has to do with the very structure of the folk system of interpersonal spatiality. Specifically, I propose that as proper appearance admits of two modes—singular and contrastive—so, too, does man as a sort of interpersonal object. As singular, man is taken for granted and, as such, constitutes the default version of a folk person in general. Once female moral sex becomes explicit in thought—either through sensory presence or through ideation—male moral sex likewise becomes explicit in thought as man now shifts into contrastive mode, ceasing to serve as the default version of folk people but, rather, serving as the correlate of woman.

Woman, however, as an interpersonal object is constituted as the exemplar of vulnerability. First, the proper appearances of man and woman are differential with regard to the concealment/exposure dynamic itself. Aside from cue-affording differences in clothing, style, and grooming, in the West, woman's proper appearance tends to involve fewer artifacts of concealment than does male proper appearance, with the consequence that the former, in contrast to the latter, involves greater "exposure" or lesser "concealment."[47] Second, woman's proper appearance will therefore already be in contrastive mode, or at least have a greater tendency to be in that mode and, therefore, to yield ideational vulnerability. Finally, women are situated as vulnerable in the very intimate interpretation that gives both proper and intimate appearance their meanings.

As woman becomes the exemplar of vulnerability, contrastive man becomes the exemplar of self-containment—of dignity as captured in this folk definition of *person*:

In emphatic use: a human being, as distinguished from an animal, thing, etc. In later use also: an individual regarded as having human rights, dignity, or worth.[48]

What I'm claiming is that the so-called dignity of man is merely the effect of differentially rendering women vulnerable.

For so-called primitive males, however, there was no contrast between dignity and vulnerability precisely because primitive females were not constituted as vulnerable in the first place. For the former, there could be no singular and contrastive mode. Rather, they were paired with enslaved and colonized females—alike ideationally intimized. To be sure, *primitive man* had a generic form (i.e., "primitive man roamed the earth"). However, it was due not to the standardization of his appearance but, rather, to his being marked "primitive" in contrast to the standard civilized man.

If what I've argued is correct, then the denial of humanity to those who were colonized and enslaved was not merely of a piece with the new worldview ushered in by philosophers and other intellectuals. Rather, as the very ideology that placed them prior to culture was part of their constitution as vestorgs, they were literally constituted as a new kind of vestorg—one that, rather than being the vestorgs man and woman, was what made man and woman possible in the first place.

Against the Universality of Gender

Instead of regarding moral sex as equivalent to Lugones's notion of the coloniality of gender, I locate it in one of Quijano's "areas of basic existence"—the area that he calls "subjectivity/intersubjectivity" and that I call "interpersonal space." In other words, I regard moral sex as the form of interpersonal space under the colonial/modern gender system.

It is, however, an area that I regard as fundamental in the sense that interpersonal objects themselves and the very modality by which the world is perceived at all are constituted through it. By this I mean that, in the colonial/modern gender system, collective authority, labor, and reproduction are differentially distributed on the basis of moral sex. Here, moral sex almost seems to serve as the substrate that underlies (the rest of) what Lugones calls "gender." I say "almost" since the constitution of moral sex is mediated through other areas of existence. For instance, the creation and maintenance of vestorgs requires the production of clothing every bit as much as it requires the reproduction of organisms. In this respect, moral sex is wrapped up in and dependent upon the other areas of existence.

In this view, at any rate, moral sex is not universal and so, consequently, neither is gender in the broad sense. Gender is also obviously not universal in the narrow sense that Lugones uses to say that, for those who were colonized and enslaved, "sex stands alone." The contrast between culture as clothing and nature as naked is merely part of the secular mythology that comes to replace the Christian one.

While neither sex nor gender are universal, however, interpersonal spatiality is. Or, at least, it can be presumed to be. And while the claim that interpersonal space is universal is, admittedly, only a presumption, it's also a presumption I share with Lugones. Attentive readers of Lugones know just how much her work concerns intimacy and distance. Indeed, in "Toward a Decolonial Feminism," Lugones explicitly aims "to figure out how to think about intimate, everyday resistant interactions to the colonial difference."[49] She clarifies, "When I think of intimacy here, I am not thinking exclusively or mainly about sexual relations. I am thinking of the interwoven social life among people who are not acting as representatives or officials."[50] I don't know how to think resistance without intimacy. And I don't think that Lugones does either.

One upshot is that, rather than regarding moral sex as something entirely new that was imposed on those who were colonized and enslaved, it ought to be regarded as the form of a system based on something they already had—namely, closeness and distance. And if this is so, then it may be the case that woman and man can be reappropriated and moral sex can be turned against itself.

To illustrate this claim, let's turn to Deborah A. Miranda's "Extermination of the *Joyas*: Gendercide in Spanish California," in which she discusses Indigenous people subsumed into the folk system as morally male yet who dressed as "women," worked with (and as) "women," married "normative men," engaged in "receptive anal intercourse," and served an important religious function in burial rites.[51] Specifically, let's consider what appears to be a straightforward case of reality enforcement—a form of reality enforcement that Miranda herself repeats.[52] The account is provided by Father Palóu:

> Among the gentile [Indian] women (who always worked separately and without mixing with the men) there was one who, by the dress, which was decorously worn, and by the heathen headdress and ornaments displayed, as well as the manner of working, sitting, etc., had all the appearances of a woman, but judging by the face and the absence of breasts, though old enough for that, they concluded that he must be a man, but that he passed himself off always for a woman and was more ashamed than if he really had been a woman.[53]

While Miranda herself argues that such actions should be characterized as "gendercide" rather than "classic homophobia (fear of people with same-sex orientation)," defining *gendercide* "as an act of violence committed against a victim's primary gender identity," we should exercise more caution since we are expressly not presuming the universality of gender (and moral sex).[54] Specifically, we should take seriously the following sorts of questions: Were joyas men who acted like women? Were there women and men at all? Were joyas male? Was the difference in labor determined on the basis of moral sex? Did the system of interpersonal space of the Chumash even have moral sex in the first place? Did forms of eroticism involve the eroticization of intimacy and was eroticism even regarded as intimate? Did differentiated proper appearance communicate differentiated intimate appearance? Was there an appearance–reality contrast? Was this joya in a proper appearance? If so, in what way did this proper appearance operate in interpersonal space? In what ways was the artifact-organism bound up with the system? Was there nakedness? If so, how was it structured, if at all? What was the content of the intimate interpretations necessary for intimate cognition? How did it relate to a cosmology? What was the intimate significance of genitalia? How was actual space—land—incorporated into interpersonal space, and how did that relate to the constitution of interpersonal objects? I could go on, of course. But the radical character of these questions suggests to me two things.

First, once moral sex is recognized as the form of colonial/modern interpersonal space and once it is recognized that intimacy and distance are universal, the possibility of resistant reclaimings of all the trappings of moral sex becomes apparent. This does not merely concern words like *man* and *woman* and their various different uses. On the contrary, it concerns proper and intimate appearance, artifacts and artifact configurations, reappropriated, their intimate interpretation altered. It concerns portions of pathways and intimate gestures recoded. Indeed, it includes vestorgs themselves, disassembled, rebuilt, and possibly abandoned. Above all, however, it concerns new forms of intimacy and distance, new formations of interpersonal space, new interpersonal objects.

Second, while, reality enforcement of the type I have hitherto discussed in this essay involves the erasure of the individual's own conception of the world and their relation to it, the instance cited by Miranda far exceeds such a scope, as I hope to have made plain in this chapter. Reality enforcement here is one among many strategies deployed in the attempted eradication or enslavement of Indigenous people and the appropriation of their land. It is embedded in the very constitution of folk personhood that itself is constituted in racist terms.

This requires those of us on the light side of gender to recognize the colonial difference. And it also raises the question of our own political involvements, our own daily contestations of reality enforcement, the underlying commitments of the resistant worlds in which we exist. In what way do they, if at all, acknowledge the colonial difference? In what way are we complicit in the colonial/modern gender system? These questions are not always easy. But they're necessary. If what I have argued is correct, then to truly break free of reality enforcement, we must undermine the colonial/modern gender system in its entirety. And to do so, we need answers to the question of what we are, or at least might be, beyond the colonial/modern gender system.

Chapter 8
The Enslaving Self

I SAID AT THE OUTSET OF THIS ESSAY that interpersonal spatiality theory overturns the key assumptions underlying the deployment of the concepts *person, self,* and *subject.* In this way, it is a theory come to replace an older one. As this essay winds down, I make good on this idea. To organize the discussion, I focus on two equivalences that are crucial in the deployment of these concepts—namely, the equivalence of *person* and *self* and the equivalence of *self* and *subject.* In this chapter, I focus on the first, and in the final chapter, I focus on the second.

My aim is not merely to reject the concepts. My aim is also to understand why the concepts arrived and how they serve the interests of the colonial/modern gender system. In this respect, these concluding chapters are continuous with chapter 7.

In this chapter, I examine the emergence of the philosophical concepts *person* and *self* through the work of John Locke. The two assumptions I consider are that morphology and species membership are irrelevant to moral status and that, by contrast, self-awareness is central to one's moral status. Much of this chapter shows how these concepts and assumptions serve as Locke's justification of chattel slavery—a justification grounded in a deep anti-Black racism. (Because this chapter includes detailed historical exegesis, those uninterested in that sort of scholarship should feel free to skim or skip those sections. Most of it, however, has been submerged into notes.)

After introducing the two assumptions and showing how interpersonal spatiality theory contests them, I provide necessary historical background. Then I show how a commitment to the two assumptions enables Locke to resolve an apparent inconsistency between his involvement in the institution of chattel slavery and his "just war" justification of slavery in the *Second Treatise.* I conclude by considering the significance of Locke's work with regard to what Sylvia Wynter calls the "two conceptions of Man."

Two Assumptions

The equation of *person* and *self* is underwritten by at least the following two assumptions: First, morphology and species membership are irrelevant to moral status (***morpho-species irrelevance***). Second, moral status derives from self-awareness (***centrality of self-awareness***). These days, it is common to formulate the first in terms of species membership alone. For instance, one might say that it is speciesist to link moral status to sheer membership within the species *Homo sapiens*. Should it turn out that a species other than *Homo sapiens*—say, *Corvus brachyrhynchos*—is self-aware, then they would bear the same moral status that members of the species *Homo sapiens* do, at least those humans who were likewise self-aware.

While species membership is, from the perspective of biological science, a more precise way of framing the matter, morphology is actually more relevant for our purposes because it's a key aspect of my theory as well as Locke's, whose biology was meager and who, in any event, harbored worries about our capacity to access the true nature of a species. I should also note that I'm purposefully vague in speaking of "self-awareness." What I mean, roughly, is the capacity to self-reflect. However, for the purposes of this current discussion, I leave the notion rather open in order to include other cognitive features associated with personhood, such as autonomy.

While some of the assumptions we'll eventually discuss are well hidden, these assumptions are not. Indeed, they're well known for leading to ableist conclusions. This is certainly so in the most traditional version of the view that self-awareness confers moral status. This traditional version is exemplified by the Argentinian court's 2015 determination that Sandra the orangutan is "una persona non-humana" (a nonhuman person) and therefore a "subject of rights"—this sets the threshold for personhood very high.[1] In this position, personhood could only be applied to a few animals: humans, some other great apes, and possibly dolphins.[2] Such a position clearly leads to ableist conclusions, as it would deny the moral status of people deemed not to pass the threshold. Indeed, it's subject to an unintentional reductio through Peter Singer's notorious ethical legitimation of the killing of cognitively disabled infants.[3]

The irony is that it's not even clear how some particular form of self-awareness is supposed to deliver moral status in the first place. After all, many animals are quite intelligent, and it's likely that there are various degrees of cognitive capacity for self-awareness and therefore different degrees of moral value (on this view). This recognition forces us to question what is so special about the one deemed to deliver personhood.[4] Or, rather, how is it—why is it—that some grand value is bestowed upon this form of cognition specifically?

Meanwhile, even versions that lower the threshold are invariably ableist. Ones that endorse such a scale of degrees of moral status will still rank people with cognitive disabilities at a lower level, and ones that set the level as low as possible—at sheer sentience, say—have surely departed from the notion of personhood altogether. Of course, none can explain the moral value of people who have permanently lost sentience.

To be clear, I have no interest in defending the moral status of people with cognitive disabilities, as I take this moral status as a starting point. Further, in case one did want to establish this starting point, I have no interest in insisting that one moral theory that does so is better than another. My aim, rather, is to show how and why interpersonal spatiality undermines these assumptions as both false and abusive.

Interpersonal spatiality undermines morphological irrelevance by restoring the link between morphology and moral value. This is not to grant morphology some magical power. It is, rather, to recognize that interpersonal objects are subsumed on the basis of morphological cues and that interpersonal objects are subject to morally binding boundaries. Regardless of cognitive status, folk people can be violated and abused, and the character of boundaries is the same—namely, ones that facilitate intimacy and distance. People with cognitive disabilities, like all folk people, are valuable within the context of relational connectedness, a complex fabric of society. To put it differently, no interpersonal object possesses moral status as some independent entity. The value is instituted, rather, through the relations that constitute an expansive universe of interpersonal space. In light of this, the centrality of self-awareness must be rejected too.

In response to the worry that I have effectively endorsed a kind of morpho-centrism that, while broad enough to accommodate different species such as Vulcans and Kryptonians, excludes morphologically distinct beings, let me note the following. First, nothing I have said denies that morphologically distinct animals—say, dolphins—have their own systems of interpersonal spatiality. Second, nothing I have said denies that the folk system itself makes room for certain animals—dogs and cats, say—by bestowing a certain sort of interpersonal boundary distinct from the one governing folk people. Finally, nothing I have said affirms that interpersonal spatiality exhaustively accounts for morality. If it accounts for anything—or, rather, if it replaces anything—it is the misguided notion of *person* as articulated in the typical version above.

Let me also be clear that just because interpersonal spatiality theory rules out certain ableist assumptions doesn't mean that the folk system itself isn't ableist. In fact, we've already discussed the abuses of individuals with intersex conditions—the mundane sensory violations, the surgical violations. No doubt such supposedly medically justified violations against folks with disabilities are legion. More than this, however, the folk system institutes a normative morphology that is then implicated in normative strips and pathways, raising questions about the exclusion of folks with disabilities from various forms of interpersonal spatiality. Further, the centralization of bounded-governed visual access—the constitution of nakedness largely in terms of that—marginalizes or excludes those with loss of vision. While I am not providing a thorough analysis here, it should be plain that one is possible. With the assumptions in hand, at any rate, let's now turn to the historical emergence of these assumptions and the emergence of the concepts *person* and *self*.

Historical Emergence

The interrelated philosophical concepts of *person, self,* and *subject* are central organizing categories in contemporary philosophy and theory more generally: they define the terrain of investigation and organize how we think about the issues that pertain principally to "us." To a very large extent, they have a taken-for-granted quality, so much so that they might seem to be perennial concepts, concepts without a birth or history. Yet they are not.

While the question "What are we?" can lay a good claim to being perennial, the question "What is a person?" can't. The thought that to answer the latter is to answer the former is already an assumption that can be questioned. Historically speaking, there have been many ways of answering the first question that do not appeal to *person* or *self* at all—approaches that avail themselves of different concepts, such as *human being, soul, spirit,* and so forth.

The fact is, while some philosophical issues might be perennial, over the course of its long history, philosophy can also shift. Issues that were considered important at one time disappear years later. While sometimes the issues reappear in new ways, sometimes they don't. And as philosophical questions shift, new concepts often come into existence to accommodate new, emerging philosophical problems, while old ones slip into the past.

These concepts are not merely ones central to this system or that—concepts such as Immanuel Kant's synthetic a priori or Martin Heidegger's being-in-the world. Rather, these are concepts that come to occupy a presumed, communal philosophical terrain, an expanse that is replete with questions, concerns, and claims, and the ideas that are taken for granted in the formulation thereof. Characteristic of these concepts is the deployment of a term—either entirely invented or repurposed from a folk use—whose significance is assumed in its uses by the various philosophers to be uniform. Whether or not its significance is actually uniform, underlying the deployments of the term lurk various more-or-less shared assumptions and commitments that constitute the grounds for the deployment.

The concepts of *person* and *self* are of this sort. They emerge during the period known as the Enlightenment. As Therese Scarpelli Cory explains:

> The philosopher paging through medieval scholastic philosophical and theological works in search of treatises on "the self" or "the I" is doomed to disappointment. Even the technical vocabulary of "self" or "Ego," as it would be used in later thinkers, is absent from medieval scholasticism. . . . The Latin term *ego* is nothing more than a pronoun naming a substance in the first person. . . . Nor is there any noun corresponding to "self." . . . Scholastic treatments of "person" (*persona*) emphasize individuality, incommunicability, and rational

nature—considerations that seem to have little in common with post-Lockean concepts of the person as a locus of moral responsibility and self-consciousness.[5]

This isn't to deny that philosophers were interested in self-awareness, or what Cory calls "the subjective dimension of human experience," before then.[6] It is, however, to claim that self-awareness came to play an important role in metaphysical, epistemological, and ethical questions that it had not hitherto enjoyed with such taken-for-granted systematicity involving the creation of new philosophical concepts, a shift in philosophical perspective, the adoption of new starting points, new assumptions.

The *Oxford English Dictionary* says that *person* starts to be used in a "general philosophical sense" as "a conscious or rational being" around 1659.[7] This is a departure from what I call the ordinary sense of *person* and *people* (circa 1200 and 1330, respectively) defined by the *Oxford English Dictionary* as "an individual human being; a man, woman, or child. In ordinary usage, the unmarked plural is expressed by the word *people*; *persons* emphasizes the plurality and individuality of the referent" and "men or women; men, women, and children; folk."[8] It's also a departure from the theological senses "each of the three modes of being of God (Father, Son, and Holy Spirit) which together constitute the Trinity" (c. 1325) and "the personality of Christ, esp. as uniting divine and human natures" (1357).[9]

Meanwhile *self* is first used in its philosophical sense in 1641.[10] Although *self* had been used as a noun before this time, it is in this new philosophical deployment that we get the link with self-consciousness. Indeed, it is just around this time that the term *self-consciousness* ("Consciousness of one's own existence, identity, sensations, etc.; self-awareness") itself emerges (1646).[11] The *Oxford English Dictionary* defines this philosophical sense of *self* as follows:

> Chiefly *Philosophy*. The ego (often identified with the soul or mind as distinct from the body); the subject of all that one does and experiences during one's existence; a true or enduring personal identity. Also: a person as the object of introspection; that to which a person refers by singular first-person pronouns (as opposed to other persons or things).[12]

Of course, the philosopher who epitomizes the emergence of the philosophical concepts *person* and *self* is John Locke. While Thomas Hobbes is one of the earliest English thinkers to use *person* philosophically (an individual whose behavior counts as an action—either of itself or some other thing), Locke is the first to define it in terms of self-consciousness.[13]

Locke's key move is to pull the term *person* away from its ordinary meaning, giving it a new philosophical one—one provided for by *self* and therefore self-consciousness. In the ordinary use, according to Locke *person* and *man* are used interchangeably. He claims, however, that this ordinary use involves the conflation of distinct ideas:

> I know that, in the ordinary way of speaking, the same Person, and the same Man, stand for one and the same thing. . . . But yet, when we will enquire what makes the same *Spirit, Man,* or *Person,* we must fix the ideas of *Spirit, Man,* or *Person* in our Minds.[14]

It is worth noting, however, that rather than outright rejecting the ordinary way of speaking, Locke distinguishes between "civil" and "philosophical" uses of the terms. The latter aims "to convey the precise Notion of Things," while the former serves "for the upholding common Conversation and Commerce, about the ordinary Affairs and Conveniences of civil Life, in the Societies of Men, one amongst another."[15] In this way, I imagine Locke initiates a specifically philosophical deployment of *person* and *self.* They become technical, philosophical terms, playing roles in various philosophical enterprises of metaphysical, epistemological, and ethical import.

Locke defines *person* as "a thinking, intelligent being that has reason and reflection and can consider itself as itself, the same thinking thing in different times and places."[16] He defines *self* as "that conscious thinking thing, (whatever Substance made up of whether Spiritual, or Material, Simple, or Compounded, it matters not), which is sensible, or conscious of pleasure and pain, capable of happiness or misery, and so is concern'd for it *self,* as far as that consciousness extends."[17] And he claims that a person just is a self: "*Person,* as I take it, is the name for this *self.* Where-ever a Man finds, what he calls *himself,* there I think another may say is the same *Person.*"[18]

Meanwhile, Locke writes of man:

> Ingenuous observation puts it past doubt, that the *Idea* in our
> Minds, of which the Sound *Man* in our Mouths is the Sign, is
> nothing else but of an Animal of such a certain Form: Since I
> think I may be confident, that whoever should see a Creature
> of his own Shape and Make, though it has no more reason all
> its Life, than a *Cat* or a *Parrot,* would call him still a *Man.*[19]

All of this occurs in a larger historical context, of course. When
Locke's notion of *person* arrives on the scene, the older Aristotelian,
hylomorphic worldview is giving way to the rise of the new mechanical sciences: philosophers are trying to negotiate their way between the
two competing visions—the former of which had provided the philosophical underpinnings of the prevailing Christian worldview since
the Renaissance. The very question "What are we?" is up for grabs.
Certainly, the abandonment of Aristotelian hylomorphism (form and
matter) in favor of the corpuscularian hypothesis (matter as tiny particles) had profound consequences for the conceptualization of the
human and, as Christianity was the law of the land, the soul.

It is also important to recognize, however, that this was a crucial
period in European colonial expansion. Consequently, it is also true
that answers to the question "What are we?" had political relevance.
According to Charles W. Mills, the Enlightenment saw the development of a herrenvolk ethics according to which nonwhites were
Untermenschen (subpersons) who did not qualify as those men who
were created equal.[20] In his view, while Africans were classified as
human in species, they were regarded as nonpersons. Mills writes,
"So 'person' may extend far beyond the human. But my concern here
is, so to speak . . . not . . . the demarcation and adjudication of the
non-human person but rather the demarcation and adjudication of
the human non-person."[21] And:

> "Person" is not co-extensive with "human" because to be
> human is neither necessary nor sufficient for personhood.
> Non-human entities exist that count as persons while human
> entities exist that do not count as persons. Not all humans
> have been granted the moral status to which their presump-
> tive personhood should have entitled them.[22]

In what follows, I want to argue that Locke's distinction between *man* and *person* is designed, in part, to accomplish precisely what Mills suggests. More specifically, I argue that the distinction allows Locke to deny that Africans are rational, while still supporting their baptism. To set the stage for this, I want to place Locke's work within the context of Morgan Godwyn's *The Negro's and Indians Advocate, Suing for Their Admission into the Church* (1680)—a work recognized by Frederick Douglass as the opening salvo in the fight for abolition.[23] Let's begin with some background.

At the beginning of the English institution of slavery there was some question as to whether allowing those who were enslaved to be baptized would require their liberation on the grounds that Christians could not be enslaved. So, in 1667, Charles II declared that the baptism of those who were enslaved would not lead to their liberation. This is notably reflected in the first of the two mentions of slavery in *The Fundamental Constitutions of Carolina* (Article 107), of which Locke was a coauthor. Nonetheless, there continued to be a reluctance to allow the conversion of those who were enslaved. After all, the grounds for baptism would also appear to be grounds for outright liberation.

Morgan Godwyn, an Anglican clergyman and former student of Locke, stirred up controversy in Virginia by urging the plantation owners to promote Christianity and to convert those who were enslaved. He was met with such hostility that he fled to Barbados, where he continued promoting his message, which, of course, was again met with resistance. He also began composing what would become *The Negro's and Indians Advocate*.[24] In 1685, he delivered (and subsequently published) a fiery sermon at Westminster condemning the institution of slavery and denouncing those who supported it both abroad and in England and, by implication, the soon-to-be crowned James II, Duke of York and director of the Royal African Company, for effectively making a pact with the devil.[25] At the beginning of the sermon, Godwyn acknowledged the risks he was undertaking. And Godwyn shortly thereafter mysteriously disappeared until his death in 1686.

As to the question of whether Locke had even read Godwyn's *Negro's and Indians Advocate,* it's certainly hard to believe that he hadn't. We know that he had a copy in his library, and the commotion that Godwyn created would have been hard not to notice—particularly given Locke's investments and other interests.[26] Never mind that Godwyn was Locke's former student. However, it's not necessary to assume that Locke had read Godwyn for my approach to be effective. The sheer contrast between the two of them will suffice for my purpose—namely, to clarify Locke's position.

In the first chapter, Godwyn aims to establish the following:

1. *First,* That *naturally* there is in every Man an equal *Right to Religion.*
2. *Secondly,* That *Negro's* are Men, and therefore are invested with the *same Right.*
3. *Thirdly,* That being thus qualified and invested, to deprive them of this *Right* is the *highest injustice.*[27]

We'll focus on the first two, since they virtually serve as premises for the last. Godwyn says of the first:

> Of all Creatures here below, Man only hath the notion of a *Deity,* and a propriety in *Religion.* Which *Right and Propriety* doth belong unto him only upon the account of his being Man; that is, because he is endued with a reasonable and immortal Soul, which alone constitutes him *a Man,* and capacitates him for *Religion.*[28]

Let's call the claim that possession of a rational soul is required to be a man and that this alone is what qualifies man for religion "Godwyn's presupposition."

Godwyn's central thesis, of course, is that Africans are men. While this may seem obvious, Godwyn is battling statements he has heard both abroad and in England, sometimes expressed privately and "in the dark"—namely, that while Africans resemble men in their appearance, they lack souls and are therefore not men.[29] Obviously, in such a view it would be pointless to baptize Africans. Let's call this the "plantation thesis." Obviously, then, the plantation thesis is Godwyn's main target.

The question I ask is this: What was Locke's position? Did he agree with Godwyn? The plantation owners? In my view, Locke's new distinction between *man* and *person* enabled him to hold a third position—one that committed to the spirit of the planation thesis while allowing for the possibility of baptism. To put it differently, Locke's distinction between *man* and *person* enabled him to deny that Africans were rational and that they had any moral status, while simultaneously allowing him to commit to their baptism.

An Inconsistency in Locke

As Robert Bernasconi and Anika Maaza Mann argue, Locke played a guiding role in shaping the English version of chattel slavery.[30] They note, "Few Englishmen who had not visited North America and the Caribbean knew more about the extent, nature, and impact of slavery than Locke."[31] In 1663, he invested in the Company of Royal Adventurers, which became the Royal African Company when it was given a monopoly in the slave trade on the West African Coast—a monopoly marked by the advent of English involvement in slavery. The Royal African Company was succeeded by the Royal African Company of England due to financial difficulties in 1671, and Locke increased his investments in it in 1674. Meanwhile, he invested in a company of merchant adventurers that traded with the Bahamas, which, of course, was using slave labor in its production of goods.

Beyond investment, Locke served as the secretary for the Lord Proprietors of Carolina from 1668 to 1675. The Lord Proprietors were eight men—one of them, Anthony Ashley Cooper, first Earl of Shaftesbury—who had been granted a huge swath of land in 1663. Notably, Locke was involved in the writing of *The Fundamental Constitutions of Carolina* (1669)—a document to which I'll return in due course. In 1673, shortly after Shaftesbury was appointed to the Council of Trade and Plantations, a body that advised Charles II on matters pertaining to its colonies in America and the West Indies, Locke began to serve as its secretary. And he continued to serve until 1676. Finally, Locke served as one of eight officers in "His Majesty's Commissioners for Promoting the Trade of This Kingdom and for Inspecting and Improving His Plantations in America and Elsewhere," which advised the king on matters pertaining to the colonies (e.g., production, government) from 1696 to 1701.

Notoriously, then, Locke's heavy involvement in the transatlantic slave trade stands in acute tension with the claims he makes in his *Two Treatises of Government*.[32] Overall, the *Second Treatise* articulates what appears to be a limited defense of slavery. Specifically, it appears justified only when captives are taken in a just war.[33] "And thus *Captives,* taken in a just and lawful War, and such only, are *subject to a Despotical Power.*"[34] In light of this, Locke expressly disavows hereditary slavery: "So that the Children, whatever may have happened to the Fathers, are Free-men, and the Absolute Power of the *Conquerour* reaches no farther than the Persons of the Men, that were subdued by him."[35] One wonders, therefore, what he might have to say about chattel slavery that was expressly hereditary.[36]

While there have been many ways of addressing this apparent contradiction, it seems to me that if Locke did intend this argument to apply to chattel slavery, there must be something like a missing claim that resolves the contradiction.[37] I propose the following:

> Racist thesis (RT): Africans lack reason and are therefore incapable of upholding the principles of human nature. They live in a perpetual state of war.[38]

This solves the contradiction. If Locke held RT, rather than endorsing the view that the crimes of the father pass on to the child, he would maintain that Africans as a whole group were incapable of upholding the principles of human nature and therefore perpetually enslaveable. While he wouldn't commit to hereditary slavery per se, his racism would make the difference irrelevant.

The early portions of the *Second Treatise* provide the context for attributing RT to Locke. While Locke ultimately justifies slavery on the basis of a just war later (in the chapter "Of Conquest"), the groundwork for this begins much earlier. Locke prepares the way in "Of the State of Nature" and "Of the State of War." Locke introduces "the Crime which consists in violating the Law, and varying from the right Rule of Reason, whereby a Man so far becomes degenerate, and declares himself to quit the Principles of Human Nature, and to be a noxious creature."[39] Locke says that this man, "having renounced Reason, the common Rule and Measure, God hath given to Mankind, hath by the unjust Violence and Slaughter he hath committed upon one, declared War against all Mankind, and therefore may be destroyed as a *Lyon* or a *Tyger,* one of those wild Savage Beasts, with whom Men can have no Society nor Security."[40] If Locke held that Africans lacked reason and could not abide by the principles of human nature, then he would have also held that they could be destroyed as "one of those wild Savage Beasts" and that, consequently, they could be enslaved.

However, this solution seems, in turn, to raise a second tension. If Locke followed the plantation owners in denying that Africans were men and that they had souls, why would Locke support the baptism of Africans? To address this, I proceed as follows: First, I ask whether Locke thought that Africans were men (i.e., what he would have thought of Godwyn's thesis). Second, I ask about his views on the afterlife and baptism (i.e., what he would have said about Godwyn's presupposition). Each question bears on the two underlying assumptions with which we began, respectively.

The *Essay*: Morpho-Species Irrelevance

Aristotle is one of Locke's main opponents in the *Essay Concerning Human Understanding*. And this is certainly so when it comes to an account of man. In the Aristotelian view, men are animals, differentiated from other species by rationality. Crucially, this species membership involves a corresponding substantial form. (Any composite substance is constituted through a distinctive value-laden form that actualizes potential matter.) We must therefore be careful not to conflate this view with the contemporary one that characterizes the human being in terms of the species *Homo sapiens*. In the Aristotelian view, morphology and rationality are wedded together in the value-conferring form(s). For Aristotle, it wouldn't be possible for a man to entirely lack reason and still be a man.

Locke rejects this. He aims to decouple rationality—the alleged distinctive value of man—from physical morphology and species membership. This leaves open the possibility that there are beings that share in our physical morphology and are members of the same species as us and yet fail to possess rationality at all, fail to partake in the value that is the alleged distinctiveness of man. To put it differently, while cognitive capacity is still taken to confer value, this value is not mediated through hylomorphism, nor does it have any connection to morphology and membership within any particular species. (Rather, the moral value is based on personhood.)

Locke's rejection of the Aristotelian view of man is part of a more general attack on hylomorphism that consists largely in arguing that nature doesn't conform to substantial forms. Specifically, by pointing to in-between cases, Locke tries to undermine the view that things in the universe can be exhaustively divided into exclusive sorts and to show that how we draw the line between species is somewhat arbitrary. Locke often uses the Aristotelian account of man as rational animal to make this move.[41]

> There are Creatures in the World, that have shapes like ours, but are hairy, and want Language and Reason. *There are Naturals amongst us that have perfectly our shape, but want reason, and some of them Language too.* There are Creatures, as 'tis said, that, with Language and Reason, and a shape in other Things agreeing with ours, have hairy Tails; others where the Males have no Beards, and others where the Females have. . . . *Shall the difference of Hair only on the Skin, be a mark of a different internal specifick constitution between a Changeling and a Drill, when they agree in Shape, and want of Reason and Speech?*[42]

Locke also writes:

> 'Twould possibly be thought a bold Paradox, if not a very dangerous Falshood, if I should say, that that some *Changelings* who have lived forty years together, without any appearance of Reason, are something between a Man and Beast. Which prejudice is founded upon nothing else but a false Supposition, that these two Names, *Man* and *Beast,* stand for distinct Species so set out by real Essences, that there can come no other Species between them.[43]

And:

> For if History lie not, Women have conceived by Drills; and what real *Species,* by that measure, such a Production will be in Nature, will be a new Question; and we have Reason to think this not impossible, since Mules and Gimars, the one from the mixture of an Ass and a Mare, the other from the mixture of a Bull and a Mare, are so frequent in the World.[44]

Now, if we put Locke's musings about a changeling species aside, it's likely that Locke would have, according to his own definition, affirmed that Africans were men. However, this rejection yields entirely different upshots for the two men. While for Godwyn this rejection would be of considerable consequence, for Locke it would mean virtually nothing. Man, for Locke, isn't the locus of moral value. A person is.

Notably, Locke mentions race several times in the *Essay*.[45] Indeed, he expressly takes up the question of whether Africans are men, although somewhat obliquely. (I say "obliquely" since the discussion ostensibly concerns his critique of the usefulness of maxims such as "Whatever is, is.")

In the passage in question, Locke examines three positions, all of which he finds wanting. This is the first:

> A Child having framed the *Idea* of a *Man*, it is probable, that his *Idea* is just like that Picture, which the Painter makes of the visible Appearances joyned together. . . . The Child can demonstrate to you, that *a Negro is not a Man*, because White-colour was one of the constant simple *Ideas* of the complex *Idea* he calls *Man*.[46]

His tone is critical. I imagine he would have regarded the child as lacking sufficient experience to abstract from white skin color to arrive at the idea that most speakers have in mind. He then goes on to use two other accounts of man to make his case. The last of these is a Platonic account that would require man to have reason and some body or other, leaving morphology entirely open. Locke obviously rejects this. The middle one, however, is particularly interesting:

> Another that hath gone farther in framing and collecting the *Idea* he calls *Man*, and to the outward shape adds *Laughter* and *Rational Discourse*, may demonstrate, that Infants, and Changelings are no Men.[47]

It's interesting because this is precisely the argument Godwyn provides to establish that Africans are men:

> The consideration of the shape and figure of our *Negro's* Bodies, their Limbs and Members; their Voice and Countenance, in all things according with other Mens; together with their *Risibility* and *Discourse* (Man's *peculiar* Faculties) should be a sufficient Conviction.[48]

Locke rejects Godwyn's argument on the grounds that this account of man would end up excluding infants and changelings. That is, Locke does not make risibility and rational discourse a requirement for being a man. To repeat: while Locke affirms Godwyn's thesis, he also guts it of any significance.

The *Essay*: The Centrality of Self-Awareness

Let's now turn to Godwyn's presupposition: the view that possession of a soul is requisite for religion. We'll start with some more background context. With the rejection of Aristotelianism, the status of the soul was placed into question. In Aquinas's hands, the Aristotelian view had provided a framework: the human soul was the (immortal) substantial form, and the human was the composite of form (soul) and matter (body). With the abandonment of hylomorphism, however, two questions became pressing: What *is* the soul, and how is the soul related to the body?

Consider: If the soul isn't a substantial form, what is it? A sheer collection of matter? And if so, what hopes could it have for lasting much longer than the body? If it isn't composed of matter, what is it composed of, and how is it related to the body, which is composed of matter? Certainly, René Descartes attempted to provide a new way of thinking about an immaterial soul as conscious thought itself, and he viewed the human being as the substantial union of soul and body (the latter now understood as a machine made of matter).[49] Unfortunately, the union proved notoriously difficult to secure, given Descartes's unsatisfying explanation of the causal interaction between the two.

For Locke, Descartes's account of the soul also depended on the empirically dubious claim that the soul was always engaged in conscious thought, including during deep sleep (otherwise a soul would cease to exist every time we slept, and so we would have many souls).[50] Rather, Locke regarded the soul as the unknown source of one's capacity for thought and capacity to move one's body.[51] Indeed, he claimed that it was possible for God to "superadd" the power of thought to matter and that we could never know with certainty if the soul was immaterial.[52]

Instead, Locke introduces the philosophical concept of a person, in part, to solve what were ostensibly theological problems: The scriptures promise a resurrection on Judgment Day. How could we make sense of an agent who is responsible for various rights and wrongs being the same agent who gets suitably rewarded or punished come Judgment Day? If we can't appeal to an immaterial soul to provide the continuity, then what should we do? The body itself can't do the trick, since the material of a living body changes over time, so it wouldn't make any sense to try to put a bunch of matter together later on. And once a living organism dies, it can't come back, says Locke, since it's nothing more than a particular sort of organization of parts.[53] What to do? Enter the person.

Locke's famous idea is that whether A and B are the same person hinges on whether they are the same self (i.e., that there is a shared consciousness over time). That is, continuity of (self-)consciousness secures continuity of the person. In this way, the question of moral responsibility is answered as follows: Is A conscious of having done the deeds of B? Yes? Then they're the same person, and the reward is deserved.

Neither continuity of body nor continuity of the soul, in his view, turn out to be necessary for the survival of a person over time. Instead, consciousness of the past is all that matters regarding moral responsibility of past deeds. Locke writes of *person*:

> It is a Forensic Term appropriating Actions and their Merit; and so belongs only to intelligent Agents capable of a Law, and Happiness and Misery. . . . And therefore conformable to this, the Apostle tells us, that, at the Great Day, when every one shall "*receive according to his doings, the secrets of all Hearts shall be laid open.*" The Sentence shall be justified by the consciousness all Persons shall have, that they **themselves** in what Bodies soever they appear, or what Substances soever that consciousness adheres to, are the *same,* that committed those Actions, and deserve that Punishment for them.[54]

In Locke's view, the immateriality, and therefore immortality, of the soul, becomes entirely irrelevant.[55]

Crucial for our purposes, this constitutes a rejection of Godwyn's presupposition. While Godwyn says:

For without this [a rational soul] he were not *a Man*; could
neither be *subject* to Laws or *Discipline*, nor capable of *Rewards*
or Punishments after this Life.[56]

Locke says:

All the great Ends of Morality and Religion, are well enough secured, without philosophical Proofs of the Soul's Immateriality;
since it is evident, that he who made us at first begin to subsist
here, sensible intelligent Beings, and for several years continued us in such a state, can and will restore us to the like state
of Sensibility in another World, and make us capable there to
receive the Retribution he has designed to Men.[57]

To put it differently, just as Locke is not denying that Africans are
men, neither is he denying that they possess souls. But as membership in the species "man" comes to nothing, so, too, does this question about souls. We simply don't know much about souls. We don't
know whether they're immaterial and therefore immortal. The crucial upshot of Locke's position is that he can reject the plantation thesis that Africans, while resembling men, are not men and lack souls,
while gutting this rejection of any significance.

This of course leaves us with a final, crucial question. Bernasconi
and Mann argue that since Locke allows for the baptism of those
who were enslaved, he obviously believes that Africans are human
and, consequently, have souls.[58] Although we have already seen that
Locke pleads agnosticism about the immateriality and therefore the
immortality of the soul, their argument can be refined. In my view,
since Locke held RT, he would not have regarded Africans as persons.
Locke says that personhood "belongs only to intelligent Agents capable of a Law" and, according to RT, Africans would not be capable
of law.[59] Why, then, would Locke support the baptism of those who
were enslaved?

The answer is that Locke doesn't require personhood for baptism.
Locke claims that the question of whether somebody should be baptized is, in practice, settled on the basis of their appearance and morphology alone rather than on the basis of their rationality. He writes,
in defending his own account of man as determined by outward
appearance:

It has been more than once debated, whether several human *Foetus* should be preserved, or received to Baptism, or no, only because of the difference of their outward Configuration, from the ordinary Make of Children, without knowing whether they were not as a capable of Reason, as Infants cast in another Mould: Some whereof, though of an approved shape, are never capable of as much appearance of Reason, all their Lives, as is to be found in an Ape, or an Elephant; and never give any signs of being acted by a rational Soul. Whereby it is evident, that the outward Figure, which only was found wanting, and not the Faculty of Reason, which no body could know would be wanting in its due Season, was made essential to the humane *Species*.[60]

Meanwhile, it's precisely his agnosticism about the soul and his appeal to the self that allows him to say of changelings, in answer to the question about their fate in the afterlife:

It concerns me not to know or enquire. To their own Master they stand or fall. . . . They are in the hands of a faithful Creator and a bountiful Father, who disposes not of his Creatures according to our narrow Thoughts or Opinions. . . . It may suffice us, that he hath made known to all those, who are capable of Instruction, Discourse, and Reasoning, that they shall come to an account, and receive according to what they have done in this Body.[61]

What happens to changelings? We don't know. It's up to God. My conclusion: Locke's distinction between man and person allows him to support the baptism of those who were enslaved while harboring profoundly racist views about them.

Locke's Significance

In "Unsettling the Coloniality of Being/Power/Truth/Freedom," Sylvia Wynter distinguishes between two conceptions of Man—two answers to the question "What and who are we?"—that reflect two different phases of colonial expansion.[62] The first is the Renaissance's humanist conception of rational man. The second is the Darwinian conception of the evolutionary, biological man. What I propose is that the Enlightenment also witnesses a key shift—a shift necessary for the movement from the Renaissance conception into the Darwinian one. Specifically, two things had to occur before the Darwinian conception of man could emerge. First, the line between beast and man had to be breached, ushering in the possibility of a far more profound animalization of those who were enslaved. Second, the notion of the soul had to disappear altogether. Locke accomplishes both.

Locke's introduction of the concepts *person* and *self* represents a critical phase of the colonial/modern gender system, perhaps as significant as the consequences of the Valladolid debate, which included replacing the enslavement of those indigenous to the land with the enslavement of Africans. To see what I have in mind, let's contrast Locke's account of slavery with that of Aristotle. Aristotle's was grounded in the notion of natural slavery, and it played a significant role in the Valladolid debate, with Juan Ginés de Sepúlveda relying heavily on it as a justification for enslaving those indigenous to the land.[63] Locke's is a more brutal form of slavery. Consider, for instance, this Aristotelian view:

> The abuse of this authority is injurious to both [master and slave]; for the interests of part and whole, of body and soul, are the same, and the slave is a part of the master, a living but separated part of his bodily frame. Hence, where the relation of master and slave between them is natural they are friends and have a common interest, but where it rests merely on convention and force the reverse is true.[64]

While Aristotle allows that the enslaver has authority over those who were enslaved but insists that this authority ought not be abused, Locke affirms the enslaver's absolute power over those who were enslaved—that is, the power to kill them with impunity. And while Aristotle speaks of "friendship" between enslaver and those who were enslaved, for Locke, the relationship is antagonistic insofar as it begins with a threat of violence.

The most important difference, however, concerns the moral value of those who were enslaved. Aristotle writes of the "lower sort" of men:

> [They] are by nature slaves, and it is better for them as for
> all inferiors that they should be under the rule of a master.
> For he who can be, and therefore is, another's, and he who
> participates in reason enough to apprehend, but not to have,
> is a slave by nature. Whereas the lower animals cannot even
> apprehend reason; they obey their passions.[65]

For Aristotle, the "lower sort" continue to participate in "rational principle." While they cannot actively engage in deliberative reasoning, they can still understand the reasoning. Aristotle says that this is precisely what distinguishes the lower sort of men from the lower animals. Of course, this is in line with a metaphysics that strictly divides nature into different sorts of things and does not, therefore, admit of in-between cases. Locke, in his attack on substantial forms, does admit such cases.

According to Locke, there are some beasts that are more rational than some men. Indeed, there can be some animals that are in between man and beast. Consequently, in contrast to Aristotle, Locke affirms that there exist men who do not partake in "the rational principle." Such men are outright excluded from personhood and are therefore inherently enslaveable. (In an odd respect, then, Locke affirms his own account of natural slavery specifically when it comes to Africans.)

To be clear, I don't mean to insist here that differences between the version of slavery created by the Spanish and the version created by the English were due to the theoretical contrast between Sepúlveda's justification of colonial slavery and Locke's. It certainly may be the case that the differences between the two men are of a piece with different cultural and intellectual milieus—such as that between Catholicism and Protestantism. My point, rather, is that Locke promotes and epitomizes an important conceptual shift during the Enlightenment that now serves as an inheritance. Locke initiates a shift away from the Christian soul to the secular self. Today the Christian soul and the metaphysical and epistemological questions that surround it are scarcely philosophically relevant, whereas the related concepts of *person* and *self* remain central in philosophy and in theory more generally. It's a key philosophical shift that helped usher in a new phase of colonial expansion.

While I have spent most of this chapter defending the view that Locke's distinction between *man* and *person* is used to ground his justification for English slavery, it is also plain by his consistent use of *idiots, naturals,* and *changelings*—not only in the examples I provided but throughout the entirety of the *Essay*—that Locke's position not only is ableist but, indeed, deploys instances of cognitive disability to secure his distinction between *man* and *person* and, therefore, his grounds for the enslavement of Africans.[66] These consequences of this further conclusion can then be framed in terms of the dark and light sides of the colonial/modern gender system. For while those on the light side have the potential of becoming cognitively disabled, those on the dark side are constitutively deficient.

Hiding Sex/Hiding Race

There is a final consequence of the worldview that Locke helps usher in—one that is far less evident—namely, the obfuscation of moral sex (or, if you prefer, "gender"). I'll conclude this chapter with a discussion of it.

To understand what I have in mind, we ought to imagine Locke theorizing from within the folk system without avail to interpersonal spatiality theory. This means we need to regard him as an interpersonal object with interpersonal awareness. It also means that in addition to asking about the relationship between his views and Aristotle's, we need to consider the relationship of both theories to folk personhood.

Locke begins with the ordinary way of speaking that, in his view, conflates *person* and *man*. If we put the words aside, we can see how Locke is actually concerned with the generic form of a folk person in the system. This is just to say, his awareness of others and himself is in standard mode. Note that Aristotelianism captures the notion of generic man by wedding morphology to the value delivered through the forms. Further, it captures moral sex through the alleged deficiency of women. When Locke rejects the Aristotelian view, however, he does not provide a new one that accommodates the generic folk person. Rather, he attempts to dissolve it. His move, as I have discussed, is to divide *man* and *person* in a way that obscures moral sex entirely.

Its elision can be brought into plain view by turning to some of Locke's arguments. While I have been looking at the broader philosophical shifts and the theoretical and political reasons for them, Locke's well-known strategy is to consider various complex problem cases, proposing several thought experiments. Let's consider one— the one that is perhaps the most well known:

> For should the Soul of a Prince, carrying with it the consciousness of the Prince's past Life, enter and inform the Body of a Cobler as soon as deserted by his own Soul, every one sees, he would be the same Person with the Prince, accountable only for the Prince's Actions: But who would say it was the same Man? The Body too goes to the making the Man, and would, I guess, to every Body determine the Man in this case.[67]

Locke's argument is that if the prince's consciousness were transferred to the body of the cobbler, the prince would be the same person, but he would not be the same man. We need only switch out the prince for a princess and the cobbler for his wife (or make the cobbler a woman) to see how the argument fails. Were Princess Elisabeth's soul, carrying the consciousness of the princess's past life, to enter the body of the female cobbler, whose own soul had departed, it is hardly obvious that this newly embodied princess would not be the same woman.

The idea that a woman or man could survive such a change in body is well accepted in science fiction and fantasy stories such as *Buffy the Vampire Slayer*. In one episode, two vampire slayers (Buffy and Faith) switch bodies.[68] The story sets it up so that that we know that Buffy herself is put into the body of Faith, and conversely. But what is recognized as obviously true in this story is that even though Buffy gets a different body, she is still the same woman (namely, Buffy). That is, sameness of woman needn't require sameness of body.

Part of the reason Locke's argument fails is purely conceptual, of course. Just as one needn't be human to be a woman, it also turns out that it is conceptually possible for a woman to survive a change of body. However, the elision of folk personhood runs deeper (as does the fact that a woman needn't be human). If we regard the princess as a "who" constituted through an interpersonal identity, then we must recognize that that identity is itself subject to a structural differentiation in boundaries on access.

Specifically, the identity is itself morally female. Because of that, the female identity demands a particular nakedness structure, a particular interpersonal constitution of the physical person. This means that in case she is transferred into the body of man, she would be a woman trapped inside the body of man. And in cases in which she does not continue on as a human at all (e.g., she's transferred into the body of a bird), while one would be hard pressed to say that she survived as a woman, one would still recognize that she was morally female and that she had survived with a moral structure that is at odds with her body.[69]

To be clear, then, Locke can certainly deliver a distinction between woman and Lockean person through considering other odd cases (e.g., putting the soul of the princess into the body of a bird). The point, however, is simply that Locke elides moral sex. And this erasure constitutes an important aspect of the prevailing worldview. It arises because the contrast between *person* (as self-aware being) and *human* (as animal organism) is taken for granted as an unchallenged presumption. Reconsider the following quote from Harry G. Frankfurt:

> There is a sense in which the word "person" is merely the singular form of "people" and in which both terms connote no more than membership in a certain biological species. In those senses of the word which are of greater philosophical interest . . . [they] are designed to capture those attributes which are the subject of our most humane concern with ourselves and the source of what we regard as most important and most problematical in our lives.[70]

Note that the way Frankfurt draws the distinction between the philosophical and ordinary senses is different from the way that Locke drew it. Whereas Locke takes the ordinary sense to conflate *human* and *person*, Frankfurt takes that separation for granted, the ordinary sense now designating membership within a particular species only. Folk personhood has disappeared. That is to say, men and women as moral entities have disappeared.

Under this obfuscation, men and women are falsely taken to reduce to "adult male members of the species *Homo sapiens*" and "adult female member of the species *Homo sapiens*," respectively. The possibility that moral sex and therefore race might be bound up with moral status is thereby obscured. Meanwhile, the moral value of dignity that was once borne by man—secured through the contrast with female vulnerability—has been allocated to the person/self, as if some certain degree of cognitive sophistication had now acquired the capacity to draw down grand status.

In this picture, sex and race are irrelevant to personhood—which, of course, would be nice if it were true. But it isn't. Instead, the fundamental relation of sex and race to folk personhood is simply hidden from the worldview altogether, free to go about its business. Meanwhile, the work of the philosophical concepts *person* and *self* and *subject* is hidden. In chapter 9, I will continue this examination, turning to the concept *subject*.

Chapter 9
Return of the Object

IN CHAPTER 8, I examined the origins of the concepts *person* and *self*. Identifying two assumptions underlying the equivalence of these concepts as false and abusive, I showed their historical emergence through the work of Locke. In this concluding chapter, I show how interpersonal spatiality theory reveals and overturns the assumptions underlying the equivalence of *self* and *subject*. These assumptions are considerably less obvious than those discussed in the previous chapter. Consequently, much of this chapter aims simply to make them obvious *as* assumptions and to show why they're false and abusive. Further, while much of the previous chapter was devoted to the historical emergence of the assumptions from the folk system, only a little bit of this chapter is similarly devoted. This is partly because no one figure really plays a central role in these assumptions.

In the first part of this chapter, I introduce the fungibility assumption and the **table-gazing model** it creates. Then, I discuss the subject–self equivalence that follows from it. This includes a return to our discussion of trans phoria from chapter 5. I conclude the section by discussing a corollary of the two equivalences—namely, the priority of the self over the social.

In the second part, I consider the work of the self–subject equivalence. First, I consider how interpersonal objects were formed into subjects and "mere" objects through the implementation of fungibility in real time. Second, I show how the table-gazing model, enshrined as the natural way of cognizing, reflects the experiences of the colonizers while serving the interests of the colonial/modern gender system.

Before we begin, however, let's briefly discuss the historical development of the philosophical term *subject*. In contrast to the departures from folk usage characterizing the terms *person* and *self,* this development involves a transformation from one technical philo-sophical meaning to another—namely, from:[1]

> *Metaphysics.* The underlying substance or essence of a thing, as distinguished from its non-essential properties; an individ-ual thing, as opposed to its properties. Frequently contrasted with *accident.* Now chiefly *historical.*[2]

to:

> A being (or power) that thinks, knows, or perceives (more fully **conscious subject, thinking subject**); the conscious mind, esp. as opposed to any objects external to it. In later use also more broadly: the person or self considered as a conscious agent.[3]

The older sense derives from Aristotelian philosophy, according to which "the subject [*hypokeimenon*] is that of which the other things are said, but which itself is never [said] of any other thing."[4] And the modern one is nicely captured by Bertrand Russell's definition of a "subject" as "any entity which is acquainted with something" and an "object" as "any entity with which something is acquainted."[5] While the older sense contrasts subjects with those things that are said of other things—properties and, more technically, accidents—the mod-ern contrasts subjects with objects:

> *Philosophy.* A thing which is perceived, thought of, known, etc.; *spec.* a thing which is external to or distinct from the ap-prehending mind, subject, or self. Opposed to **subject** *n.* II.9.[6]

It's important to keep in mind, however, that the modern notion has, in some respects, retained the older conception of a being on which properties depend, with a notable change—namely, that *sub-ject* is often restricted to thinking beings alone.[7] Thus, in speaking of "a being that thinks, knows, or perceives," we might also speak of the thoughts or thinking, perceptions or perceiving that depend on this being for their existence. (Here, we're at risk of collapsing the two senses, thereby facilitating an identification between the men-tal states and the objects.) Finally, sometimes *subject* is used as a simple synonym for *self* (as in *self-conscious being*) in a way that does not include any further content (e.g., *subject* versus *accident*, *subject* versus *object*).[8]

While in chapter 8 I was concerned with the philosophical emergence of the terms, I am not, in this chapter, concerned about when and how the meaning began to shift and who shifted it. In this case, it's far less clear. Further, I think the terms are less important than the underlying metaphysical, epistemological, and political shifts that were occurring, and it's those basic shifts that I want to bring to the surface.

Fungibility of Objects

TABLE-GAZING

Begin by looking at the nearest available table. Notice that you are aware of the table. Notice, also, that you are likewise aware that *you* are aware of the table. Now, notice that, to this extent, you are aware of something in addition to the table—namely, yourself. Notice, also, that this awareness of yourself is very different from your awareness of the table in that you don't see yourself. I call this "table-gazing," and I call the model of awareness based on this the "table-gazing model."

I use the expression *table-gazing* only because it evokes *navel-gazing* and thus serves as a way of making fun of a model that makes too big a deal of this sort of awareness. Table-gazing needn't involve a philosophically hypnotized staring at a table. It need only involve the regular perception that one has of a table in the ordinary course of life—for instance, as one heads into one's living room and places a cup of coffee on the table, hoping to quickly enjoy some quiet time before work. This means that the various steps outlined above need only occur implicitly. One needn't think to oneself, "Oh, yes, I am aware of myself seeing a table." Rather, one need only be implicitly aware of *oneself* perceiving the *table*. Oneself and table. That's the key.

Further, let me point out that this alleged *self*-awareness provided by the table-gazing model ought to seem a little sketchy. Here's one worry: just because one is aware that one's neighbor's lights are on doesn't mean that one is aware of one's neighbor. Similarly, just because one is aware that one is thinking doesn't mean that one is aware of oneself.[9] Concerns like this—and many others—over the status of self-awareness in this model have led to much discussion about the nature (and existence) of this awareness, starting with David Hume's announcement that he could find no such thing when he turned "reflection on himself."[10] Immanuel Kant worried that the "I think" was merely a constituent of any thought and, hence, was useless in delivering substantive information about oneself.[11]

These various disputes about the status of self-awareness ought to be viewed as, in some ways, constitutive of the model itself. In the end, it doesn't matter whether this awareness delivers up a self or, more impressively, some persisting entity behind that awareness. The point is that this table-gazing model of awareness has itself come to typify subjectivity per se. That is, it is taken for granted as the underlying picture.

According to interpersonal spatiality theory, however, table-gazing is merely one form of interpersonal awareness among several others. Typically, table-gazing will come into prominence when one is alone, since it is less likely that one will experience awareness of oneself as an object for a potential other, as one is not aware of any interpersonal objects and, indeed, does not anticipate the possibility of any.

However, this doesn't mean that one couldn't have different sorts of self-awareness should another interpersonal object come onto the scene or should, even, one anticipate the possibility. One might become aware of one's possible appearance for another, as a "subject looking at a table." And even without the intrusion, there are other possibilities. While looking at the table, one might also see one's arms and legs. Further, one might experience various affective valences of object self-awareness, such as shame or self-containment.

The point is that table-gazing is experienced in a larger context of interpersonal awareness in which awareness of oneself as an object is a constituent. According to interpersonal spatiality theory, the table-gazing model is a misrepresentation of actual experience. It is a philosopher's invention got by extracting table-gazing from the larger phenomenological context and then treating it as the basis for the entirety of the context.

Even the awareness one has of one's mental states, in this model, is framed in terms of this awareness of oneself as a table-gazing subject. Either the thoughts and feelings play the role of tables themselves or else they serve as the vehicles through which one experiences and thinks about tables. Either way, however, the model distorts how one experiences one's thoughts and feelings as shareable with others and as shared with others and, further, how one experiences one's physical person, in comportment to another as a necessary condition of this sharing.

Fungibility

The table-gazing model is created by a crucial hidden assumption—namely, the assumption of object fungibility. In this assumption, there is no distinction between interpersonal and nonpersonal objects regarding sensory and informational access. That is, it is assumed that there are no moral boundaries governing access to objects at all. By treating all objects as nonpersonal objects, table-gazing becomes ubiquitous.

This assumption of fungibility is false, however. One's perception of another interpersonal object is always determined by boundaries. One must always either observe or cross a boundary. By contrast, perception of a nonpersonal object, such as a table, does not admit of the same constraint. To treat perception of interpersonal and nonpersonal objects as if they were on par is therefore to make a serious mistake.

More than that, it's simply abusive to treat interpersonal objects as if they were nonpersonal objects. To spell this out, consider the roughly Kantian dictum that one ought treat another not as a mere object but, rather, as a subject. Despite its wide endorsement—an endorsement that speaks volumes about the wide commitment to fungibility—the dictum is abusive.

The key problem is the devaluation of the object—that is, the assumption of fungibility. Specifically, it's the erasure of the interpersonal object. This object—the agent object—displays itself to others, and it's through this display that the object reveals itself as an agent in the first place. So, it's not wrong to treat somebody as an object. In fact, it's required. To be sure, there are different ways of treating such an object, and some of them are wrong. Violations, for instance. Intimate disregard. However, it's not the treating of them as an object per se that's wrong. It's simply the violation or the contempt. Clearly, worst of all would be to treat an interpersonal object as though they were a nonpersonal object. Alas, this is precisely what the dictum itself does.

THE SELF–SUBJECT EQUIVALENCE

The self–subject equivalence posits a supposedly special form of self-awareness that just is an awareness of oneself as a point of view—that is, the awareness one has of oneself on the table-gazing model. So, for instance, while seeing oneself in the mirror might count as a form of self-awareness, it isn't a special form of self-awareness. The being one sees in the mirror, rather, is merely identified with oneself. By contrast, one is aware of oneself as a subject gazing into the mirror where this awareness does not involve seeing oneself. This awareness, under the equivalence, is the basic awareness. Let's call this special self-awareness *"essentially reflexive awareness."* The equivalence says that the only kind of essentially reflexive awareness of oneself is as a subject.

Rather than merely pointing out how interpersonal spatiality theory contests the self–subject equivalence, I want to show how the nonequivalence is necessitated by trans experiences of phoria. So, let's return to the hub of the essay—the account of trans phoria as resistant to trans oppression. And let's also resurrect the incongruence account—an account that has been a crucial target in this essay and that both relies upon and epitomizes the table-gazing model.

Essentially Reflexive Awareness

The falsity of this equivalence is entailed by interpersonal spatiality theory, since the theory centralizes awareness of oneself as an object for others—an awareness that ought to be essentially reflexive. And it is precisely the *essential reflexivity* of awareness of oneself as an object that helps explain the phenomena of pretransition self-recognition and loss, as well as gender phoria more generally.

When I look into a mirror, I don't identify the person I see as myself on the basis of her appearance. Rather, I know that is myself because I understand what mirrors are for and how they operate. I know that I am looking at my reflection. This is why I can be so unrecognizable to myself when I look in the mirror—ravaged by the horrors of time and yet I still know that I see myself in the mirror. Who else would I see? My judgment that I look tired and haggard surely doesn't involve any identification of this person as myself. Rather, the fact that she appears just in the way she does in the mirror is all the basis I need—that is to say, the same basis I have for judgment that somebody looks tired and haggard. Should I look into the mirror and see an entirely different face, now green and with horns, the first thing I would think is this: What the hell happened to me? Not: Am I misidentifying somebody else for myself?

The same is so in the experience of pretransition self-recognition. One simply sees oneself and experiences a profound sense of self-collection. It is not about identifying who one sees in the mirror with oneself. The experience of extinguishment involves the loss of this positive state. This is to say, the dysphoric state is not so much a failure to identify oneself in the mirror so much as the disappearance of this liminal being altogether.

When one looks into the mirror only to see a man dressed up like a woman—a mere make-believer—there's never a "not-me" moment, as one is never in doubt that one sees oneself in the mirror. Indeed, profound moments of dysphoria trade exactly on this—what one sees is "all too me." Unavoidably me. Nothing-I-can-ever-do-about-it me. The-source-of-deep-despair me.

The incongruence account, by contrast, is dependent on the table-gazing model and, therefore, committed to the equivalence of self and subject. Thus, it posits an inconsistency between one's experience of oneself as a subject and a visual awareness of oneself as an object. The falsity of this approach is obscured by the notable fact that, in the case of the mirror, technically one does not see oneself so much as one sees a reflection of oneself (left and right reversed). This allows for there to be a gap between oneself as subject and the image one sees.

The matter becomes clearer, however, when one drops the mirror and simply looks at one's torso, hands, and legs, say. One is clearly presented in a way that is entirely different from any other access to interpersonal objects. But applying the table-gazing model in advance, however, overlooks this fact, treating both modes of access as if they were on par. In doing so, one forgoes the tools for accommodating the awarenesses of oneself as object that constitutes phoria.

To help make my points clearer, I want to consider an independent ground for rejecting the self–subject equivalence. The fact that my account both predicts and explains this finding is surely yet another of its merits. So, let's turn to a literature in analytic philosophy that takes as its starting point some perplexing remarks in Ludwig Wittgenstein's *Blue Book*.[12]

There, Wittgenstein draws a contrast between what he calls the use of *I* as subject and the use of *I* as object. The examples he provides of the former include "'*I* see so-and-so,' '*I* hear so-and-so,' '*I* try to lift my arm,' '*I* think it will rain,' '*I* have a toothache.'" Examples of the latter include "'My arm is broken,' 'I have grown six inches,' 'I have a bump on my forehead,' and 'The wind is blowing my hair.'"[13] (Put aside Wittgenstein's choice of examples for now.) The former use, Wittgenstein claims, doesn't involve "recognizing a person."

In the literature that follows, thanks to Sydney S. Shoemaker, "use as subject" has been characterized in terms of immunity to error through misidentification (IEM) relative to the pronoun *I*.[14] For instance, I could not, upon feeling angry, be correct that *somebody* is angry but incorrect that *I* am that individual. In cases of IEM, the basis on which the statement "I am F" is made is such that to know that *somebody* is F is ipso facto to know that *I* am F. In other words, knowledge that I am F does not require a distinct warrant for believing the identity statement "I am identical to the person who is F." The basis on which the judgment is made is identification-free.

"Uses as object," by contrast, do involve identification and therefore aren't immune in this way. Suppose, for instance, that I am looking at a photograph and I remark, "Boy, do I look young." However, it turns out that the person in the photograph is not myself but, rather, my sister. In this case, it's possible for me to be correct that *somebody* looks young and wrong that that somebody is me. Note that in this case, my judgment that *I* look young is clearly based on me identifying the person in the photograph with myself. In this case, I make the judgment because the person in the photograph looks like me.

Gareth Evans then advances the conversation by showing that IEM can be extended to examples that don't concern thoughts and feelings—cases involving proprioceptive, kinesthetic awareness, and the like. Just as "I see a table" is identification-free, so, too, is "A table is in front of me." So, too, are "My legs are crossed," "I am standing," and so forth.[15] To undermine knowledge that it is *my* legs that are crossed is to undermine my knowledge that *anybody's* legs are crossed.[16]

The reason that philosophers had been inclined to dismiss these cases as IEM is that weird examples could be produced to show how errors of misidentification could occur. For example, it could be possible (although very unlikely) that my judgment "A table is in front of me" is wrong because the table is actually in front of somebody else. Perhaps I am really on a slab in some scientist's laboratory, my brain hooked up to a machine that relays what this other individual sees. What Evans shows is that these examples don't work. Not only does the example cast into doubt the fact that the table is in front of me, but it also casts into doubt the fact that the table is in front of *anybody*. If I'm being tricked by some scientist, then how would I know that this isn't just some form of CGI being put into my mind? As Evans says, it would just be a "shot in the dark."[17] To put it differently, if the example undermines my warrant for both "The table is in front of me" and "The table is in front of somebody," then it's not an example that can show that identification is somehow involved.

We come now to the crucial point. What has been oddly unnoticed is that many cases that seem to count quite plainly as "uses as object" exhibit the same immunity. Consider one of Wittgenstein's examples: "I have a bump on my forehead." Suppose I pull a compact mirror out of my purse and, upon looking into it to adjust my makeup, notice that I have a bump on my forehead. Does this basis for making the judgment involve an identification? Who else would I see in the compact mirror if not myself? Surely, any possibilities that undermine that knowledge are likewise possibilities that undermine my knowledge that anybody has a bump. The mirror isn't really a mirror, it's a computer screen. Or, perhaps, I'm receiving images from somebody else's brain. In such cases, to judge that anybody at all had a bump on their head would surely be—as Evans puts it—just a "shot in the dark."

To be sure, it is possible for mirror cases to involve misidentification in odd cases. Suppose, for instance, that I am having sex, looking up into a big Vegas ceiling mirror. "My leg has peanut butter on it," I say. I am wrong, however, as it turns out that one of my partner's legs has the peanut butter, not my own. Here, I obviously did make a misidentification—I mistook their leg for my own. That this can occur in such uncommon cases, however, shows little about the usual ones. Specifically, I fail to see how the misidentification in this case goes any distance to showing that when I judge I have a bump on my forehead upon looking in my compact, I have somehow made a judgment that is identification-dependent.

The point becomes even clearer when we drop mirrors altogether and consider the simple fact that one can typically see oneself by merely deciding to turn away from the table to examine one's torso, legs, and arms. One could perceive one's hair framing ones face, as well as one's own nose, should one turn one's eyes just so. "There's coffee on my blouse," I judge. Again, the knowledge that the blouse is my own is simply part and parcel of the way I know that somebody's blouse is coffee-stained in this case. There is no identification involved. Indeed, the warrant for my judgment that it is *I* who see the stained blouse is surely the same as the warrant for my judgment that it is *myself* that I see. Such examples pull the phenomenon of IEM apart from uses of *I* "as subject," since these examples so obviously concern the object, not the subject, and they lead to the following conclusion: What is at stake is not awareness of oneself as a point of view but, rather, an awareness of oneself that is essentially reflexive—that is, is identification-free.

Admittedly, identification-freedom in the case of mirrors requires that one know what a mirror is and how it operates. So, one might argue that in order to know this, one would have to, at least at some point, have identified the image in the mirror as an image of oneself. Even if this is so, it is irrelevant to the case at hand since we are to presume a typical awareness of the social world in which we operate. More deeply, I doubt that this is how one learns what mirrors are and how they work (typically, an adult simply explains it to a child), and even if this point were conceded, it would not undermine more basic sorts of sensory perception of oneself outlined above (e.g., looking at one's torso). These examples are essentially reflexive modes of awareness and, crucially, they would be necessary for any identification of the image in the mirror with oneself. To put it differently, one would need to be aware of one's own appearance *as* one's appearance.

This necessity can be brought out in a different way by noting that, in the literature, modes of self-awareness that have been deemed special have been internal in character. By this I mean that in cases of access to one's mental states from the inside or of the disposition of one's body through proprioceptive awareness from the inside, the access is only ever to oneself. One cannot access another being in those ways, and another cannot access oneself in those ways.

By contrast, one can indeed access both oneself and others by vision. Vision is not internal.

What we have learned is that in the case of vision (and touch, I would add), while the content may be the same, it is not accessed in the same way.[18] Access, rather, is bifurcated into reflexive and irreflexive modes. Such an essentially reflexive modality of awareness is necessary to properly explain the phenomena to which interpersonal spatiality theory attends. When a person is staring at me and I feel vulnerable, I might check my blouse to see if anything is amiss. Here, I am assuming that they can see what I see—that is, I assume that we see the same content. It seems important, however, that the way I perceive it is essentially reflexive. How else, after all, would I even know that somebody was staring at me. I'd need to know that I had a visual appearance. And to know this, I'd need visual access to myself that was essentially reflexive.

Consequences
Although there isn't a systematic deployment of these expressions in philosophy, it is nonetheless true that the expressions *first-person stance* and *third-person stance* have a philosophical resonance, while the second-person perspective operates in a peripheral and under-discussed way.[19] The former are often used with respect to mental states. David Chalmers, for instance, contrasts mental activity as "inner life"—that is, regarded from the "first person (or subjective) view" with activity regarded from "the third person (or objective) view," which "looks at consciousness as it exists in others."[20] The latter, he explains, "is the domain of neurophysiologists and psychologists."[21] However, these expressions can also be deployed with respect to awareness of bodies. For instance, José Luis Bermúdez writes:

> The body is a physical object, and we can be aware of it in much the same ways that we can be aware of any other physical object. The body can be the object of vision, smell, or touch, for example. I will call these *third-person forms of bodily awareness*. These forms of bodily awareness involve the normal exercise of our ordinary, outward-directed sensory modalities. At the same time, we have special ways of finding out how things are with our bodies—ways that do not extend

to any other physical object. Each of us is aware of their body "from the inside," as it is standardly put. There are several different forms of awareness here. I will term them collectively *first-person forms of bodily awareness.*[22]

Here, Bermúdez is, of course, merely fixing the meaning of the expressions. However, the stipulation isn't entirely arbitrary either, drawing, as it does, on a philosopher's sense of the lay of the land. Bermúdez's stipulation resonates with standard philosophical sensibilities.

In light of interpersonal spatiality theory, however, we must reject these sensibilities. First, we must deny that one typically has a third-person visual access to oneself at all. Rather, one has first-person (essentially reflexive) access to oneself through vision and touch. Third-person visual access is therefore restricted to those other than oneself. That is, third-person access is essentially irreflexive. To put it differently, interpersonal spatiality theory says that sensory access to others must be subject to boundaries, while sensory access to oneself must not be similarly bounded. That is, it requires that the two modes of sensory access be structurally distinct.

This can again be illustrated by an application of an Evans-style argument: if I do not need to identify the individual I see *as* myself, then, presumably, I needn't distinguish the other individuals I see *from* myself. I see somebody walking in the distance or, rather, somebody *else* walking in the distance. In this case, the basis on which I judge that somebody is walking is the very same as that on which I judge that this individual is not identical to myself. For should it turn out that I am so confused that, somehow, this actually is myself, then surely the judgment that anybody at all is walking would merely be a "shot in the dark."

This yields a further consequence, closely related to the denial that one typically possesses third-person access to oneself. This is that there is no such thing as a neutral third-person access of the sort Bermúdez posits. To put it differently, in the normal course of things, the only third-person access there is is third-person access to another. So, to take a third-person perspective on oneself is to access oneself as though one were another. Unlike the neutral third-person visual access envisioned by Bermúdez, this access requires a flight of fancy as its starting point, calling into question not only its neutrality but its regularity. To put it differently, should someone continue to perceive themself in this way once they have put the mirror away, we ought to regard them as inhabiting some sort of dissociated state. This has illuminating results for our understanding of trans phoria. To alleviate painful interpersonal sentiments—dysphoric experiences of objecthood—some of us trans people engage in *dissociation* by replacing reflexive access to our sensory appearances with irreflexive access so that we become someone other than the person with that appearance. It's a sort of retreat.[23] And this, in turn, suggests a perverse respect in which the incongruence account almost seems to get it right. In the dysphoric state, dissociation may lead to the adoption of a table-gazing perspective that, in turn, requires a gap between the viewer and the viewed—even when one is looking at one's person without a mirror. While this may characterize a "before" mirror experience, however, it does not characterize the "after" experience. The experience is not one of continued dissociation with one disowned appearance being replaced by a more acceptable one. Rather, self-recognition, in this case, involves the shift from a dissociated state into a centered awareness of oneself as an object, whereby one stops feigning to be somebody else, whereby one becomes who one sees, whereby the very somebody else one was pretending to be—the distant subject—ceases to exist.

Some final remarks. If we wish to continue using expressions such as *first-person perspective* and the like, it would be useful to afford more precision in our characterization of these perspectives. First, I would call the interpersonal awareness one has in dialogical interaction the "second-person perspective," and I would make it central. Second, it might be helpful to distinguish between third-person access to interpersonal objects and third-person access to nonpersonal objects. For instance, we could speak of the "third-person bounded" and the "third-person unbounded." We should also recognize that third-person bounded is not discontinuous from the second-person perspective but necessary to it. Finally, we could distinguish between the first-person awareness one has of oneself in relation to one's unbounded third-person access of something else and the first-person awareness one has of oneself in relation to another interpersonal object—principally dialogical but also in third-person. That said, we needn't adopt this way of talking. We might forgo it altogether, simply using the terminology deployed in interpersonal spatiality theory.

TWO COROLLARIES: THE PRIORITY OF REFLEXIVITY AND THE PRIORITY OF THE INDIVIDUAL

Due to the identification of *person* with *self* that we discussed in chapter 8, *self*-awareness is privileged as the most important access one has to a person. In other words, as self-consciousness is one's source of moral status, one only has preeminent access to this sort of moral being through reflexive access. (Note that not only does interpersonal spatiality theory reject this, but it also inverts it. Irreflexive awareness is the primary way one accesses interpersonal objects, since even the awareness one has of oneself is an awareness of oneself as an object for another.)

Crucially, the self–subject equivalence is also necessary for this privileging because, as I have shown, one's appearance is accessed through both essentially reflexive and essentially irreflexive modes. This undermines the elevation of reflexive access as the sole mode by which a person can be properly accessed. By restricting essentially reflexive awareness of oneself to awareness of oneself as a point of view (via the fungibility assumption), however, this problem is eliminated. To put it differently, only by illegitimately limiting it through self–subject equivalence can essentially reflexive access appear special.

It's precisely this privileging of reflexive access that leads, in turn, to the privileging of the individual self over the sociomoral. Since reflexive awareness involves one self-aware individual at the outset, to capture some form of sociality, one must put two selves into interaction with each other. In interpersonal spatiality theory, by contrast, we proceed with two individuals distinguished by the boundary. Or, rather, we proceed with the boundary itself, yielding a prioritization of the sociomoral over the individual.

This is not merely a phenomenological point about interpersonal awareness. It's the claim that interpersonal awareness is underwritten by an interpersonal structure that makes possible the former. In other words, the existence of the boundary and the intimate gestures in which the boundary inheres constitute a necessary condition for one's having interpersonal experience at all. In this respect, interpersonal spatiality theory is antecedent to any phenomenology, since, to put it metaphorically, the phenomenology rides atop the underlying structure—a structure that constitutes objects.

One might object, of course: Doesn't the agent object require subjectivity to engage in self-display? According to interpersonal spatiality theory, one must first be constituted as an interpersonal object to have what is misleadingly called "subjectivity" (i.e., interpersonal awareness). First, in order to be aware of oneself as a self-sharing object, one must first have the capacity for engaging in self-sharing, and one does not have this without boundaries. Second, the very capacity for having socially recognizable feelings and thoughts depends upon access to a repertoire of avowals—discursive devices by which one, as an object, shares these feelings and thoughts with others. Third, the very capacity for avowing to another requires the capacity to comport oneself to another—to move from passive to dialogical presence—as a self-displaying object.

Yet surely one requires cognition and consciousness prior to immersion in these social structures, one might insist. Perhaps. But I doubt that whatever precedes these social structures would be recognizable as social feelings and thoughts, anyway. More importantly, this capacity can't be the heart of the matter unless we're prepared to endorse morpho-species irrelevance and the centrality of self-consciousness. No doubt, some cognition dispersed among participants is required for the system to operate. However, all interpersonal objects are constituted as agent objects. And what matters are the ways in which we are constituted through and in interpersonal space.

Finally, one might press: Isn't the interpersonal object itself just a subject in the sense that it is an agent? Only if one begs the question about agency or changes the meaning of the word *subject*. The key feature of the interpersonal object is that it is an object of bounded access. It is precisely this feature that allows it to display itself to another as an agent. Again, sharing of reasons, mental states, and so forth involves being an object to another. To call the agent object a "subject" is, at the very least, highly misleading.[24]

The priority of the sociomoral over the phenomenological has profound consequences, of course. It can enable useful analyses that were not hitherto possible. For instance, it allows us to expose and invert Locke's famous account of land appropriation. In the *Second*

Treatise, Locke deploys a notion of *person* that closely resembles the physical person, the person one has. He writes:

> Though the Earth and all inferior Creatures be common to all Men, yet every Man has a *Property* in his own "person." This nobody has any right to but himself. The "labour" of his body and the "work" of his hands, we may say, are properly his.[25]

Locke uses *person* in a quasi-technical way to designate the "body as moral entity." For Locke, self-consciousness appropriates a body to itself, as one experiences the world through that body. It's just this feature that permits him to speak of the physical person as a moral entity. And it is through this moral entity that land becomes property. As the physical person is deployed to cultivate the land (in an English way!), the land comes to belong to the individual who possesses that physical person.

According to interpersonal spatiality theory, however, the physical person is already worked up. One's sex-differentiated physical person is constituted within the folk system of interpersonal spatiality before consciousness arrives on the scene. What gives the physical person moral import is its role within the folk system, not self-consciousness. So, it's not because of self-consciousness that one comes to possess a physical person. It is, rather, in light of the physical person that interpersonal awareness is made possible, shaped by the structure of the physical person.

Once we recognize this fact, we can also recognize that this structure of folk personhood is that through which land is appropriated well before Locke thinks it is. The constitution of his physical person is already one that, within the folk system, weds boundaries to location, linking people to land. Locke's account gets its backward.

This priority of the sociomoral over the individual is, of course, also key to our understanding of trans gender phoria. Awareness of oneself as an object presupposes the gesture of self-display, which is only possible interpersonally. Perhaps most importantly, the pre-transition self-recognition that occurs in the blank open is not only a transformation of a prior social state but also a liminal state that is fundamentally interpersonal in character—reaching out for a sociality that demands a recognitional pause as a condition for subsumption and that thereby seeks to open the door for the interpersonal creation of new forms of intimacy and distance.

To appreciate the significance of the shift I'm proposing, I'll conclude the section by considering another incongruence account of trans phoria—namely, the account of Henry S. Rubin, an early and often unfairly ignored trailblazer in what will later be called "critical phenomenology." Rubin provides a preliminary account that appeals to Jean-Paul Sartre's three dimensions of bodily ontology.[26] The first dimension (the body-for-itself) is the body-as-point-of-view-on-the-world. The second dimension (the body-for-others) is the body as sensorily accessible to others—that is, the body as object. The third dimension is one's experience of oneself as being an object to another. It's an awareness of oneself as being looked at or in some other way sensorily accessed.

For Rubin, the first dimension concerns trans experience of one's body from the inside (the body-for-itself), as sexed one way—say, male. The second dimension concerns the fact that one's body, as accessible to others (the body-for-others), is sexed a different way—say, female. The third dimension, one of profound alienation, is characterized by the first-person experience of one's body as an object for others, which Rubin uses to understand "a transsexual's painful realization that his flesh, his body-for-others is . . . not what he sees in his body image."[27] For Rubin, then, the root of trans gender dysphoria is the incongruence between the first and the third levels of bodily ontology.

According to interpersonal spatiality theory, however, this is to get it all backward. The second dimension is our starting point. We must begin with one's appearance for others—the conditions under which one is subsumed into boundaries—as determined within a specific system of interpersonal spatiality. That is, we must begin with one's constitution as an object. The third dimension follows immediately thereafter. It reflects the way one is aware of oneself as an object for others. It is for this reason that satisfaction, if it is to be found, requires the institution of interpersonal gestures that accommodate one's pretransition self-recognition. The first dimension, by contrast, is the last dimension, as it involves the temporary recession of any awareness of oneself as an object for others through dissociation.[28]

Fungibility in the Colonial/Modern Gender System

ON SUBJECTS AND OBJECTS

Thus far, I've discussed the abstract assumption of object fungibility, the table-gazing model, the self–subject equivalence, and the prioritizing of the self over the social. Together these constitute what can be regarded as a distorted philosophical model. Just as we found that the assumptions underwriting the self–person equivalence were due to important intellectual shifts, so, too, we will find that this model is due to similar changes, and I'll discuss them in due course. More than that, we'll see how the model is useful in covering up the true character of abuse in the system—an abuse I now introduce.

As we saw in chapter 8, the emergence of the self–person equivalence was bound up with the structure of society itself—and particularly bound up with the English version of chattel slavery. That is, it was not merely that the morpho-species irrelevance and the centrality of consciousness were endorsed as a theoretical way of looking at the universe. It was that, on the basis of this view, enslaved Africans were treated as though they lacked some cognitive capacity and therefore moral status. To put it otherwise, the theoretical view was actualized in real time.

It is perhaps unsurprising, then, that we should find something similar in the case of the table-gazing model and the self–subject equivalence. What we find, in particular, is that some interpersonal objects were structurally formed into "subjects" and others into "mere objects." To put it differently, the interpersonal objects of the colonial/modern gender system were ordered so as to conform to the table-gazing model.

Begin by noting that if we take *subject* as the correlative of *object,* there are two instances in which this contrast has salience in a system of interpersonal spatiality. The first is when there is an asymmetry in intimate access between two interpersonal objects. In this case, we would speak of the intimate subject and the intimate object. The second is when there is a contrast between the interpersonal subject and the nonpersonal object.

Now the different instances in which a subject–object contrast is salient are instantiated in the different ways in which white and Black women are constituted as objects. Drawing a distinction between (white female) objects and (Black female) animals, Patricia Hill Collins writes:

> Within the mind/body, culture/nature, male/female binaries in Western social thought, objects occupy an uncertain interim position. As objects, White women become creations of culture—in this case, the mind of White men—using the materials of nature—in this case, uncontrolled female sexuality. In contrast, as animals Black women receive no such redeeming dose of culture and remain open to the type of exploitation visited on nature overall. Black women's portrayal in pornography as caged, chained, and naked creatures who possess "panther-like," savage, and exotic sexual qualities . . . reinforces this theme of Black women's "wildness" as symbolic of an unbridled female sexuality.[29]

I take Collins to mean, among other things, that white women were constituted as objects of desire where this desire was constituted by the eroticization of the increasing intimization through the interplay of clothing and exposed flesh. By contrast, to be constituted as an animal is to be constituted as incapable of being intimized because one is already entirely exposed. Here the eroticization is of the complete foreclosure of intimization through maximal exposure. To put it differently, white women were constituted as compromised agent objects capable of self-display, albeit if often compelled and manipulated. Black women, by contrast, were constituted as nonagential objects, foreclosed from such self-intimization in the first place. They were incapable of self-intimization because they had already been exhaustively intimized.

Notably, in the first case, the subject contrasts with the object with regard to its dignity, in its lack of vulnerability. It's a contrast that ultimately takes place in dialogical engagement, through the second-person. This affords the subject some degree of self-awareness as an interpersonal object—if only by way of contrasting itself with the vulnerable object and experiencing an interpersonal sentiment. That said, this awareness easily disappears when the sole focus is on the self-intimizing object. After all, most interpersonal sentiments concern the latter, not the former.

In the second case, by contrast, the subject and object differ with regard to agency. Here, no such dialogical engagement can occur. Here access occurs in the third-person only. And while this third-person is bounded, the capacity of comportment—movement into second-person—is undermined through repeated boundary violations. That is, rather than intimizing the other dialogically, in this case, the other is foreclosed from dialogical interaction altogether. As such, the awareness the subject has of itself involves no awareness of oneself as an object at all. That is, it becomes entirely ignorant to how it appears to those one is abusing.

Unsurprisingly, this denial of agency is accomplished through the real-time institution of fungibility within the colonial/modern gender system. Thus, Snorton speaks of "an onto-epistemological framework premised on the fungibility of captive bodies, wherein the flesh functioned as a disarticulation of the human form from its anatomical features and their claims to humanity were controverted in favor of the production and perpetuation of cultural institutions."[30] And Hortense J. Spillers writes of the South Carolina Civil Code (Article 461), "Everywhere in the descriptive document, we are stunned by the simultaneity of disparate items in a grammatical series: 'Slave' appears in the same context with beasts of burden, *all* and *any* animal(s), various livestock, and virtually endless profusions of domestic content from the culinary item to the book."[31]

Spillers says the process by which this occurs involves the following "externally imposed meanings and uses":

> (1) The captive body as the source of an irresistible, destructive
> sensuality; (2) at the same time—in stunning contrast—
> it is reduced to a thing, to *being* for the captor; (3) in this
> distance *from* a subject position, the captured sexualities
> provide a physical and biological expression of "otherness";
> (4) as category of "otherness," the captive body translates into
> a potential for pornotroping and embodies sheer physical
> powerlessness that slides into a more general "powerlessness,"
> resonating through various centers of human and social
> meaning.[32]

(As Amber Jamilla Musser notes, "The violence and projection that produce the pornotrope require at their core a subject who desires and who thereby objectifies and possesses others through this desire.")[33] And to provide further precision in her account, Spillers then introduces the notion of "flesh." She writes:

> I would make a distinction in this case between "body" and "flesh" and impose that distinction as the central one between captive and liberated subject-positions. In that sense, before the "body" there is the "flesh." . . . Even though the European hegemonies stole bodies . . . we regard this human and social irreparability as high crimes against the *flesh,* as the person of African females and males registered the wounding.[34]

Crucially, Spillers speaks of crimes against the flesh and associates it with the physical person—the person one has. And this raises the possibility that interpersonal spatiality theory may be useful in elaborating the concept *flesh.* This possibility is further strengthened when Andrea Warmack wonders in her brilliant essay "We Flesh":

> What if prior to theft, flesh was the primordial status of all *homo sapiens?* What if when the bewildering encounter transformed freely relational African flesh/body into the captive/stolen body and flesh, it also transformed relational pre-european flesh into the European, then white, subject? This transformation instigates a subject-object relation in which the human subject/thief maintains its subjectivity by fleeing from its fleshiness and turning toward surface, transparency, and determination.[35]

In such a view, the white European subject is an interpersonal object that, in its abusiveness, has lost contact with what it actually is. That is, it is a highly distorted interpersonal object—twisted through both its crimes and its flight. Likewise, the abused object is an interpersonal object. It is, however, a nonpersonal interpersonal object. That is, it's an interpersonal object that has had its capacity for self-display undermined.

Admittedly, the notion of a nonpersonal interpersonal object might seem to be a contradiction in terms. However, it echoes what Spillers calls the "stunning contrast" between, on the one hand, being viewed as a source of powerful sexuality and, on the other, being reduced to a thing. And it is a useful concept, as we shall now see, in outlining just how the institution of African fungibility was perpetrated.

In my view, enslaved Africans were constituted as interpersonal objects—as vestorgs—within the system. Thus, they were clothed by the Europeans, on the dark side of gender. To be sure, they were constituted as interpersonal objects that were highly sexual in nature, objects that served as the morality tale to ensure the vulnerability of white women. But they were constituted as interpersonal objects, nonetheless.

That said, they were a particular sort of interpersonal object—namely, nonagential. And they were constituted this way through their institutionalized treatment as nonpersonal objects. That is, owing to perpetual boundary violations, their capacity for self-display and, therefore, dialogical interaction was foreclosed in the overworld. Perhaps this is what Spillers has in mind when she speaks of "a *willful* and violent . . . severing of the captive body from its motive will."[36]

Crucially, a self-perpetuating cycle of abuse was then enabled precisely by the Lockean notion of personhood—that is, the separation of morphology from moral status and the latter's strict allocation to consciousness (alluded to by Snorton above). On the one hand, the view that enslaved Africans were not subject-selves seemed to excuse the inexorable subjection to extreme boundary violations. On the other hand, such violation would thereby appear to undermine the capacity for comportment and, therefore, the capacity for dialogical engagement and avowal in the overworld, thereby effecting an illusion of nonselfhood. (Note that, as Spillers writes, "under these conditions, we lose at least *gender* difference *in the outcome,* and the female body and the male body become a territory of cultural and political maneuver, not at all gender-related, gender-specific."[37] No doubt, since to treat interpersonal objects as though they were nonpersonal objects in the folk system is to treat them as lacking moral sex altogether.)

PHILOSOPHY, POWER, AND OBFUSCATION

Having discussed the abusive mechanism by which subjects and mere objects were constituted in the colonial/modern system, I'd like to now discuss how the abuse through which this was instituted was entirely hidden. For Aníbal Quijano, modernity involves the naturalization of modes of thinking that reflect the experiences of the ruling class (Europeans) while serving the necessities of the colonial/modern system.[38] It's with this in mind that I want to return to the impoverished table-gazing model of the philosophers and the self–subject equivalence and its work in both reflecting the experiences of the colonizers while obfuscating social reality. We'll discuss these in order.

In chapter 8, recall, I discussed the origin of the assumptions sustaining the person–self equivalence by considering the changing worldview—the collapse of Aristotelianism in the face of the rising mechanical science, as well as the necessities of the colonial/modern gender system. A similar account can be provided for the origin of object fungibility and the table-gazing model (putting aside the fact that the assumption of object fungibility may have been partially based in the literal institution of the fungibility of those who were enslaved).

In the Aristotelian view, sense perception is understood in terms of value-bearing forms that are propagated to the senses and ultimately delivered to the understanding. Forms are value-bearing because they constitute real being—something positive in reality rather than mere privation of reality. In such a view, it is possible to *see* a man—where the form is closely wed to man's specific morphology. While this view hardly captures all the details of interpersonal spatiality and the folk system, it does allow for a value-laden distinction between the perception of man and the perception of anything else. Further, as we saw earlier, it captures the way woman is rendered marked and deficient in the folk system. (Of course, it also, unfortunately, endorses it.) The modern, mechanistic vision rejects these forms, endorsing, rather, matter as tiny particles. Since there are no value-bearing forms, in this view, the senses won't be able to deliver value-laden differentiations, and any value-laden differences between the perception of man and of something else will be lost, since all the various sensations are on par.[39]

Once Aristotelianism is rejected, it is little wonder that object fungibility should be adopted, particularly once we recall that philosophers tend to philosophize alone, among nonpersonal objects. The sort of interpersonal awareness one would have in such a context is already not so far removed from the table-gazing model that follows from object fungibility. This yields a crucial upshot—namely, it turns out that this table-gazing mode of awareness is simply a

philosophical refinement of the typical mode of interpersonal awareness to be expected from men on the light side of gender.

The presumed self-awareness from which theorizing proceeds
is one in which there are very few experiences of self as object, no
vulnerability. Indeed, the only occasion in which one might be aware
of oneself as an object is during movement from passive presence
to dialogical presence, and here—particularly, without a broader
context—the experience is unremarkable. Robust forms of awareness
of oneself as an object are formally excluded from the model altogether or else disregarded as marginal.

By contrast, since females on the light side of gender and females and males on the dark side of gender must invariably inject
intimacy into an interpersonal context, albeit in different ways—the
former as vulnerable object, the latter as an interpersonal-reduced-
to-nonpersonal one—their own forms of interpersonal awareness
will involve greater and more frequent forms of object self-awareness
than standard forms. In the table-gazing model, these forms of interpersonal awareness are erased. In other words, while we've already recognized fungibility as the extraction of table-gazing from
the richer panoply of modes of interpersonal awareness to yield an
impoverished model of awareness, we must now also recognize the
table-gazing model as an artificial refinement of standard/male interpersonal awareness on the light side of the colonial/modern gender system.

This fact ought to leave us with deep concerns about current phenomenological accounts of gender or racial embodiment. Specifically,
as these accounts invariably take for granted fungibility and the table-
gazing model, they cannot explain what they aim to explain, since
they have already taken for granted, in the very model they use, an
implicitly male-structured model of interpersonal awareness. The
hiddenness of gender in the table-gazing model thereby infects any
attempt to elucidate gendered or racialized experiences. In other
words, if there is to be something like trans phenomenology, it can't
be one that proceeds from Edmund Husserl's desk.[40]

In addition to reflecting the experiences of the ruling class,
the table-gazing model eliminates the resources to even elucidate
the abuses perpetrated in the system, thereby serving the interests
of the system. What the model lacks is a full-blooded account of the

second-person perspective in which two active objects are delivered to each other in reciprocal object comportment, revealed to each other in overlapping modes of interpersonal awareness, engaged in the mirroring dialectic of call and reply. Such an account simply isn't possible under the fungibility assumption. Rather, it leaves us with only first- and third-person perspectives, distorted by the presumption of dissociation, no less.

Consider a simple case of an individual behaving in the world as though fungibility were true. María Lugones provides an example:

> Many times people act in front of their maids as if there were no one in the room. They say things and behave in ways that one can imagine are said or done only in private. When people behave this way, they do not see themselves as the maid sees them and they do not want to remember or recognize the persons who are seen by the maids, of whom the maids are witnesses.[41]

Suppose some woman acts as though she were entirely alone in front of a second woman who is employed by her as a maid. The first woman, in this situation, does not recognize a distinction between interpersonal and nonpersonal objects in her apartment, say, as she takes herself to be alone. The problem here, in my view, is that she treats the second woman as a nonpersonal object rather than an interpersonal one. To do so is abusive, as it means treating her as though she has no boundaries, thereby rendering her incapable of intimate agency and intrinsic intimacy.

The salient fact is that a table-gazing model that centralizes the subject cannot properly diagnose the abusive behavior of this woman. That is, while the abusive behavior of the first woman can be registered in the very table-gazing model she dramatizes, such an approach gets it all wrong. In such a view, dialogical interaction is construed in terms of conscious subjects alone. Typically, in this approach, one must use one's awareness of one's own self as a model to understand the other, since one cannot directly access this subject. Accordingly, the first woman could be characterized as failing to recognize the second woman as a subject, thereby rendering her part of the furniture—one among the mere objects. One might say that the first woman fails to use her own self-awareness to understand the second woman as a subject and thereby fails to recognize that the second woman sees her as an object. So, what the first woman needs to do is treat the second as a subject.

But now consider the extraordinary interpersonal distance maintained in this version. The first woman is not aware of herself as the second woman sees her precisely because she lacks awareness of herself as an object at all. To be aware of herself as an object present to the second woman would require her to recognize the second woman as an active interpersonal object in the first place. Instead, she's aware of herself as a table-gazing subject only. This protects her from recognizing her own abusiveness.

What the first woman does not experience, after all, is a painful presence to the second woman. She does not feel exposed to her. Neither can the first woman recognize the close presence of the second woman to her. The second woman is not some hidden subject, accessible only to herself. She is right there, present with the first woman—an active object. She has the capacity to open herself up to the first woman. Indeed, she has the capacity to call the first woman through a gesture of self-display, a call that, if heeded, would require the first woman to be aware of her own capacity for self-display. Alas, the first woman is not there.

It's a dysfunctional relational state oddly touted in the table-gazing model as a paradigm instance of intersubjectivity. It is the appropriate mode to adopt when one wants to be polite, nice, distant, unengaged. It is a very thin form of interaction that has any possibilities of intimacy gutted. In this model, both women are self-invisible subjects. But this model is wrong. Only the first woman is in this state—a state that is useful for avoiding accountability. It is typically the way one relates to those one has oppressed and that one has made a habit of not interacting with to avoid facing who one is. Indeed, relational detachment bespeaks distinct pathways of intimacy that segregate—by race, say. What the table-gazing model doesn't capture is the depth of full relationality and the ways it can be absent.

Of course, on a much larger scale, this is precisely why the colonial/modern gender system afforded no resources for registering the abuse of fungibility that remade society into subjects and mere objects. As I've noted, the abuse was not in treating those who were enslaved as if they weren't "subject-selves." The abuse, rather, was in first treating them like nonpersonal objects rather than interpersonal ones. This is just what undermined the capacity for dialogical interaction in the overworld in the first place, thereby facilitating the subsequent denial of subjectivity.

The incapacity of this distorted philosophical model to properly capture the abuses perpetrated in the colonial/modern gender system is not especially surprising, of course. Indeed, this is just what one should expect from the hegemonic way of thinking—namely, that the character of those abuses should be hidden and, further, that the true character of the colonizing subjects as distorted interpersonal objects be entirely obfuscated. My hope, however, is that interpersonal spatiality theory helps tear away the curtain to not only reveal the nature of these abuses but also expose these taken-for-granted ways of knowing—subjects and objects, table-gazing, and the like—as false, abusive, and in the service of empire.

If I'm right, at any rate, the concepts *person, self,* and *subject* no longer have play. Of what use is the self, after all, when self-awareness doesn't secure moral status and, further, reflexive access isn't even privileged? And once we have dispensed with the table-gazing model, the very philosophical content of *subject* drains away, and the philosophical notion of *object* that presupposes fungibility is demolished. Given this, what use is defining *person* in terms of *self* and *subject*?

To be sure, it may still be useful to talk about these concepts so as to identify the harmful work they perform. And, of course, there is nothing wrong with using words such as *subject* and *object* in case we can stipulate some useful philosophical application. This is a far cry from deploying the original concepts themselves, which depend upon the assumptions I have rejected.

That said, the words themselves may simply be too painful for some of us to use anymore. If so, we ought to find different words. For instance, while *object* played an important role in my theory, my only reason for choosing that word was to help put that theory into conversation with the framework I was critiquing. Now that it's been rejected, other words may easily be used, such as *appearance* and the like. The most important thing, however, is the rejection of a model that has impaired our understanding for too long.

Conclusion

PERHAPS IT SEEMS LIKE WE ARE, by now, far away from where this essay began—my original account of trans oppression long behind us. It's worth reviewing how we got here. My efforts, recall, were first directed at providing accounts of trans oppression and trans phoria. To do so, however, I needed to appeal to interpersonal spatiality theory.

It's worth dwelling on this accomplishment. While trans people have had available only two relatively positive accounts—the wrong-body account and the beyond-the-binary account—I have demonstrated the inadequacy of both, and I've provided a new one. This account is notable in that it provides an underlying framework that finally departs from the more-or-less Butlerian basis that much of trans theory has taken for granted. That is, it provides a trans basis for trans theory for perhaps the first time.

One consequence of my theory was that key assumptions underlying the concepts *person, self,* and *subject* had to be rejected. No doubt, it will always be possible to say, "Well, the philosopher so-and-so didn't commit to this or that assumption. They broke free of it altogether." Or "The philosopher so-and-so never used this term because of this and that." And, certainly, it isn't possible, at least not within the purview of this essay, to show how the assumptions are built into virtually all the views that compose philosophical engagements from the eighteenth century onward. However, an honest look at the departure I'm proposing will reveal it to be a novel one—one that ultimately brings to the surface several false and abusive presumptions that have been taken for granted for a long time.

Finally, I had wanted to situate my account of trans oppression and phoria within a much larger account of oppression. And I did so by showing how the folk system of interpersonal spatiality is part of the colonial/modern gender system. The consequence is that trans politics and theory need to be embedded within a much larger political project. They cannot be thought alone. Further, given the nature of this work, it also may be that the ideas in this essay are useful well beyond trans studies—in decolonial feminist theory, for instance. That is my hope.

I want to say now that the very fact that a relatively humble beginning could lead to such an ambitious result is a testament to the sort of philosophy I have aimed to practice. I had wanted to produce a work that, while deeply grounded in everyday life, could discover deep and expansive ways of looking at the worlds—a work in which there was no line between high theory and life experience.

This is to say, I have demonstrated the power of trans philosophy to execute philosophy per se. While this essay certainly concerns trans people—indeed, it is by a trans person, for trans people—it is also a philosophy that is broad and far reaching. It's a philosophy about personhood, intimacy, and oppression. It's not a philosophy that renders transness its subject matter but one that takes transness as its approach.

Let me also say that what we have witnessed is the extraordinary way in which philosophical presuppositions, buried in history, make it virtually impossible for ground-bound philosophy to do its work. With the meager resources provided by the concepts *person, self,* and *subject,* it was literally impossible to make any sense of trans phoria. New tools needed to be developed, almost out of whole cloth, for that to happen. Consider, for instance, that while there has been steady work toward the notion of a relational, rather than solitary, self-subject, what I've shown is that full relationality can never be represented through the concepts of *person, self,* or *subject* at all. These concepts must be abandoned to situate relationality prior to the individual.

What lessons might we draw from this? First, philosophy as practiced, with its long, proud traditions, ought to be viewed as absolutely chilling from the perspective of ground-bound philosophy. Its underlying assumptions run deep, and the contribution of these assumptions to the colonial/modern gender system are extensive.

Second, the question as to what degree philosophy remains committed to fungibility is a pressing one. Recall that, according to Aníbal Quijano, modernity involves the production and centralization of ways of knowing that satisfy the needs of the colonial capitalist system.[1] The table-gazing model is, of course, foundational to these ways of knowing, and it endorses full unfettered access to everything. Nothing is subject to boundaries. All must be stripped bare. In what ways is philosophy like that? To what degree does it confuse solitary investigation with dialogue and nonpersonal objects with interpersonal ones?

To the extent that philosophy remains a vibrant force in the world, it must be one that is a ground-bound practice. I say this out of necessity not only of resisting oppression but also of discovering deep truth. Or, rather, I regard both as the same. In my view, much of mainstream philosophy as currently practiced has little interest in liberation or truth. On the contrary, it aims to maintain the status quo, providing adequate employment for thinkers—highly intelligent thinkers—to add to a literature that, for the most part, traffics in philosophical problems largely of its own making. Only by getting outside the presuppositions that sustain philosophy as it currently stands can the spirit of philosophy be unleashed.

Further, only through complex, third-order communication across differences can anything like transformative philosophical conversation occur. And that requires some vulnerability, which is terrifying—particularly for those of us who have been abused or annihilated in the overworlds.

Nonetheless, it can be good to be an interpersonal object for another. And it can be good to be aware of oneself as an interpersonal object for another, even in those cases in which one is laid utterly bare. It can feel tender to be received in this way. If what I've argued is correct, however, this vulnerability requires intimacies made in new interpersonal spaces—spaces that afford as yet unfathomed creative possibilities and, above all else, spaces that move well beyond the catastrophe we call "personhood."

Glossary

affective account: An account of trans gender phoria according to which feeling bad and feeling good are central.

affective makeup: An individual's disposition to experience certain interpersonal sentiments in various interpersonal scenarios. Probably a joint function of prior engagements with the world and bodily dispositions.

agent object: An interpersonal object with an emphasis on the object's capacity for self-display.

animation: The process through which an act of self-display is attributed to the "who."

anticipatory vulnerability: The anticipation of exposure to another.

apparitional liminality: The state of being in between make-believe and complex interpersonal engagement.

aspirational account: An account of trans gender phoria according to which desires are central.

attention: An intimate gesture that invites self-display in another, responds to self-display of another, or communicatively traverses the boundary of another.

awareness of oneself as an object for others: An aspect of interpersonal awareness. Awareness of oneself as a sensory and discursive appearance for another.

beyond-the-binary account (BTBA): An account of trans and nonbinary oppression according to which all such oppression is to be explained by appeal to the dichotomies between male and female, man and woman, and masculine and feminine, as well as the mandated alignment between the three pairs.

blank open: A state of liminality secured through infraintimate self-containment and that reaches out for new ways of relating in interpersonal space.

boundary crossing: A form of sensory or discursive access. Boundary traversal or violation.

boundary observation: A sensory or discursive access that does not involve boundary crossing.

boundary system: An integration of various pathways into an overarching whole.

boundary traversal: An authorized boundary crossing.

boundary violation: A nonauthorized boundary crossing.

calamities of intimacy: The risks associated with playing along with trans people: taking it too far, the risk of alleged males being in female-segregated space, the risk of having sex with the supposed wrong sex.

centrality of self-awareness: One of two assumptions key to the person–self equivalence. A sophisticated form of self-awareness is central to moral status.

closeness: A spatial metaphor for characterizing intimacy between two or more individuals in a given encounter.

complex intimacy: Intimacy that occurs across multiple boundary systems. World-making intimacy. Intimacy that requires the other to understand one's vulnerability to a specific boundary system among multiple boundary systems.

comportment: A fundamental form of self-display by which one moves from passive presence to dialogical presence.

conscious gender identity: A conscious sense of oneself as a gendered being.

contrastive mode: Proper appearance accompanied by intimate thought juxtaposing it with intimate appearance.

deceiver–make-believer bind: An aspect of reality enforcement. Either come out as trans (admit one is a "make-believer") or refrain from doing so and risk exposure as a "deceiver."

dialogical presence: Two interpersonal objects are dialogically present to each other when they are bound together in mutual engagement through intimate gesture.

dignity: A type of self-collection. Often contrasted with vulnerability.

dissociation: A state of viewing oneself from the perspective of another.

distance: A lack of closeness.

essential reflexivity: The defining feature of those reflexive relations that are identifiably reflexive owing to their very character (rather than through the identification of the two relata).

essentially reflexive awareness: Self-awareness that does not involve identification of somebody with oneself.

existential depth: The capacity of an interpersonal identity to admit of the question "Who are they, really?"

existential identity: An interpersonal identity at significant existential depth.

existential WTF: The perplexity that arises when the common sense of a world makes no sense at all. An experience by those oppressed in a world.

folk person: An interpersonal object in the folk system that is a man, woman, boy, or girl.

folk system of interpersonal spatiality: The hegemonic system of interpersonal spatiality within the colonial/modern gender system. *Folk system* is no doubt a somewhat distorted simplification of multiple systems.

form of nakedness: A ruse of the system. A structure of boundaries as applied to body parts.

gender phoria: Gender dysphoria, euphoria, and like experiences in between these extremes. Presumed to be multifaceted and capable of ambiguity.

gesture of intimacy: A communicative act that makes another or oneself vulnerable.

ground-bound philosophy: Philosophy as responsive to oppression. Philosophy that takes the existential WTF as its starting point.

heterorelational complex: Integration of the sexual pathway and the romantic/affective pathway into a larger system of pathways. A feature of the folk system.

ideational intimization: The process by which the salience of one's boundaries and their intimate meaning (whether crossed or not) becomes uniquely evident within a context composed of other interpersonal objects.

imputation: The attribution of an interpersonal identity to an interpersonal object.

incongruence account: An account of trans phoria that posits conflict between internal experience of sex/gender and outward sex/gendered appearance (or sex/gendered materiality).

infraintimacy: A freedom from vulnerability due to the other's failure to understand the multiworldly character of one's intimate gestures or boundaries. Protection through the obliviousness of the other.

interpersonal account: A version of the affective account of trans gender phoria that appeals to interpersonal sentiments—modalities of awareness of oneself as an object for others.

interpersonal awareness: Awareness of oneself and others in relation to each other as interpersonal objects. All forms of awareness: awareness of oneself and another in dialogical engagement; awareness of oneself and another as passively present; awareness of oneself as alone. Also, awareness of nonpersonal objects within any of the three preceding configurations.

interpersonal boundaries: Boundaries between interpersonal objects. Boundaries that make possible traversal and self-display.

interpersonal identity: A biographic account of interpersonal objects—including past and anticipated futures and the background conception of the world. Interpersonal identity is accessible to the object itself as well as to other objects. It is subject to boundaries and is imputed to interpersonal objects upon subsumption.

interpersonal object: An object of sensory or discursive access where the access is subject to boundaries. An interpersonal object possesses an interpersonal identity.

interpersonal sentiments: Modes of awareness of oneself as vulnerable to another.

interpersonal space: Closeness and distance between interpersonal objects.

interpersonal spatiality: The characteristic of admitting of closeness and distance. Attributed to sensory and discursive forms of access.

interpersonal spatiality hypothesis: The hypothesis that folk people are interpersonal objects. Made in light of the Superman argument.

intimate appearance: The sensory appearance of interpersonal objects allocated to intimate pathways.

intimate cognition: The coming into consciousness of intimate content or the intimate content itself.

intimate deadening: The incapacity to experience vulnerability.

intimate disregard: The intentional failure to respond to gestures of intimacy.

intimate hemorrhaging: The experience of constant, often increasing, exposure to others. The experience of an inability to prevent exposure.

intimate meaning: Intimate content taken to elucidate and justify specific boundaries. Part of the mythology that makes interpersonal identity possible.

intimate movement: Boundary crossing, including self-display.

intimate recoding practices: Practices of intimacy whereby the assigned boundaries of a system are, at least provisionally, replaced with ones that are constituted in reciprocal engagement.

intimization: A rendering of an interpersonal object that is increasingly available. Can be sensory, discursive, or ideational.

intrinsic intimacy: Intimacy for the sake of intimacy; communicative intimacy; intimacy that is not merely instrumental (e.g., intimate access during a physical exam).

irregular interpersonal sentiments: Interpersonal sentiments experienced in atypical configurations.

Lockean personhood: *Person* defined as a "self." Presumption of the table-gazing model.

material genitalia: The morphological appearance of genital flesh.

moral genitalia: Genitalia provided for by an attributed nakedness structure (e.g., a male nakedness structure includes a penis as a structural component, regardless of the current material state of the genitalia).

moral maturity: A boundary-structured difference with regard to appropriateness for sexual pathways. A subdifference in moral sex.

moral sex: A boundary-structured difference between men and women (and boys and girls). Difference in nakedness structures; difference in pathway positions; difference in the modality of sensory of access (analogous to the difference in the modality of access between interpersonal and nonpersonal objects—as a feature of subsumption, allocated to differences above); difference in forms of self-awareness. Substrate upon which gendered considerations are differentially allocated (e.g., labor, material resources, evaluative norms of conduct).

moral status: Something like the status that we typically associate with humanity or personhood without being too specific about it. An individual who possesses this status is capable of being dehumanized. Alternatively, different sorts of statuses ranked with humanity on top. Each status dictates appropriate moral interactions.

morpho-species irrelevance: One of two assumptions key to the person–self equivalence. Morphology and species membership are irrelevant to moral status.

naked body: That which exists underneath clothing, demanding concealment. The body as naked, where the moral significance is supposed to exist prior to societal implementation. A fiction.

nakedness: A social mode of appearance in the folk system. The intimate appearance in the folk system.

naturalization of nakedness: A ruse of the folk system whereby nakedness appears capable of preexisting societal implementation. The mode of nakedness falsely viewed as the naked body.

nonpersonal object: An object of sensory or discursive access that is not subject to interpersonal boundaries.

object fungibility assumption: The false view that there is no distinction between interpersonal and nonpersonal objects. Underlies the self–subject equivalence. Yields the table-gazing model.

ordinary notion of personhood: Personhood in which folk personhood and membership within the genus *Homo* are conflated.

passive presence: Sensory accessibility subject to a boundary and yet prior to comportment.

pathway: A prestructured arrangement of gestures of intimacy leading to increased intimacy.

people-as-folk: People regarded as men, women, boys, and girls.

people-as-human: People regarded as members of the species *Homo sapiens.*

physical person: The person one has. The body viewed as a moral entity. The sensory appearance of interpersonal objects in the folk system. Proper and intimate appearances considered together.

physical strip: The strip ordering organism-artifact configurations in the folk system.

playing along: Acting as if a trans person's self-identifications were true while not actually accepting the self-identifications as such.

proper appearance: The taken-for-granted sensory appearance of interpersonal objects in the folk system. Unmarked appearance. Clothed appearance.

reality enforcement: A structured form of violence that includes misgendering, the deceiver–make-believer bind, and genital verification.

realization: The process by which the experience of self-recognition (self-collection) in the blank open is made actual through integration into interpersonal space.

selective targeting: Holding an oppressed group accountable for some undesirable act or attitude while simultaneously failing to hold an oppressing group accountable for the same act or attitude and failing to recognize the possibility of resistance on the part of the oppressed group.

self-collection: An interpersonal sentiment. The experience of a lack of vulnerability as a consequence of one's agency. Dignity and poise.

self-containment: An interpersonal sentiment. The experience of a lack of vulnerability regardless of agency.

self-display: A gesture of intimacy whereby another is provided with greater access to an interpersonal object's boundaries.

self-revelation: A form of self-display whereby one discloses "who one really is." Can be discursive or sensory.

sex-representational system: A system of interpersonal spatiality in which proper appearance provides information about intimate appearance in advance of an intimate encounter.

singular mode: Proper appearance without intimate cognition. Proper appearance as taken for granted. Proper appearance without contrast with intimate appearance.

strip: The moral and temporal ordering of boundaries determining access to a single interpersonal object. Immanent in pathways.

subsumption: The process of sensory access already in accord with a boundary (e.g., boundary observation).

Superman argument: An argument concluding that men, women, boys, and girls needn't be members of the species *Homo sapiens.*

table-gazing model: A model that treats the awareness one has when sensorily accessing a nonpersonal object (alone) as the basis for all forms of awareness.

vestorg: An interpersonal object that is composed of an organism and clothing.

vulnerability: The state of being more exposed to another than they are to oneself and being aware of it.

"who": The protagonist of an interpersonal identity.

wrong-body account (WBA): An account of trans gender phoria that uses the incongruence account, affirms the innateness of sense of self or internal body image, and validates trans identities on the basis of the preceding.

Notes

Introduction

1. While *gender dysphoria* is a common term in the trans community, I call into question its usefulness in detail in chapter 1. I use the term here with considerable skepticism.

2. As I shall discuss in chapter 7, notions such as *man, woman, person,* and *human* are profoundly implicated in colonial impositions. They are philosophically and politically charged terms, making it controversial to deploy them straightforwardly in this essay. María Lugones tends to use expressions such as *the colonized* presumably to avoid this problem. However, one might worry that this move risks reducing those who were colonized to colonized constructions. I considered using the term *individual* to avoid this concern. Unfortunately, this goes against my aim of moving away from the notion of the individual, towards that of the relationship. In the end, I have settled on the locution *those who were colonized* because it resists reduction while avoiding the use of the very terms I intend to analyze. María Lugones, "Toward a Decolonial Feminism," *Hypatia: A Journal of Feminist Philosophy* 25, no. 4 (Fall 2010): 742–59.

3. Lugones, "Toward a Decolonial Feminism."

4. María Lugones, *Pilgrimages/Peregrinajes: Theorizing Coalition against Multiple Oppressions* (Lanham, Md.: Rowman and Littlefield, 2003), 17.

1. Getting "Real"

1. Judith Butler, *Gender Trouble: Feminism and the Subversion of Identity* (1990; repr., New York: Routledge, 1999).

2. I won't be using the expressions *cis, cissexual,* or *cisgender,* sticking rather with the old-fashioned *nontrans,* which is not used to indicate a specific identity but to indicate the lack of a trans identity. I do think that *cis* can be useful as a term of self-identification. However, the uncritical deployment of *cis* seems to already involve tacit acceptance of a specific trans politics, and one might want some distance to be critical of such a view. A. Finn Enke, "The Education of Little Cis: Cisgender and the Discipline of Opposing Bodies," in *The Transgender Studies Reader 2,* ed. Susan Stryker and Aren Z. Aizura

(New York: Routledge, 2013), 234–47. See also B. Aultman, "Cisgender," *TSQ: Transgender Studies Quarterly* 1, no. 1–2 (May 2014): 61–62. For more on the presumed whiteness necessary for the intelligibility of the notion, see Che Gossett, "Blackness and the Trouble of Trans Visibility," in *Trap Door: Trans Cultural Production and the Politics of Visibility*, ed. Reina Gossett, Eric A. Stanley, and Johanna Burton (Cambridge, Mass.: MIT Press, 2017), 183–90; Elías Cosenza Krell, "Is Transmisogyny Killing Trans Women of Color? Black Trans Feminisms and the Exigencies of White Femininity," *TSQ: Transgender Studies Quarterly* 4, no. 2 (May 2017): 226–42, 234; V. Varun Chaudry, "Trans/Coalitional Love-Politics: Black Feminism and the Radical Possibilities of Transgender Studies," *TSQ: Transgender Studies Quarterly* 6, no. 4 (November 2019): 521–38.

3. I am grateful to Jake Hale, who tries to remind people of this point—a point that keeps wanting to culturally evaporate.

4. American Psychiatric Association, *Diagnostic and Statistical Manual of Mental Disorders*, 5th ed. (Arlington, Va.: American Psychiatric Association, 2013), 453–59.

5. Simone de Beauvoir, *The Second Sex*, ed. and trans. H. M. Parshley (New York: Random House, 1952), 201.

6. For further discussion, see Talia Mae Bettcher, "Trapped in the Wrong Theory: Rethinking Trans Oppression and Resistance," *Signs: Journal of Women in Culture and Society* 39, no. 2 (Winter 2014): 383–406.

7. These ideas were first developed in Talia Mae Bettcher, "Evil Deceivers and Make-Believers: Transphobic Violence and the Politics of Illusion," *Hypatia: A Journal of Feminist Philosophy* 22, no. 3 (Summer 2007): 43–65.

8. Of course, there are complexities. The distinction between the two sides of the bind isn't always sharp: a trans person who doesn't pass may still be viewed as a potential deceiver (why else wear this costume). Similarly, a trans person exposed as a deceiver may find themself represented as pretending. Consequently, the make-believer may be subject to moral judgment, while the deceiver may be subject to concerns about mental stability. Further, deception requires that a trans person pass as nontrans for at least a brief period, so those who don't pass will invariably be represented according to the one side of the bind (as "make-believers") and hence not subject to a bind at all. Finally, passing isn't all or nothing, as one may pass from a distance only to be read up close or pass up close only to be read when one speaks. Consequently, one might find oneself effecting disclosures on a regular basis.

9. Marilyn Frye, *The Politics of Reality: Essays in Feminist Theory* (Freedom, Calif.: Crossing Press, 1983).

10. Bettcher, "Evil Deceivers and Make-Believers," 48.

11. Loren Cannon, *The Politicization of Trans Identity: An Analysis of Back-*

lash, Scapegoating, and Dog-Whistling from Obergefell to Bostock (London: Lexington Books, 2022), 163.

12. It's also no surprise that in case the secret becomes public, such men can deploy the deceiver representations ("He tricked me") to lie and possibly murder their way out of what is, for them, a highly embarrassing situation.

13. See Kimberlé Crenshaw, "Demarginalizing the Intersection of Race and Sex: A Black Feminist Critique of Antidiscrimination Doctrine, Feminist Theory and Antiracist Politics," *University of Chicago Legal Forum* (1989): 139–67; Combahee River Collective, "A Black Feminist Statement," in *This Bridge Called My Back: Writing by Radical Women of Color,* ed. Cherríe Moraga and Gloria Anzaldúa (New York: Kitchen Table, 1981), 210–18.

14. María Lugones calls this the "intermeshing of oppressions." *Pilgrimages/Peregrinajes: Theorizing Coalition against Multiple Oppressions* (Lanham, Md.: Rowman and Littlefield, 2003), 223.

15. Angela Y. Davis, "Rape, Racism, and the Myth of the Black Rapist," in *Women, Race, and Class* (New York: Random House, 1981), 172–201, 175.

16. Lugones calls this phenomenon the "interlocking of oppressions." She writes, "Oppressions interlock when the social mechanisms of oppression fragment the oppressed both as individuals and collectivities." Lugones, *Pilgrimages/Peregrinajes,* 223.

17. Crenshaw, "Demarginalizing the Intersection of Race and Sex," 149.

18. Note, again, that my move away from category-based vectors is crucial here in both allowing that trans men can be subject to sexual violence without having to count them as women and recognizing how trans women can be subject to sexual violence even when they are not regarded as women.

19. Frye, *Politics of Reality.*

20. Talia Mae Bettcher, "Understanding Transphobia: Authenticity and Sexual Violence," in *Trans/Forming Feminisms: Transfeminist Voices Speak Out,* ed. Krista Scott-Dixon (Toronto: Sumach Press, 2006), 203–10.

21. Moreover, the psychological damage inflicted through pervasive reality enforcement may lead to substance use that requires the kind of money that only sex work can provide. More than this, the specific needs that many trans women have (access to technologies), in this system, require capital to which trans women don't have access (again grounded in transphobia, again grounded in reality enforcement). Furthermore, there are personal reasons that hinge on reality enforcement. Trans women may well turn to commercial sex as a form of identity validation in the face of constant reality enforcement. Or it may simply seem like the smart move in light of the economy of intimacy. (If one must be a dirty secret, why not get some cash?) Finally, it's often simply a part of trans subcultural experience—an aspect of life and, therefore, a form of resistance to reality enforcement.

22. Aníbal Quijano, "Coloniality of Power, Eurocentrism, and Latin America," *Nepantla: Views from South* 1, no. 3 (2000): 533–80. While this discussion focuses on trans women, it's notable that trans men and other transmasculine people likewise do sex work. See Jaime M. Grant et al., *Injustice at Every Turn: A Report of the National Transgender Discrimination Survey* (Washington, D.C.: National Center for Transgender Equality and National Gay and Lesbian Task Force, 2011); Nihils Rev and Fiona Maeve Geist, "Staging the Trans Sex Worker," *TSQ: Transgender Studies Quarterly* 4, no. 1 (February 2017): 112–27, 116.

23. Quijano, "Coloniality of Power, Eurocentrism, and Latin America," 535.

24. Treva Ellison, Kai M. Green, Matt Richardson, and C. Riley Snorton, "We Got Issues: Toward a Black Trans*/Studies," *TSQ: Transgender Studies Quarterly* 4, no. 2 (May 2017): 162–69, 163.

25. Tom Boellstorff, Mauro Cabral, Micha Cárdenas, Trystan Cotton, Eric A. Stanley, Kalaniopua Young, and Aren Z. Aizura, "Decolonizing Transgender: A Roundtable Discussion," *TSQ: Transgender Studies Quarterly* 1, no. 3 (August 2014): 419–39, 422.

26. C. Riley Snorton, *Black on Both Sides: A Racial History of Trans Identity* (Minneapolis: University of Minnesota Press, 2017), 57; Chaudry, "Trans/Coalitional Love-Politics," 525.

27. Francisco J. Galarte, *Brown Trans Figurations: Rethinking Race, Gender, and Sexuality in Chicanx/Latinx Studies* (Austin: University of Texas Press, 2021), 32.

28. Andrea J. Pitts, *Nos/Otras: Gloria E. Anzaldúa, Multiplicitous Agency, and Resistance* (Albany: State University of New York Press, 2022), 144.

29. Pitts, *Nos/Otras*, 144.

30. Pitts, 144.

31. María Lugones, "Toward a Decolonial Feminism," *Hypatia: A Journal of Feminist Philosophy* 25, no. 4 (Summer 2010): 742–59, 742.

32. *Oxford English Dictionary*, s.v. "person (*n*.), sense II.2.a," February 2024, https://doi.org/10.1093/OED/1152482240; *Oxford English Dictionary*, s.v. "people (*n*.), sense I.2.a," March 2024, https://doi.org/10.1093/OED/7290 165651.

33. Harry G. Frankfurt, "Freedom of the Will and the Concept of a Person," *Journal of Philosophy* 68, no. 1 (January 14, 1972): 5–20, 6.

2. On Intimacy and Distance

1. I also avoid the words *constructionism* and *constructivism* to prevent association with the position of moral constructivism.

2. The idea of an "if-can" test is from Candace West and Don H. Zimmerman, "Doing Gender," in *Doing Gender, Doing Difference: Inequality, Power, and*

Institutional Change, ed. Sarah Fenstermaker and Candace West (New York: Routledge, 2002), 3–23, 9.

3. Of course, in difficult cases that prevent smooth subsumption, more explicit processes and methods—some that cite criteria—may be deployed to make a determination. These cases are uncommon. We can understand the capacity to differentiate as grounded in the allocation of different forms of sensory access to pathways and the dispositional mastery thereof.

4. One can be visually present to another without being "in person"—that is, without there being tactile access, as in the case of Zoom. Further, one can be auditorily present (as when one speaks to another on the phone).

5. For further discussion, see Talia Mae Bettcher, "Trans Identities and First-Person Authority," in *"You've Changed": Sex Reassignment and Personal Identity,* ed. Laurie J. Shrage (Oxford: Oxford University Press, 2009), 98–120.

6. For accounts of the narrative self, see Marya Schechtman, *The Constitution of Selves* (Ithaca, N.Y.: Cornell University Press, 1996); Marya Schechtman, "The Narrative Self," in *The Oxford Handbook of the Self,* ed. Shaun Gallagher (Oxford: Oxford University Press, 2011), 394–416.

7. *Oxford English Dictionary,* s.v. "person (*n.*), Etymology," February 2024, https://doi.org/10.1093/OED/1152482240.

8. *Oxford English Dictionary,* s.v. "person (*n.*), sense I.1," February 2024, https://doi.org/10.1093/OED/7798840322.

9. *Oxford English Dictionary,* s.v. "person (*n.*), sense II.4.b," February 2024, https://doi.org/10.1093/OED/5963113790.

10. *Oxford English Dictionary,* s.v. "person (*n.*), sense II.3.b," February 2024, https://doi.org/10.1093/OED/3072702980.

11. *Oxford English Dictionary,* s.v. "person (*n.*), sense II.4.a," February 2024, https://doi.org/10.1093/OED/1018211809.

12. *Oxford English Dictionary,* s.v. "person (*n.*), sense II.4.c," February 2024, https://doi.org/10.1093/OED/1112118541.

3. The Multiplicity of Meaning

1. María Lugones, *Pilgrimages/Peregrinajes: Theorizing Coalition against Multiple Oppressions* (Lanham, Md.: Rowman and Littlefield, 2003), 21.

2. Lugones, *Pilgrimages/Peregrinajes,* 89.

3. For a discussion of some of the complexities, see Mariana Ortega, *In-Between: Latina Feminist Phenomenology, Multiplicity, and the Self* (Albany: State University of New York Press, 2016), 96–102.

4. Lugones, *Pilgrimages/Peregrinajes,* 89.

5. Lugones, 86.

6. Lugones, 89.

7. Lugones, 55.

8. Lugones, 55.

9. Lugones, 55.

10. For examples of the ameliorative approach, see Sally Haslanger, *Resisting Reality: Social Construction and Social Critique* (Oxford: Oxford University Press, 2012), 221–47; Katharine Jenkins, "Amelioration and Inclusion: Gender Identity and the Concept of *Woman*," *Ethics* 126, no. 2 (January 2016): 394–421, https://doi.org/10.1086/683535. For a view that misreads my own as ameliorative, see Elizabeth Barnes, "Gender without Gender Identity: The Case of Cognitive Disability," *Mind* 131, no. 523 (July 2022): 836–62. There, she suggests that my position—outlined below and originally in "Trans Women and the Meaning of 'Woman,'" in *The Philosophy of Sex: Contemporary Readings*, 6th ed., ed. Nicholas Power, Raja Halwani, and Alan Soble (Lanham, Md.: Rowman and Littlefield, 2013), 233–50—is prescriptive (Barnes, "Gender without Gender Identity," 853). However, I am describing the practices that operate in trans underworlds—practices that already exist. I have not made the claim that overworlds *should* adopt this practice. Rather, I'm interested in describing oppressive and resistant practices so that we can better know how to navigate and oppose them. So, when Barnes critiques my view as disallowing cognitively disabled individuals from having genders (since in my account gender seems to require self-identification), this ought to be taken less as a criticism of my view and more as a criticism of the discursive and extradiscursive practices that exist in trans underworlds that I describe. That said, as a matter of fact, such practices would typically lead one to say that we do not know what this individual's gender is. Or else, the gender would simply default to sex assigned at birth. Barnes insists that because I have offered a "self-identification account," such possibilities are off the table. I suspect this is because she regards me as offering an ameliorative account rather than a description of the underworld practices. Meanwhile, of course, gender would continue to be assigned in the overworld in the way that it normally is—say, based on sex assigned at birth. Barnes misses this aspect of my account as well because she misses my commitment to ontological pluralism.

11. C. Riley Snorton, *Black on Both Sides: A Racial History of Trans Identity* (Minneapolis: University of Minnesota Press, 2017), 175.

12. Ludwig Wittgenstein, *Philosophical Investigations*, trans. G. E. M. Anscombe (1953; repr., Oxford: Blackwell Publishing, 2001).

13. In what I think is the earliest paper in trans philosophy of language, "Are Lesbians Women?," C. Jacob Hale argues for this position. Hale similarly draws on Lugones's notion of multiple worlds. C. Jacob Hale, "Are Lesbians Women?," *Hypatia: A Journal of Feminist Philosophy* 11, no. 2 (May 1996): 94–121; C. Jacob Hale, "Consuming the Living, Dis(re)membering the Dead in the Butch/Ftm Borderlands," *GLQ: A Journal of Lesbian and Gay Studies* 4,

no. 2 (April 1998): 311–48; C. Jacob Hale, "Tracing a Ghostly Memory in My Throat: Reflections on Ftm Feminist Voice and Agency," in *Men Doing Feminism,* ed. Tom Digby (New York: Routledge, 1998), 99–129.

14. There have been many appeals to a family-resemblance account in analyzing trans identities. See Natalie Stoljar, "Essence, Identity, and the Concept of Woman," *Philosophical Topics* 23, no. 2 (Fall 1995): 261–93; Cressida J. Heyes, *Line Drawings: Defining Women through Feminist Practice* (Ithaca, N.Y.: Cornell University Press, 2000); Jennifer McKitrick, "Gender Identity Disorder," in *Establishing Medical Reality: Essays in the Metaphysics and Epistemology of Biomedical Science,* ed. Harold Kincaid and Jennifer McKitrick (Dordrecht, Netherlands: Springer, 2007), 137–48. For more discussion of these accounts, see Stephanie Kapusta, "Misgendering and Its Moral Contestability," *Hypatia: A Journal of Feminist Philosophy* 31, no. 3 (Summer 2016): 502–19.

15. For further critique, see Kapusta, "Misgendering and Its Moral Contestability."

16. Jennifer Mather Saul, "Politically Significant Terms and Philosophy of Language: Methodological Issues," in *Out from the Shadows: Analytical Feminist Contributions to Traditional Philosophy,* ed. Sharon L. Crasnow and Anita M. Superson (Oxford: Oxford University Press, 2012), 195–216.

17. Saul, "Politically Significant Terms," 203.

18. E. Díaz-León, "*Woman* as a Politically Significant Term: A Solution to the Puzzle," *Hypatia: A Journal of Feminist Philosophy* 31, no. 2 (2016): 245–58.

19. Díaz-León, "*Woman* as a Politically Significant Term," 249.

20. Díaz-León, 247.

21. Perhaps with this concern in mind, Díaz-León allows, in endnote 6, that the relevant contextual moral and political considerations might determine that trans women are women even in the medical context of screening for vaginal disease. However, this allowance highlights a bind confronting the contextualist account. On the one hand, it's difficult to imagine any context in which trans identity invalidation would be acceptable. On the other hand, the appeal to a contextual account to validate trans identities requires there be contexts in which sex is salient and therefore contexts that are invalidating to trans identities. I say "requires" because if the contextualist view posits the empirical claim that it just so happens that every context validates trans identities, then the entire appeal to semantic contextualism to validate trans identities seems pointless. Worse, the position is clearly ad hoc. It mandates an empirical claim about the world—a claim that may or may not be true—to evade the criticism that some contexts will invalidate trans identities.

22. I originally provided this sort of account in "Trans Women and the Meaning of 'Woman.'" Hopefully this is an improvement.

23. In this view, orientation would count as a special case of gender expression.

24. In some cases, failure to sufficiently conform to these norms can yield assessments about what's "natural."

25. For instance, what's considered masculine in a woman may well be considered somewhat feminine in a man. Femininity and masculinity are relative to assigned gender category.

26. It doesn't follow from this that the norms can't play a semantic role in gender terms. *Woman*, for instance, might name a normative status much in the way that *U.S. citizen* does. It does mean that conformity to the norms should not be conflated with the criteria on the basis of which the status is conferred.

27. I first made this point in Talia Mae Bettcher, "Trans 101," in *The Philosophy of Sex: Contemporary Readings*, 7th ed., ed. Raja Halwani, Alan Soble, Sarah Hoffman, and Jacob M. Held (New York: Rowman and Littlefield, 2017), 119–37, 120. Marcus Arvan makes a similar point and goes on to make arguments similar to the ones I provide here about moral sex. Because I became aware of this article during production, I was not able to engage with it to explore the differences. Marcus Arvan, "Trans Women, Cis Women, Alien Women, and Robot Women Are Women: They Are All (Simply) Adults Gendered Female," *Hypatia: A Journal of Feminist Philosophy* 38, no. 2 (2023): 373–89.

28. In Appendix A, "Durin's Folk," J. R. R. Tolkien speaks of "dwarf-women" and "dwarf-men" (1,053). He also refers to the former as "the women-folk" (1,050n2). J. R. R. Tolkien, *The Lord of the Rings* (New York: Houghton Mifflin Company, 1994).

29. To press this last point, imagine a "twin earth" almost entirely qualitatively identical to our own. The only difference is that the individuals concerned aren't members of the species *Homo sapiens*. As we regard Kal-El as a man, however, we would surely regard these people on twin earth as properly men and women as well. And we would consider them to be men and women in the same way of speaking—the same idiolect—as our own. This stands in notable contrast to Hilary Putnam's well-known example of water. In that case, should we suppose that what folks called "water" was in fact composed of XYZ rather than H_2O, we should not regard what they were speaking of as water at all. The reason for this difference is that while *water* rigidly designates the natural kind H_2O, the terms *man* and *woman* do not rigidly designate the natural kinds "adult male member of the species *Homo sapiens*" and "adult female member of the species *Homo sapiens*," respectively. Hilary Putnam, "Meaning and Reference," *Journal of Philosophy* 70, no. 19 (November 8, 1973): 699–711.

30. Admittedly, one might protest that gender terms don't apply to these imaginary beings without qualification: one might say that a Martian woman isn't a woman simpliciter. Even if this was true (which I doubt), these gen-

der concepts still can be applied to imagined individuals who don't belong to human species, so we should conclude that the concepts *man*, *woman*, and *people* don't require species membership.

31. *Oxford English Dictionary*, s.v. "person (*n.*), sense II.2.a," February 2024, https://doi.org/10.1093/OED/1152482240; *Oxford English Dictionary*, s.v. "people (*n.*), sense I.2.a," March 2024, https://doi.org/10.1093/OED/7290165651.

32. This distinct folk sense is more than a mere stipulation. There's a use of *people* that applies to nonhumans such as Vulcans, Klingons, and the like in much the same way the terms *men* and *women* apply to them. Yet *people* does not apply to all intelligent beings that would count as Lockean persons. Consider, for instance, the Horta from the original *Star Trek* television series. The Horta is a rocklike, silicon-based life-form that is, while at least as cognitively sophisticated as humans, shaped more or less like a blob. In a philosophical sense, the Horta will no doubt be recognized as a person in the sense that she possesses a high degree of cognitive sophistication and is therefore a bearer of rights. By contrast, one would certainly not say, "Hey, there's a bunch of people outside my apartment," meaning to speak of a group of Horta milling about. A Horta, while a person in some philosophical sense, isn't a (folk) person in the sense that Vulcans and Klingons are.

33. Note that on this hypothesis, we can say that what's under contestation between trans underworlds and the overworld are precisely the underlying practices of interpersonal spatiality. This has the benefit of avoiding positing disconnected discursive practices in different worlds that then have little in common. It's not that *knight* now refers to something entirely equivocal (a toaster, say). Instead, the rules of the game are altered in this underworld so that a knight can move differently. That is, the extradiscursive practices constitute the (new) social kind differently.

34. Joan Roughgarden, *Evolution's Rainbow: Diversity, Gender, and Sexuality in Nature and People* (Berkeley: University of California Press, 2004), 24–26.

35. *Female* is used ca. 1350. *Oxford English Dictionary*, s.v. "female (*n. & adj.*)," July 2023, https://doi.org/10.1093/OED/8097376973. *Male* is used ca. 1383. *Oxford English Dictionary*, s.v. "male (*adj. & n.*)," July 2023, https://doi.org/10.1093/OED/5152231266.

36. By contrast, moral sex does not typically implicate moral maturity. And because of this, moral maturity ought to be regarded as subsidiary to—an aspect of—moral sex.

37. Lugones, *Pilgrimages/Peregrinajes*, 60–62.

38. Lugones, 60.

39. Another objection to this type of thought—certainly one found in the work of Judith Butler—is that the assumption that whatever underlies a social construction can be studied, discussed, etc., in a way that isn't already

culturally laden is false. So, to talk about this "precultural" animal organism would already be a dubious proposition. See, for example, Judith Butler, *Gender Trouble: Feminism and the Subversion of Identity* (New York: Routledge, 1990).

40. See, for example, Lugones, *Pilgrimages/Peregrinajes,* 14, 88.

41. It's in this sense, I believe, that Lugones also speaks of the multiplicitous self (in addition to the multiple selves). Lugones, *Pilgrimages/Peregrinajes,* 121–48.

42. Lugones, 61–62.

43. Lugones, 103–18.

44. Lugones, 112.

45. Alfred Arteaga, ed., *An Other Tongue: Nation and Ethnicity in the Linguistic Borderlands* (Durham, N.C.: Duke University Press, 1996), cited in María Lugones, "On Complex Communication," *Hypatia: A Journal of Feminist Philosophy* 21, no. 3 (Summer 2006): 75–85, 82.

46. Arteaga, "An Other Tongue," in Arteaga, *Other Tongue,* 12–13, 27.

4. The Politics of Pretense

1. María Lugones, "Heterosexualism and the Colonial/Modern Gender System," *Hypatia: A Journal of Feminist Philosophy* 22, no. 1 (February 2007): 186–219, 187.

2. *Red pill* and *blue pill* are expressions from the film *The Matrix* (dir. Lana Wachowski and Lilly Wachowski, 1999). While the latter enables the user to return to a state of computer-generated illusion and ignorance, the former enables the user to perceive social reality free from such illusion.

3. I do not take up Kenneth Clark's famous distinction of "nakedness" and "nude" in art. Kenneth Clark, *The Nude: A Study of Ideal Art* (Harmondsworth, U.K.: Penguin, 1956). However, see Ruth Barcan, *Nudity: A Cultural Anatomy* (New York: Berg, 2004), 143.

4. For related discussion, see Barcan, *Nudity,* 1–2.

5. Of course, this echoes Donna J. Haraway's "A Cyborg Manifesto," in *Simians, Cyborgs, and Women: The Reinvention of Nature* (New York: Routledge, 1991), 149–82.

6. *Oxford English Dictionary,* s.v. "person (*n.*), sense II.4.a," February 2024, https://doi.org/10.1093/OED/1018211809. Emphasis added.

7. In some respects, the physical person is like one's body, and just what a body is and what it is to have one are extraordinary philosophical questions. I touch on them by asking other questions such as the following: What would it be to view the body as an appearance? Is the "physical or outward appearance" of an individual the same thing as a body? What of clothes and adornments? Are they included or not included?

8. Crucially, at this point in my account, no significant correlation with morphological differences has yet been assigned. So *male* and *female* need not be taken to refer to anything other than this difference in strip and pathway position.

9. Thomas Nagel, *Concealment and Exposure and Other Essays* (New York: Oxford University Press, 2002), 4. I would add "at a standard interpersonal distance," as nakedness isn't disqualifying in the right intimate context.

10. For a related discussion, see J. David Velleman, "The Genesis of Shame," in *Self-to-Self: Selected Essays* (Cambridge: Cambridge University Press, 2006), 170–202.

11. For different representations of the naked body as truth, see Barcan, *Nudity,* 97–106. For nakedness and the metaphor of truth, see Barcan, 98.

12. To better understand what I have in mind, consider a scenario that some analytic philosophers enjoy posing when pondering the notion of social construction. When we consider the Salem witch trials, as no woman found guilty was actually endowed with supernatural powers, we should deny that there were any witches. Witches don't exist. Should we not then say that same thing in the case of clothing and the naked body? Since clothing can't conceal something that doesn't exist, shouldn't we deny that it exists at all? This is plainly different from the alleged Salem witches in that there were not even any organized practices that these women engaged in. Rather, the allegation in question was entirely false. Were it the case that these women practiced something that they called "witchcraft," then there would certainly be some respect in which these witches did exist even though their beliefs about witchcraft were false.

13. This is precisely why a man's access to a woman's intimate appearance would constitute a violation of privacy, while the converse would constitute an offense of decency against her. What's wrongly framed through the idea that the supposedly precultural female body (and eyes) is vulnerable to violation is simply the fact that female intimate disregard is built into the (hetero)sexuality-relation complex.

14. Gottlob Frege, "On Sense and Nominatum," in *The Philosophy of Language,* ed. A. P. Martinich (Oxford: Oxford University Press, 1996), 186–98.

15. Kathleen Stock, "Reply to Professor Talia Mae Bettcher," Medium, May 31, 2018, archived October 31, 2018, at the Wayback Machine, https://web.archive.org/web/20181031025424/https://medium.com/@kathleenstock/response-to-professor-talia-mae-bettcher-21263ffd87c8.

16. My thanks to C. Jacob Hale for this enlightening discussion.

17. None of this is to exclude trans people who have not had genital reconstruction surgery. It's simply to make a point. Ultimately, such alterations are far less relevant than some might suppose. For example, nothing stands

or falls on these trans men discussed above as having had phalloplasty. So long as their intimate appearance could be taken as morally male, it wouldn't matter for precisely the reasons already discussed. Indeed, this fact that attributed moral structure can outstrip material genitalia opens up further possibilities.

18. Talia Mae Bettcher, Sharon Brown, Shirin Buckman, Masen Davis, and Francisco Dueñas, "Recommended Models and Policies for LAPD Interactions with Trans Individuals," City of Los Angeles, Human Relations Commission, July 2010.

19. C. Jacob Hale, "Leatherdyke Boys and Their Daddies: How to Have Sex without Women or Men," *Social Text* 15, nos. 3/4 (Fall/Winter 1997): 223–36; Julia M. Serano, "The Case against Autogynephilia," *International Journal of Transgenderism* 12, no. 3 (2010): 176–87.

20. Hale, "Leatherdyke Boys and Their Daddies," 230.

21. Suzanne J. Kessler and Wendy McKenna, *Gender: An Ethnomethodological Approach* (New York: John Wiley and Sons, 1978); Candace West and Don H. Zimmerman, "Doing Gender," in *Doing Gender, Doing Difference: Inequality, Power, and Institutional Change,* ed. Sarah Fenstermaker and Candace West (New York: Routledge, 2002), 3–23; Kate Bornstein, *Gender Outlaw: On Men, Women, and the Rest of Us* (New York: Routledge, 1994); C. Jacob Hale, "Are Lesbians Women?," *Hypatia: A Journal of Feminist Philosophy* 11, no. 2 (May 1996): 94–121.

22. Harold Garfinkel, *Studies in Ethnomethodology* (Cambridge: Polity Press, 1967), 118–85.

23. Kessler and McKenna, *Gender,* 5.

24. Edmund Husserl, *Ideas for a Pure Phenomenology and Phenomenological Philosophy 1,* trans. Daniel O. Dahlstrom (Indianapolis: Hackett, 2014), sec. 27–30, 4–5.

25. Garfinkel, *Studies in Ethnomethodology,* 122.

26. Garfinkel, 122.

27. Garfinkel, 123–24.

28. Garfinkel, 125.

29. My argument against the family-resemblance account in chapter 3 also shows why exclusiveness can't be used to explain reality enforcement.

30. Garfinkel, 116.

31. Garfinkel, 122.

32. Garfinkel, 122–23.

33. Garfinkel, 127.

34. Garfinkel, 127.

35. Jay Prosser explains, "The stigmatization of transsexuals as not 'real men' and 'real women,' turns on this conception of transsexuals as con-

structed in some more literal way than nontranssexuals—the Frankensteins of modern technology's experiments with sexual difference." Jay Prosser, *Second Skins: The Body Narratives of Transsexuality* (New York: Columbia University Press, 1998), 8–9. Alas, Prosser does not recognize that this is merely an extension of the reality enforcement that confronts trans people who have not availed themselves of modern technology.

36. Sharon E. Preves, *Intersex and Identity: The Contested Self* (New Brunswick, N.J.: Rutgers University Press, 2003), 60–86.

37. Preves, *Intersex and Identity*, 73.

38. Cheryl Chase, "What Is the Agenda of the Intersex Patient Advocacy Movement?," *Endocrinologist* 13, no. 3 (June 2003): 240–42, 240.

39. For further discussion and references, see my "Intersexuality, Transsexuality, Transgender," in *The Oxford Handbook of Feminist Theory*, ed. Lisa Jane Disch and Mary Hawkesworth (Oxford: Oxford University Press, 2016), 407–27, esp. 408–9.

40. Judith Butler, "Imitation and Gender Insubordination," in *Inside/Out: Lesbian Theories, Gay Theories,* ed. Diana Fuss (New York: Routledge, 1991), 13–31, provides the best summary of their account. I draw on it here.

41. Judith Butler, *Gender Trouble: Feminism and the Subversion of Identity* (New York: Routledge, 1990), 137–38.

42. Butler, "Imitation and Gender Insubordination," 25.

43. Judith Butler, "Gender Is Burning: Questions of Appropriation and Subversion," in *Bodies That Matter: On the Discursive Limits of "Sex"* (New York: Routledge, 1993), 121–40, esp. 126–27.

44. Butler "Imitation and Gender Insubordination," 21.

45. Butler, *Gender Trouble*, 148–49.

46. Francisco J. Galarte, *Brown Trans Figurations: Rethinking Race, Gender, and Sexuality in Chicanx/Latinx Studies* (Austin: University of Texas, 2021), 45.

47. Prosser, *Second Skins*, 21–60; Viviane K. Namaste, "'Tragic Misreadings': Queer Theory's Erasure of Transgender Subjectivity," in *Invisible Lives: The Erasure of Transsexual and Transgendered People* (Chicago: University of Chicago Press, 2000), 9–23.

48. According to Prosser, by focusing on gender performativity and the body as mere surface, rather than narrative and the materiality of the body (as he will do in his own account), Butler cannot account for transsexual experience. According to Namaste, Butler illicitly takes one example of a specific practice (drag) and then uses it to represent all contexts in which gender operates, thereby departing from the poststructuralist underpinnings of their approach. Prosser, *Second Skins*, 6; Namaste, "'Tragic Misreadings,'" 21–23.

49. Butler, "Imitation and Gender Insubordination," 20.

50. Butler, *Gender Trouble*, 136.

51. bell hooks, "Is Paris Burning?," in *Black Looks: Race and Representation* (Boston: South End Press, 1992), 145–56.

52. Butler, "Gender Is Burning," 124.

53. Butler, "Gender Is Burning," 137.

54. Butler, "Gender Is Burning," 130.

55. Butler, "Gender Is Burning," 131.

56. Besides arguing that Butler uses Xtravaganza's murder as an allegory by which to motivate their own theory, both Prosser and Namaste argue the following: First, Butler elides the fact that Xtravaganza is murdered because she is a transsexual sex worker of color by suggesting that she is treated in "the ways in which women of color are treated" (Butler, "Gender Is Burning," 131; Prosser, *Second Skins*, 47; Namaste, "'Tragic Misreadings,'" 13). Second, in Butler's account, Xtravaganza's desire to become a suburban housewife is to be regarded as nonsubversive, deluded by the mechanisms of heterosexuality (Butler, "Gender Is Burning," 130; Prosser, *Second Skins*, 48; Namaste, "'Tragic Misreadings,'" 14). Namaste also worries that Butler's account forces a split between drag queens (subversive) and transsexuals (reactive), while Prosser points out that, in Butler's view, Xtravaganza is at her most subversive the moment she is murdered—presumably because her "little secret" is revealed and the relationship between sex and gender is thereby "denaturalized" (Namaste, "'Tragic Misreadings,'" 14; Prosser, *Second Skins*, 49).

57. Butler, "Gender Is Burning," 130.

58. Prosser, *Second Skins*, 46; Namaste, "'Tragic Misreadings,'" 13.

59. Butler, 129.

60. Butler, 131.

61. The ability of my account to elucidate trans oppression where Butler's account fails is, of course, due to its deep theoretical departures from their view. Butler, some may recall, is interested in debunking a common view that runs something like this: (hetero)sexual desire and masculine and feminine behavior arise from—are expressions of—a stable psychological core. Further, these cores, and therefore the desires and behaviors they express, are proper to—belong to—anatomically distinct bodies, male and female. There's a causal claim here, according to which sex-differential bodies give rise to sex-differential cores, which give rise to sex-differentiated forms of behavior and desire. That is, in a female body resides a feminine core from whence feminine behavior and desires flow.

This is wrong, says Butler. There is no necessary alignment of sexuality, gendered behavior, and sex in the way imagined above. Indeed, this is to get the causation backward. There is no such core from whence these behaviors flow—not really. Rather, there's nothing but behavior that's falsely taken to express such a core. Through constant repetition, the illusion of a stable core

is created. Further, neither do sexual desires and feminine or masculine behaviors belong to any one anatomical sex. Rather, this sense of propriety is
likewise an illusion generated through repetition. Indeed, sex as that to which
a specific set of desires and behaviors belong is itself an effect of the repetition—an effect of treating the behavior *as if* it were expressive.

One obvious difference between our views concerns sex. Because the relevance of sex in Butler's view principally concerns its being "that to which
gender belongs," it is not much more than the train's caboose, merely the location to which gendered behavior is ascribed (Butler, "Imitation and Gender
Insubordination," 21). However, in my theory, it is the central focus. There is
far more to sex than the site at which norms governing gendered behavior are
assigned. Moral sex is also the basic differentiation between men and women.
Indeed, it is the very form by which one's experience of oneself and others
is structured. Note here, also, that Butler's account requires an appeal to the
psychological (constitution of the psychological core), while mine does not.
Although I'll discuss the relevant psychological matter in the following two
chapters, my discussion of the constitution of the physical person sans mind is
important in my overturning of core assumptions underlying the deployment
of the concepts *person* and *self,* to which I will return in chapters 8 and 9.

Another difference is that whereas Butler sees the fiction of the original,
"natural" gendered beings (men and women) as constituted through the repetition of as-if behavior, I regard them as the effect of a representational relation
between proper and intimate appearances that casts the illusion of morally
saturated naked bodies existing prior to any cultural intervention. Further, I
regard the constitution of gender make-believe as necessary to the preservation of that illusion.

A final difference worth mentioning: since Butler is steeped in the psychoanalytic tradition, it is perhaps unsurprising that they should point to the
importance of the incest taboo as well as the presupposed taboo against homosexuality (Butler, *Gender Trouble,* 42–43). For Butler, because the presupposed
homosexuality taboo requires that "the boy" give up desire for his father—
a desire that can't even be articulated—he must, through melancholia, incorporate the lost father into his own identity instead of mourning the loss (Butler, *Gender Trouble,* 68–69).

By contrast, I do not focus on any one taboo. Rather, I centralize "the
boundary" in general, which is the basis for all taboos of this sort. Meanwhile,
I account for the prohibition against homosexuality specifically through the
naturalization of structures of nakedness, as well as a specific eroticism (as
I outlined earlier). Further, because of my approach, I don't focus on sexuality alone. Instead, I adopt a larger view that encompasses intimacy more
broadly, and, beyond that, distance. Finally, and because of the preceding, my

discussion concerning the psychological aspects of gender depart significantly from their psychoanalytic approach.

5. The Phenomenology of Illusion

1. Jay Prosser, *Second Skins: The Body Narratives of Transsexuality* (New York: Columbia University Press, 1998), 69.

2. Prosser, *Second Skins*, 100.

3. Prosser, 100.

4. Gayle Salamon, *Assuming a Body: Transgender and Rhetorics of Materiality* (New York: Columbia University Press, 2010), 4.

5. Salamon, *Assuming a Body*, 47.

6. Henry S. Rubin, "Phenomenology as Method in Trans Studies," *GLQ: A Journal of Lesbian and Gay Studies* 4, no. 2 (April 1998): 263–81, 270.

7. For example, see Christine Overall, "Sex/Gender Transitions and Life-Changing Aspirations," in *"You've Changed": Sex Reassignment and Personal Identity,* ed. Laurie J. Shrage (Oxford: Oxford University Press, 2009), 11–27.

8. Julia Serano, *Whipping Girl: A Transsexual Woman on Sexism and the Scapegoating of Femininity* (Emeryville, Calif.: Seal Press, 2007), 78.

9. What I mean is not far from Florence Ashley's view that "gender identity is constituted [and yet underdetermined] by gender subjectivity through a process of phenomenological synthesis." Florence Ashley, "What Is It like to Have a Gender Identity?," *Mind* 132, no. 528 (October 2023): 1,053–73, 1,054 (my insert). Ashley's account is particularly useful in capturing the overall stability of a gender identity, the way it not only interprets gender experiences but integrates them so that experience and identity are a virtual unity. One difference worth noting is that while Ashley understands gender identity in the broad sense "that includes the grounds of gender self-categorization, the strength of one's identification, and the totality of feelings about self-categorization," I go a step further in situating gender identity within a larger conception of oneself in the world at large (1,054). It is, in this way, of a piece with a more general sense of self.

10. An earlier version of the discussion that follows can be found in Talia Mae Bettcher, "Trans Phenomena," in *50 Concepts for a Critical Phenomenology,* ed. Gail Weiss, Ann V. Murphy, and Gayle Salamon (Evanston, Ill.: Northwestern University Press, 2020), 329–36.

11. Serano, *Whipping Girl,* 78.

12. Janet Mock, *Redefining Realness: My Path to Womanhood, Identity, Love & So Much More* (New York: Atria Books, 2014), 16.

13. This argument also provides the basis for an argument against the aspirational account. As many of us must develop a new self-conception that includes within it various conscious desires, these desires can't explain dys-

phoria since the desires are a consequence of the dysphoria. By analogy, consider somebody experiencing addiction. Whether or not they desire to address this addiction depends on many things. But regardless of whether any desire to be free of addiction is formed—never mind the desire to join a twelve-step program—it can also be true that this life of addiction is largely painful and unhappy. Of course, any desires for change are going to be at least partially based on the unhappiness. But the fact remains that the pain and unhappiness are prior to a desire to quit. And unlike a desire, the pain is not in itself end-directed, unless we count the cessation of pain itself as an end. Even if we do, that doesn't give us more specific desires, such as suicide or joining a twelve-step program, and, in any event, the feeling (pain) is still prior to the desire for cessation. It seems to me, at any rate, that trans phoria is like that. It is prior to any specific conscious desire. The only other possibility is to posit an unconscious desire—one that does not show up in one's self-conception. However, it is difficult to believe in unconscious desires that include well-articulated ends (e.g., transitioning), since such ends depend upon the conceptual scheme underwriting one's self-conception and often these sorts of schemes simply don't afford the necessary ends.

14. Serano, *Whipping Girl*, 78.

15. To be clear, I am not (merely) suggesting that there are trans bodies that do not fall neatly into the categories "male" and "female"—bodies that might be described as "mixed" or "in-between." Rather, I am suggesting that what counts as "mixed" or "in-between" in the first place depends upon the interpretation itself. And it's the interpretation that's an important issue in trans body dysphoria. In other words, the very description of a body as "in-between" may foreclose competing understandings of that body and thereby impose an interpretation that induces dysphoria in a trans person.

16. Serano, *Whipping Girl*, 82.

17. Salamon, *Assuming a Body*, 76–77.

18. Paul Schilder, *The Image and Appearance of the Human Body* (New York: John Wiley & Sons, 1950).

19. Salamon, *Assuming a Body*, 30.

20. Serano, *Whipping Girl*, 82.

21. Prosser, *Second Skins*, 7.

22. Schilder, *Image and Appearance of the Human Body*, 137.

23. Salamon, *Assuming a Body*, 42.

24. Prosser, *Second Skins*, 62–63.

25. The aspirational account can be ruled out immediately with respect to this phenomenon as it must deny that one already feels like one is a man or woman or what-have-you prior to transition in a positive way, in a way that could motivate transition. That is, it must say that there is nothing but the

desire alone. Why? Because the incongruence account must likewise postulate and therefore describe the experience of desire—namely, the desire for congruence, the desire to bring one's external material body into alignment with one's internal sense of self. Similarly, the affective account will likewise postulate a desire—namely, the desire to get rid of the bad feelings to find the good. In order for the aspirational account to be a distinct account, it must make the desire basic. In doing so, it must drop any sense of already being what one desires to be prior to transition. This is, however, phenomenologically inaccurate, at least for many of us.

26. Andrea Long Chu, "My New Vagina Won't Make Me Happy—And It Shouldn't Have To," *New York Times,* November 24, 2018, https://www.nytimes.com/2018/11/24/opinion/sunday/vaginoplasty-transgender-medicine.html.

27. Chu, "My New Vagina."

28. Chu.

29. Hil Malatino, *Side Affects: On Being Trans and Feeling Bad* (Minneapolis: University of Minnesota Press, 2022), 2. See also Cameron Awkward-Rich, *The Terrible We: Thinking with Trans Maladjustment* (Durham, N.C.: Duke University Press, 2022), 4.

30. I do not engage with Jacques Lacan's famous notion of the mirror stage in this essay. That discussion is for another time.

31. Gloria Anzaldúa, *Borderlands/La Frontera: The New Mestiza* (1987; repr., San Francisco: Aunt Lute Books, 1999), 64.

32. Anzaldúa, *Borderlands/La Frontera,* 66.

33. AnaLouise Keating, "Introduction: Reading Gloria Anzaldúa, Reading Ourselves . . . Complex Intimacies, Intricate Connections," in *The Gloria Anzaldúa Reader,* ed. AnaLouise Keating (Durham, N.C.: Duke University Press, 2009), 1–15, 1.

34. For discussion of the complex relation of Anzaldúa's work to Indigeneity, see Andrea J. Pitts, *Nos/Otras: Gloria E. Anzaldúa, Multiplicitous Agency, and Resistance* (Albany: State University of New York Press, 2021), 130–39. Pitts reads my own work, drawing as it does from the work of María Lugones, as a way of rereading Anzaldúa with respect to Indigenous politics and critique (139–49).

35. Anzaldúa, *Borderlands/La Frontera,* 60.

36. María Lugones, *Pilgrimages/Peregrinajes: Theorizing Coalition against Multiple Oppressions* (Lanham, Md.: Rowman and Littlefield, 2003), 1.

37. Arnold van Gennep argues that all rites to some extent exemplify a pattern found in rites of passage—rites by which an individual moves from one social status to another. The pattern, as David I. Kertzer summarizes Gennep, consists of three stages—separation (from mundane sociality), the margin (*la marge*), and reaggregation (back into mundane sociality) (David I. Kertzer,

introduction to *The Rites of Passage*, by Arnold van Gennep, 2nd ed., trans. Monika B. Vizedom and Gabrielle L. Caffee [1960; repr., Chicago: University of Chicago Press, 2019], xviii). Crucially, these "transitional periods," Gennep says, "whose generality no one seems to have noticed previously," "sometimes acquire a certain autonomy" (191–92). Victor Turner then influentially discusses the sociocultural properties of the liminal stage introduced by Gennep (Victor Turner, "Betwixt and Between: The Liminal Period in *Rites de Passage*," in *The Forest of Symbols: Aspects of Ndembu Ritual* [Ithaca, N.Y.: Cornell University Press, 1967], 93–111). Crucially among them, for our purposes—"The subject of passage ritual is, in the liminal period, *structurally*, if not physically '*invisible*'" (95, emphasis added). Lugones begins with Turner's notions of liminality, drawing specifically on Turner's "structural invisibility" to characterize the possibility of resistance. "Seeing structural invisibility as an important aspect of liminality makes clear why victims of ethnocentric racism are never seen as liminal subjects" (Lugones, *Pilgrimages/Peregrinajes*, 61). However, she departs from Turner in two crucial ways. First, she regards Turner as mistakenly appealing to some "transcendental self," instead insisting that structure constitutes persons themselves (60–61). Second, she says one can live in "more than one structure" (61). My own contribution, as I see it, is the claim that structural invisibility can secure an infraintimate state—one that stands in tension with that of oblivious foreclosure and that can thereby yield a sort of multiplicity.

38. María Lugones, "From within Germinative Status: Creating Active Subjectivity, Resistant Agency," in *Entre Mundos/Among Worlds: New Perspectives on Gloria Anzaldúa*, ed. AnaLouise Keating (New York: Palgrave Macmillan, 2005), 85–99, 92, 86.

39. Turner goes on to introduce the notion of *communitas*—an unencumbered and creative solidarity of equals that, he claims, can be experienced in liminal periods when hierarchical positions are effectively placed in limbo (Victor Turner, *The Ritual Process: Structure and Anti-structure* [New York: Routledge, 1969], 96). He juxtaposes communitas with structure, calling the former an "anti-structure." He also recognizes that liminality is not the only site of communitas, including the "outsiderhood" of the shaman, priests, drifters, and the like, as well as the "marginality" of those "who are simultaneously members . . . of two or more groups whose social definitions and cultural norms are distinct from, and often even opposed to, one another" (Victor Turner, *Dramas, Fields, and Metaphors: Symbolic Action in Human Society* [Ithaca, N.Y.: Cornell University Press, 1974], 233). Of the marginals, he writes that they "like liminars are also betwixt and between, but unlike ritual liminars they have no cultural assurance of a final stable resolution of their ambiguity" (233). By contrast, "Ritual liminars are often moving symbolically to a

higher status, and their being stripped of status temporarily is a 'ritual,' and 'as-if,' or 'make-believe' stripping dictated by cultural requirements" (233).

40. Turner draws a contrast between the liminal and the liminoid. The former can be found in societies where ceremonial rites involving liminality play a central role, whereas the latter can be found in societies where such ceremonies do not. The latter includes, instead, theater, masquerade, acting, and so forth—leisure and entertainment possibilities constituted within a capitalist society, rather than the ceremonial rites of a religious society. While the experience of self-recognition may begin in liminoid space, because it opens up into a multiplicity through the infraintimate, it also serves as a portal to other worlds. The experience, far from merely recreational, can be quite serious, as most epiphanies can. Indeed, as an event in trans development, it can be viewed as a liminal period between two identities—pretransition and posttransition. This makes it resemble la marge in a rite of passage, without the ritualistic components and therefore different from the liminoid, which does not typically involve any transition from one status to another. Victor Turner, "Liminal to Liminoid, in Play, Flow, and Ritual: An Essay in Comparative Symbology," in *From Ritual to Theatre: The Human Seriousness of Play* (New York: PAJ, 1982), 20–60.

41. Anzaldúa, *Borderlands/La Frontera*, 64–65.

42. Anzaldúa, 70.

43. Anzaldúa, 70.

44. Anzaldúa, 71.

45. I suspect that this notion of **apparitional liminality** may be found in *Borderlands/La Frontera*. Certainly, for Anzaldúa, imagination and storytelling are crucial, and it seems to me that there is, for her, a movement from make-believe into reality where that movement is so much about intimate connection. See, for example, the chapter "*Tlilli, Tlapalli*/The Path of the Red and Black Ink." If so, this provides another way of understanding liminality in her work that doesn't involve the problematic notion of *mestizaje*.

6. The Operations of Theory

1. The useful expression "coming into identity" is from Sonny Nordmarken, "Coming into Identity: How Gender Minorities Experience Identity Formation," *Gender and Society* 37, no. 4 (August 2023): 584–613.

2. Katharine Jenkins provides an account of gender identity according to which "to say that someone has a female gender identity is to say that she experiences the norms that are associated with women in her social context as relevant to her." Katharine Jenkins, "Toward an Account of Gender Identity," *Ergo: An Open Access Journal of Philosophy* 5, no. 27 (2018): 713–44, 728. The account was originally developed to provide an ameliorative analysis of *woman* that did

not exclude trans women. While I have raised worries about the specifics of that account elsewhere, I wish to address a misreading of my own account. In "Through the Looking Glass," I suggested it would be cleaner to put the concept of gender identity aside in attempting to validate trans identities. Jenkins misreads me as claiming that the practices of self-identification that determine identity in trans underworlds (described later in this chapter) constitute gender identity. I had provided no account of gender identity there. I have, by contrast, provided an account of (conscious) gender identity here. Talia Mae Bettcher, "Through the Looking Glass: Trans Theory Meets Feminist Philosophy," in *The Routledge Companion to Feminist Philosophy*, ed., Ann Garry, Serene J. Khader, and Alison Stone (New York: Routledge, 2017), 393–404, 396.

3. Jay Prosser, *Second Skins: The Body Narratives of Transsexuality* (New York: Columbia University Press, 1998), 120.

4. Prosser, *Second Skins*, 4, 14.

5. Prosser, 4.

6. Prosser, 5.

7. Prosser, 101.

8. Prosser, 124.

9. Prosser, 114.

10. Prosser, 102.

11. Prosser, 117–18; quoting Jan Morris, *Conundrum* (New York: Harcourt Brace Jovanovich, 1974), 3.

12. Bernice L. Hausman, *Changing Sex: Transsexualism, Technology, and the Idea of Gender* (Durham, N.C.: Duke University Press, 1995), 173.

13. Prosser, *Second Skins*, 115.

14. For a related discussion, see also Amy Billingsley, "Technology and Narratives of Continuity in Transgender Experience," *Feminist Philosophy Quarterly* 1, no. 1 (2015): https://doi.org/10.5206/fpq/2015.1.6.

15. For a critique of the narrative self, see Galen Strawson, "Against Narrativity," *Ratio* 17, no. 4 (December 2004): 428–52.

16. Nordmarken, "Coming into Identity," 584.

17. Indeed, in some cases there is no need for transition at all, as one's life may have already changed significantly.

18. Much of what both Prosser and I say about the attitudes of clinicians has changed for the most part. Thus, some of this is more historical than anything else.

19. Harry Benjamin, *The Transsexual Phenomenon* (New York: Julian Press, 1966), 115.

20. Such invalidation of trans identities is also evidenced by the consistent use (back then) of the expression *male transsexual* to refer to transsexual women and the expression *female transsexual* to refer to transsexual men.

21. An earlier version of this discussion can be found in Talia Mae Bettcher, "Trapped in the Wrong Theory: Rethinking Trans Oppression and Resistance," *Signs: Journal of Women in Culture and Society* 39, no. 2 (Winter 2014): 383–406.

22. Henry Rubin, *Self-Made Men: Identity and Embodiment among Transsexual Men* (Nashville, Tenn.: Vanderbilt University Press, 2003), 109.

23. Prosser, *Second Skins*, 82.

24. Prosser, 62–63.

25. Prosser, 68.

26. Jan Morris, *Conundrum: An Extraordinary Narrative of Transsexualism* (New York: Holt, 1986), 19; Leslie Feinberg, *Journal of a Transsexual* (Atlanta: World View, 1980), 20; Raymond Thompson with Kitty Sewell, *What Took You So Long? A Girl's Journey to Manhood* (London: Penguin, 1995), 200; all quoted in Prosser, 68–69.

27. Prosser, 82.

28. This easily addresses the alleged conflict, cited by Hausman, between the claim to change sex and the claim to have always already been that sex (Hausman, *Changing Sex*, 173). The former concerns one's moral sex—in this case determined by one's interpersonal identity and the structure of nakedness required by that identity. The latter concerns one's material morphology that is brought into alignment with that structure.

While it's fairly standard to ground the always-already claim by appealing to biology, there are many ways to ground it. One might, for instance, appeal to a gendered soul. This is important to note because it shows that what's going on here does not concern whatever biologists mean by *biological sex*. It concerns moral sex.

29. Harold Garfinkel, *Studies in Ethnomethodology* (Oxford: Polity Press, 1967), 128.

30. Garfinkel, *Studies in Ethnomethodology*, 129.

31. Garfinkel, 131.

32. Garfinkel, 129.

33. See Kimberlé Crenshaw's discussion of 2 Live Crew in "Mapping the Margins: Intersectionality, Identity Politics, and Violence against Women of Color," *Stanford Law Review* 43, no. 6 (July 1991): 1,241–99, 1,285–90.

34. Kate Bornstein, "The Trouble with Tranny," *Out*, November 14, 2010, http://www.out.com/entertainment/2010/11/14/trouble-tranny-0.

35. It's important to recognize, here, that despite these changes, the illusion of the precultural moral body persists. The mythology of nakedness and clothing is deeply entrenched not only in our culture but in many. What changes, however, is the idea that there is a highly specific moral structure of the body that can be read off in advance. While, no doubt, a general sense of what

body parts are intimate is typically presumed, there is not much more than that. To put it otherwise, the rationales for concealment are not that specific. To some degree, even, proper appearance is still said to vaguely suggest an intimate appearance that's female or male (as suggested below). But what, exactly, that appearance involves with respect to both morphology and the moralization thereof is altogether unclear. In this way, proper appearance acquires what may be described as an opacity.

36. I first developed this view in Talia Mae Bettcher, "Trans Identities and First-Person Authority," in *"You've Changed": Sex Reassignment and Personal Identity*, ed. Laurie J. Shrage (Oxford: Oxford University Press, 2009), 98–120. My view has changed somewhat. I now suspect it's better to view the nondeep self-identification as performatives rather than avowals.

37. For a critique of my view, see Burkay Ozturk, "The Negotiative Theory of Gender Identity and the Limits of First-Person Authority," in *The Philosophy of Sex: Contemporary Readings*, 7th ed., ed. Raja Halwani, Alan Soble, Sarah Hoffman, and Jacob M. Held (Lanham, Md.: Rowman and Littlefield, 2017), 139–60. Ozturk points to cases in which avowals of self-identification can be overridden, taking this to undermine my view. It does not, as it is plain that in certain cases first-person authority can indeed be overridden. Moreover, there are even circumstances in which it is acceptable to point this out to the avower—in therapy, for instance.

38. In this description, while trans people turn out to possess ethical authority over their gender—at least in trans underworlds—I have refrained from ascribing epistemic authority over gender. No doubt, to some, this will disappoint: Shouldn't trans people know best who they are and what their gender is? Indeed, shouldn't this be so for everyone? Part of the issue turns on my own specific views about first-person authority—views I have defended elsewhere and will touch on briefly below. Part of the issue turns on the following facts.

First, as we've already discussed, many of us spent part of our lives not knowing our gender and, indeed, being wrong about who we were. Perhaps we had nagging doubts, and things felt off. But that is scarcely knowledge of our gender, never mind knowledge of who we were. Second, trans people who have had a lot of experience with other trans people often get quite good at identifying a person as trans even though that person is still unaware of this fact. Colloquially, these unwitting people are known as "eggs." If it's true that one has epistemic authority over one's gender, then why do eggs exist and how is it that other trans people can be so good at identifying them? Where's the first-person epistemic authority?

Notably, such cases aren't that different from the first-person authority people are traditionally taken to have over mental states. "I'm not sad," somebody says earnestly, even though those close to them can easily recognize the fact that they are sad. "I'm not angry," somebody claims, their hands trembling, their face flush with rage.

Perhaps these cases are not as common as cases in which the first-person gets it right. Sometimes I wonder. But, even so, we need to ask whether this ability to get it right is anything more than one's being particularly well acquainted with oneself since one is always around oneself, as it were. If it isn't anything more than that, then there's no epistemic first-person authority in the way standardly imagined, since the peculiar way in which one accesses one's mental states does not itself guarantee any epistemic advantage a priori.

Further, we still need to explain the deference we give the first-person as if their avowals were incorrigible when they aren't. The answer I've proposed is that the peculiar grammar of avowal demands deference and the first-person has ethical first-person authority over the official interpretation of their mental states and, I would add, their gender (i.e., whether they are a man, woman, etc.). See Bettcher, "Trans Identities and First-Person Authority."

39. For a related discussion, see Rachel McKinnon, "Trans*Formative Experiences," *Res Philosophica* 92, no. 2 (April 2015): 419–40.

40. Nordmarken, "Coming into Identity," 584.

41. Prosser, *Second Skins*, 4.

42. María Lugones, "On Complex Communication," *Hypatia: A Journal of Feminist Philosophy* 21, no. 3 (Summer 2006): 75–85, 77.

43. María Lugones, *Pilgrimages/Peregrinajes: Theorizing Coalition against Multiple Oppressions* (Lanham, Md.: Rowman and Littlefield, 2003), 115–16.

44. Lugones, "On Complex Communication," 84.

45. Lugones, 83.

7. The Coloniality of Intimacy

1. María Lugones, "Heterosexualism and the Colonial/Modern Gender System," *Hypatia: A Journal of Feminist Philosophy* 22, no. 1 (February 2007): 186–209.

2. Aníbal Quijano, "Colonialidad del Poder y Classificación Social," *Journal of World Research System* 6, no. 2 (Summer/Fall 2000): 342–86, repr. in *Aníbal Quijano: Cuestiones y horizontes—De la dependencia histórico-estructural a la colonialidad/descolonialidad del poder* (Buenos Aires: Latin American Council of Social Sciences, 2014), 285–327. Quijano uses the expression "ámbitos de existencia social" throughout (289). In "Heterosexualism and the Colonial/Modern Gender System," Lugones uses the expression "areas of human existence" (189). For the purposes of this essay, and in light of the political and philosophical significance of the concept *human*, I use "areas of social existence."

3. Quijano, "Colonialidad del Poder y Classificación Social," 287.

4. Lugones, "Heterosexualism and the Colonial/Modern Gender System."

5. Lugones, 195, 206.

6. Elías Cosenza Krell, "Is Transmisogyny Killing Trans Women of Color? Black Trans Feminisms and the Exigencies of White Femininity," *TSQ: Transgender Studies Quarterly* 4, no. 2 (May 2017): 226–42, 233. See Marlon B. Ross, "Beyond the Closet as Raceless Paradigm," in *Black Queer Studies: A Critical Anthology,* ed. E. Patrick Johnson and Mae G. Henderson (Durham, N.C.: Duke University Press, 2005), 161–89. See also Siobhan B. Somerville, *Queering the Color Line: Race and the Invention of Homosexuality in American Culture* (Durham, N.C.: Duke University Press, 2000).

7. María Lugones, "Toward a Decolonial Feminism," *Hypatia: A Journal of Feminist Philosophy* 25, no. 4 (Fall 2010): 742–59, 743.

8. María Lugones, "Gender and Universality in Colonial Methodology," *Critical Philosophy of Race* 8, nos. 1–2 (January 2020): 25–47, 30.

9. Tzvetan Todorov, *The Conquest of America: The Question of the Other,* trans. Richard Howard (1982; repr., New York: Harper Perennial, 1984), 34–35.

10. Christopher Columbus, *The Journal of Christopher Columbus,* trans. Cecil Jane (New York: Clarkson N. Potter, 1960), 25, 36, 41, 52, 57.

11. An early version of this analysis can be found in Talia Mae Bettcher, "Getting 'Naked' in the Colonial/Modern Gender System: A Preliminary Trans Feminist Analysis of Pornography," in *Beyond Speech: Pornography and Analytic Feminist Philosophy,* ed. Mari Mikkola (Oxford: Oxford University Press, 2017), 157–76.

12. Matthew 25:35–36 (King James Version).

13. William N. Brewster, "Christ's Methods of Missionary Work," in *The Missionary Review of the World,* vol. 11 new series, vol. 21 old series, *January–December 1898,* ed. Arthur T. Pierson (New York: Funk and Wagnalls, 1898), 771–77, 774.

14. With regard to the former, see John L. Comaroff and Jean Comaroff, "Fashioning the Colonial Subject: The Empire's Old Clothes," in *Of Revelation and Revolution,* vol. 2, *The Dialectics of Modernity on a South African Frontier* (Chicago: University of Chicago Press, 1997), 218–73, 219.

15. Thomas Laurie, *The Ely Volume: The Contributions of Our Foreign Missions to Science and Human Well-Being,* 2nd ed. (Boston: American Board of Commissioners for Foreign Missions, Congregational House, 1885), 419–20. Laurie characterizes "civilization" as a move away from nakedness through religious knowledge. This creates an initial need for commerce.

16. Lugones, "Toward a Decolonial Feminism," 744.

17. Irene Watson, "Naked Peoples: Rules and Regulations," *Law/Text/Culture* 4, no. 1 (1998): 1–17, 2.

18. Satsuki Kawano, "Japanese Bodies and Western Ways of Seeing in the

Late Nineteenth Century," in *Dirt, Undress, and Difference: Critical Perspectives on the Body's Surface*, ed. Adeline Masquelier (Bloomington: Indiana University Press, 2005), 149–67, 160.

19. Watson "Naked Peoples," 3.

20. Watson, 2.

21. For example, Comaroff and Comaroff discuss the Tswana in "Fashioning the Colonial Subject," 228. See also Lissant Bolton, "Gender, Status, and Introduced Clothing in Vanuatu," in *Clothing the Pacific*, ed. Chloe Colchester (Oxford: Berg, 2003), 119–40.

22. For example, see Comaroff and Comaroff, "Fashioning the Colonial Subject," 229; Robert Ross, "Reclothed in Rightful Minds: Christian Missions and Clothing," in *Clothing: A Global History, or The Imperialists' New Clothes* (Cambridge: Polity Press, 2008), 83–102, 87.

23. Todorov, *Conquest of America*, 48–49.

24. Todorov, 49.

25. Robert Ross, "First Colonialisms," in *Clothing*, 38–51, 45.

26. Robert Michels, *Sexual Ethics: A Study of Borderland Questions* (1914; repr., New Brunswick, N.J.: Transaction Publishers, 2002), 42.

27. Michels, *Sexual Ethics*, 42.

28. Patricia Hill Collins, "The Sexual Politics of Black Womanhood," in *Black Feminist Thought: Knowledge, Consciousness, and the Politics of Empowerment*, 2nd ed. (Routledge: New York, 2000), 123–48.

29. C. Riley Snorton, *Black on Both Sides: A Racial History of Trans Identity* (Minneapolis: University of Minnesota Press, 2017), 33.

30. Che Gossett, "Blackness and the Trouble of Trans Visibility," in *Trap Door: Trans Cultural Production and the Politics of Visibility*, ed. Reina Gossett, Eric A. Stanley, and Johanna Burton (Cambridge, Mass.: MIT Press, 2017), 183–90, 184. See Perry Zurn, "Waste Culture and Isolation: Prisons, Toilets, and Gender Segregation," *Hypatia: A Journal of Feminist Philosophy* 34, no. 4 (Fall 2019): 668–89.

31. Zurn, "Waste Culture and Isolation," 679.

32. Kimberlé Crenshaw, "Demarginalizing the Intersection of Race and Sex: A Black Feminist Critique of Antidiscrimination Doctrine, Feminist Theory, and Antiracist Politics," *University of Chicago Legal Forum* (1989): 139–67, 157.

33. Saidiya V. Hartman, *Scenes of Subjection: Terror, Slavery, and Self-Making in Nineteenth-Century America* (New York: Oxford University Press, 1997), 79–80.

34. Technically, there are many systems of interpersonal spatiality that may be described as "sex-representational." For example, both ancient Greek and

Hebrew systems were sex-representational, while differing in key respects. For a discussion of the contrast between Greek and Hebrew representations of nakedness, see Mario Perniola, "Between Clothing and Nudity," trans. Roger Friedman, in *Fragments for a History of the Human Body: Part Two,* ed. Michel Feher with Ramona Naddaff and Nadia Tazi (New York: Zone, 1989), 236–65. They were not, however, part of the colonial/modern gender system.

35. [Jacques Boileau], *A Just and Seasonable Reprehension of Naked Breasts and Shoulders Written by a Grave and Learned Papist,* trans. Edward Cooke (London: Jonathan Edwin, 1678), 49–50, cited in Efrat Tseëlon, *The Masque of Femininity: The Presentation of Woman in Everyday Life* (London: Sage Publications, 1995), 27–28.

36. Boileau, *Just and Seasonable Reprehension,* 137, cited in Tseëlon, *Masque of Femininity,* 13–14.

37. Boileau, 50.

38. Sylvia Wynter, "Unsettling the Coloniality of Being/Power/Truth/Freedom: Towards the Human, After Man, Its Overrepresentation—An Argument," *CR: The New Centennial Review* 3, no. 3 (Fall 2003): 257–337.

39. Wynter, "Unsettling the Coloniality," 292.

40. Francisco J. Galarte, *Brown Trans Figurations: Rethinking Race, Gender, and Sexuality in Chicanx/Latinx Studies* (Austin: University of Texas, 2021), 32.

41. Lugones, "Toward a Decolonial Feminism," 743–44.

42. Lugones, 744.

43. Lugones, 744.

44. Aristotle, *De Generatione Animalium,* trans. Arthur Platt, in *The Works of Aristotle Translated into English,* vol. 5, ed. J. A. Smith and W. D. Ross (Oxford: Clarendon Press, 1912), 738b.

45. Aristotle, *De Generatione Animalium,* 737a.

46. Aquinas, *Summa Theologica,* 1, Q 92, A 1, ad 1.

47. In Islamic systems, by contrast, the opposite is the case, with concealment extending to neck and face.

48. *Oxford English Dictionary,* s.v. "person (*n.*), sense II.2.c," June 2024, https://doi.org/10.1093/OED/5264867944.

49. Lugones, "Toward a Decolonial Feminism," 743.

50. Lugones, 743.

51. Deborah A. Miranda, "Extermination of the *Joyas*: Gendercide in Spanish California," *GLQ: A Journal of Lesbian and Gay Studies* 16, no. 1–2 (April 2010): 253–84.

52. For example, in introducing this text, she writes, "Father Palóu described a group of natives visiting at Mission Santa Clara; soldiers and priests noticed that one native among the women was actually a man" (264).

53. Francisco Palóu, *Palóu's Life of Fray Junipero Serra,* ed. and trans. Maynard J. Geiger (Washington, D.C.: American Academy of Franciscan History, 1955), 214–15, quoted in Miranda, "Extermination of the *Joyas,*" 264–65.

54. Miranda, "Extermination of the *Joyas,*" 258–59.

8. The Enslaving Self

1. Alaa Elassar, "Sandra the Orangutan, Freed from a Zoo after Being Granted 'Personhood,' Settles into Her New Home," CNN, November 9, 2019, https://www.cnn.com/2019/11/09/world/sandra-orangutan-florida-home -trnd/index.html. While Sandra is not recognized as a moral agent, capable of being held morally accountable for her actions (to human beings), she is nonetheless assigned the status of "personhood" and granted the right of self-determination on the basis of her capacity for self-awareness.

2. This is not to say that the Aristotelian view doesn't likewise lead to ableist consequence. However, Aristotelianism doesn't lead to the utter exclusion of cognitively disabled individuals from moral status altogether.

3. Peter Singer, *Practical Ethics* (New York: Cambridge University Press, 1979), 131–38.

4. Bob Jones in conversation with the author, around 2005.

5. Therese Scarpelli Cory, "Aquinas and 'I': A Medieval Concept of Self," in *The Self: A History,* ed. Patricia Kitcher (Oxford: Oxford University Press, 2021), 73–98, 73–74.

6. Cory, "Aquinas and 'I,'" 74.

7. *Oxford English Dictionary,* s.v. "person (*n.*), sense II.2," June 2024, https://doi.org/10.1093/OED/5545320830.

8. *Oxford English Dictionary,* s.v. "person (*n.*), sense II.2.a," June 2024, https://doi.org/10.1093/OED/7617533244; *Oxford English Dictionary,* s.v. "people (*n.*), sense I.2.a," March 2024, https://doi.org/10.1093/OED/7290165651.

9. *Oxford English Dictionary,* s.v. "person (*n.*), sense III.6.a," June 2024, https://doi.org/10.1093/OED/6880157944; *Oxford English Dictionary,* s.v. "person (*n.*), sense III.6.b," June 2024, https://doi.org/10.1093/OED/1047912806.

10. *Oxford English Dictionary,* s.v. "self (*n.*), sense I.5," June 2024, https://doi.org/10.1093/OED/6599221862.

11. *Oxford English Dictionary,* s.v. "self-consciousness (*n.*), sense 1," July 2023, https://doi.org/10.1093/OED/3941142763.

12. *Oxford English Dictionary,* s.v. "self."

13. Thomas Hobbes, *Leviathan,* ed. Christopher Brooke (London: Penguin Classics, 2017), chap. 16.

14. John Locke, *An Essay Concerning Human Understanding,* ed. Peter H. Nidditch (Oxford: Oxford University Press, 1975), 2.27.15, 340.

15. Locke, *Essay Concerning Human Understanding,* 3.9.2, 476. In the *Sec-*

ond Treatise, Locke uses *man* in a way that implies rationality as well as moral status—contrary to the distinction he draws in *An Essay Concerning Human Understanding*. For example, he characterizes the state of nature: "Men living together *according to reason* without a common superior on earth, with authority to judge between them, is properly the state of Nature." John Locke, *Second Treatise*, in *Two Treatises of Government*, student ed., ed. Peter Laslett (Cambridge: Cambridge University Press, 1988), sec. 19, 280.

16. Locke, *Essay Concerning Human Understanding*, 2.27.9, 335.

17. Locke, 2.27.17, 341.

18. Locke, 2.27.26, 346.

19. Locke, 2.27.8, 333.

20. Charles W. Mills, *The Racial Contract* (Ithaca, N.Y.: Cornell University Press, 1997); Charles W. Mills, *Blackness Visible: Essays on Philosophy and Race* (Ithaca, N.Y.: Cornell University Press, 1998).

21. Charles W. Mills, "The Political Economy of Personhood," *On the Human: A Project of the National Humanities Center* (blog), April 4, 2011, https://nationalhumanitiescenter.org/on-the-human/2011/04/political-economy-of-personhood/.

22. Mills, "Political Economy of Personhood."

23. Frederick Douglass, "The United States Cannot Remain Half-Slave and Half-Free," speech delivered in the Congregational Church, Washington, D.C., on the twenty-first anniversary of emancipation in the District of Columbia, 1883.

24. For a related discussion of Godwyn, see David Livingstone Smith, *Making Monsters: The Uncanny Power of Dehumanization* (Cambridge, Mass.: Harvard University Press, 2021), 32, 76, 146, 226.

25. Morgan Godwyn, "Trade Preferr'd before Religion and Christ Made to Give Place to Mammon Represented in a Sermon Relating to the Plantations: First Preached at Westminster-Abbey and afterwards in Divers Churches in London / by Morgan Godwyn" (London: Printed for B. Took and for Isaac Cleave, 1685), available at University of Michigan Library Digital Collections, Early English Books Online, accessed July 25, 2024, https://name.umdl.umich.edu/A42952.0001.001.

26. John Harrison and Peter Laslett, *The Library of John Locke* (Oxford: Oxford University Press, 1965), 144.

27. Morgan Godwyn, *Negro's and Indians Advocate, Suing for Their Admission into the Church* (1680; repr. Kessigner's Legacy Reprints, 2003), 9.

28. Godwyn, *Negro's and Indians Advocate*, 10–11.

29. Godwyn, 3.

30. Robert Bernasconi and Anika Maaza Mann, "The Contradictions of Racism: Locke, Slavery, and the *Two Treatises*," in *Race and Racism in Modern*

Philosophy, ed. Andrew Valls (Ithaca, N.Y.: Cornell University Press, 2005), 89–107.

31. Bernasconi and Mann, "Contradictions of Racism," 89.

32. William Uzgalis argues that the *Second Treatise* is Locke's repudiation of his earlier views about hereditary slavery. William Uzgalis, "'. . . The Same Tyrannical Principle': Locke's Legacy on Slavery," in *Subjugation and Bondage: Critical Essays on Slavery and Social Philosophy,* ed. Tommy L. Lott (Lanham, Md.: Rowman and Littlefield, 1998), 49–78, 56. As Bernasconi and Mann argue, this position does not account for Locke's continued involvement in the practice ("Contradictions of Racism," 98–99).

33. It stretches plausibility to suppose that enslaved African men, women, and children were captives in some just war. First, to my knowledge, no kingdom in Africa had declared war on England. Second, it is implausible to view enslaved women and children as enemy combatants.

34. Locke, *Second Treatise,* sec. 172, 383.

35. Locke, sec. 189, 393.

36. One possibility is that Locke's account isn't intended to apply to chattel slavery. After all, it's generally recognized that the *Two Treatises* are specifically addressed to Englishmen. Since Locke is taking direct aim at Robert Filmer's account of government as absolute monarchy according to which all men are born slaves, why think this has anything to do with chattel slavery? James Farr argues for this position in "So Vile and Miserable an Estate: The Problem of Slavery in Locke's Political Thought," *Political Theory* 14, no. 2 (May 1986): 263–89. While Farr reads Locke as concerned only with politics at home, rather than actual slavery abroad, Clarence Sholé Johnson argues that Locke denied the personhood of Africans altogether and that, therefore, Locke's account of slavery in the *Second Treatise* isn't intended to apply to them since his account concerns persons (*Cornel West and Philosophy: The Quest for Social Justice* [New York: Routledge, 2003], 166). While I agree with Johnson that Locke did not regard Africans as persons, I contend that Locke's official account of slavery was indeed intended to apply. Locke draws a distinction between "philosophical" and "civil" uses of terms. While he distinguishes *man* and *person* in the *Essay Concerning Human Understanding* (philosophical use), he does not in the *Second Treatise* (civil use). Because of this, there is no reason to think that the account was not intended to apply to Africans. I therefore defend a position stronger than that of Johnson's—namely, that the distinction between *person* and *man* is used by Locke in his justification of chattel slavery.

It is implausible to suppose that Locke would provide an account of slavery that had little to do with the sort of slavery he himself was involved in. If his defense wasn't intended to apply to chattel slavery, why would he not provide an account of the practice? Didn't he have any? The supposition of nonapplicability is particularly odd given that Locke infamously does provide a justification for the appropriation of Native Americans' land in the *Second Treatise*. If his account of property applies to Native Americans, why would his account of slavery not apply to Africans? Indeed, there are clear overlaps between the slavery defended in the *Second Treatise* and the slavery set down in *The Fundamental Constitutions of Carolina*—of which Locke was one of the authors. Specifically, in the *Second Treatise*, Locke argues that "masters" have not only "absolute authority" but "absolute power" over those who were enslaved. By this he means the power to kill those who were enslaved with impunity. For instance, in "Of Conquest," he writes, "The power a conqueror gets over those he overcomes in a just war, is perfectly despotical: he has an absolute power over the lives of those, who, by putting themselves in a state of war, have forfeited them" (sec. 180). Similarly, article 110 of the *Fundamental Constitutions* says, "Every freeman of Carolina shall have absolute power and authority over his negro slaves, of what opinion or religion soever." Crucially, while the original draft of the *Fundamental Constitutions* was in the handwriting of another, it appears that "absolute power" that was added to article 110 was in Locke's handwriting.

37. Bernasconi and Mann argue that we ought to accept that Locke simply offered a poor justification for chattel slavery. As they rightly note, "Racists often use bad arguments: it is the only kind they have" ("Contradictions of Racism," 101). The problem with this move, however, is that the argument is *too* bad. Locke is very clear that hereditary slavery is not justified. Yet, chattel slavery is hereditary slavery. It is grossly implausible to suppose that Locke did not notice this contradiction.

Charles W. Mills says of the contradiction that it "could be resolved by the supposition that Locke saw Blacks as not fully human." He also appeals to Jennifer Welchman's view, discussed below. Mills, *Racial Contract*, 68.

38. Jennifer Welchman provides a different reading. She begins by arguing that Locke would have regarded Africans as living in a state of nature and that, because of that, subject to natural law only, they would be subject to enslavement by anyone should they engage in warfare. My view is similar—however, I posit Locke as believing that Africans were in a perpetual state of war due to their alleged inherent violence and cognitive deficiency. Welchman goes on to implausibly argue that while Locke's denial of hereditary slavery would have applied to the offspring of an enslaved man prior to his enslavement, it would not apply to his offspring after his enslavement. Not only does this not account for the children who were, as a matter of fact, enslaved in the first scenario, the entire proposal goes against Locke's reasons for rejecting hereditary slavery in the first place—namely, that a father does not possess absolute authority of his offspring. Jennifer Welchman, "Locke on Slavery and Inalienable Rights," *Canadian Journal of Philosophy* 25, no. 1 (March 1995): 67–81.

39. Locke, *Second Treatise*, sec. 10, 273.

40. Locke, sec. 11, 273.

41. For a related discussion, see Robert Bernasconi, "Locke's Almost Random Talk of Man: The Double Use of Words in the Natural Law Justification of Slavery," *Perspektiven der Philosophie* 18 (1992): 293–318.

42. Locke, *Essay Concerning Human Understanding*, 3.6.22, 450–51. According to the *Oxford English Dictionary*, a changeling is "a person having a mental or intellectual disability (*offensive*)" and a natural is "a person having a low learning ability or intellectual capacity; a person born with impaired intelligence" (*Oxford English Dictionary*, s.v. "changeling (*n*.), sense I.3," July 2023, https://doi.org/10.1093/OED/7890643581; *Oxford English Dictionary*, s.v. "natural (*n*.), sense II.7," March 2024, https://doi.org/10.1093/OED/1268077511). I presume that he means roughly the same thing by them, although this is a complicated matter. A drill is "a West African species of baboon" (*Oxford English Dictionary*, s.v. "drill (*n*.3)," July 2023, https://doi.org/10.1093/OED/1161249498).

43. Locke, *Essay Concerning Human Understanding*, 4.4.13, 569.

44. Locke, 3.6.23, 451.

45. Locke, 2.25.1, 319; 2.25.10, 323; 3.8.1, 474.

46. Locke, 4.7.16, 606–7.

47. Locke, 4.7.17, 606–7.

48. Godwyn, *Negro's and Indians Advocate*, 13.

49. René Descartes, *Meditations on First Philosophy*, in *The Philosophical Writings of Descartes*, vol. 2, trans. John Cottingham, Robert Stroothoff, and Dugald Muroch (Cambridge: Cambridge University Press, 1984).

50. Locke, *Essay Concerning Human Understanding*, 2.1.10–20, 108–16.

51. Locke, 2.23.15, 305.

52. Locke, 4.3.6, 539–43.

53. Locke, 2.27.1, 328.

54. Locke, 2.27.26, 346.

55. In proposing the possibility of a changeling species, he says, "'Twould possibly be thought a bold Paradox, if not a very dangerous Falshood" (Locke, 4.4.13, 569). One reason for this is that once one allows for creatures who are in between man and beast, the notion that man has a soul while beasts do not is put under pressure. After all, whether a being possesses a soul is a yes or no question. It does not admit of gradations. But, according to Locke, the distinction between man and beast does.

56. Godwyn, *Negro's and Indians Advocate*, 11.

57. Locke, *Essay Concerning Human Understanding*, 4.3.6, 542.

58. Johnson seems oddly to identify the soul with the person in Locke's account. Given his view that Locke denied personhood of Africans, this would

lead to the conclusion that Locke denied that West Africans possess souls (Johnson, *Cornel West and Philosophy*, 153). In response, Bernasconi and Mann argue that Locke's commitment to the baptism of those who were enslaved proves that Locke did think Africans had souls ("Contradictions of Racism," 104). Both positions are incorrect, however, because Locke claims that we don't know whether the soul is immaterial.

59. Locke, *Essay Concerning Human Understanding*, 2.27.26, 346.

60. Locke, 3.6.26, 453–54.

61. Locke, 4.4.14, 570.

62. Sylvia Wynter, "Unsettling the Coloniality of Being/Power/Truth/Freedom: Towards the Human, After Man, Its Overrepresentation—An Argument," *CR: The New Centennial Review* 3, no. 3 (Fall 2003): 257–337, 309.

63. Lewis Hanke, *Aristotle and the American Indians: A Study in Race Prejudice in the Modern World* (Chicago: Henry Regnery Company, 1959), esp. 44–61; Bartolomé de Las Casas, *In Defense of the Indians*, trans. and ed. Stafford Poole (DeKalb: Northern Illinois University Press, 1992), chaps. 1–4, 25–53.

64. Aristotle, *Politics*, in *The Complete Works of Aristotle: The Revised Oxford Translation*, vol. 2, ed. Jonathan Barnes (Princeton, N.J.: Princeton University Press, 1984), 1255b10–15.

65. Aristotle, *Politics*, 1254b19–23.

66. Stacy Clifford Simplican, *The Capacity Contract: Intellectual Disability and the Question of Citizenship* (Minneapolis: University of Minnesota Press, 2015), 40–44.

67. Locke, *Essay Concerning Human Understanding*, 2.27.15, 340.

68. *Buffy the Vampire Slayer*, season 4, episode 16, "Who Are You?," written and directed by Joss Whedon, aired February 29, 2000, on the WB.

69. On this point, it is worth noting that while Locke uses *man* to mean "human," he also uses it in contrast to *woman*. He writes that when one understands "same man" in terms of "same individual, immaterial, thinking Substance," "it must be allowed possible that a Man born of different Women, and in distant times, may be the same Man." Locke, 2.27.21, 343.

70. Harry G. Frankfurt, "Freedom of the Will and the Concept of a Person," *Journal of Philosophy* 68, no. 1 (January 14, 1971): 5–20, 6.

9. Return of the Object

1. Part of this discussion comes from Talia Mae Bettcher, *Berkeley's Philosophy of Spirit: Consciousness, Ontology, and the Elusive Subject* (New York: Continuum, 2007), 117–32.

2. *Oxford English Dictionary*, s.v. "subject (*n*.), sense II.5," June 2024, https://doi.org/10.1093/OED/8449316670.

3. *Oxford English Dictionary,* s.v. "subject (*n*.), sense II.9," June 2024, https://doi.org/10.1093/OED/7719103400.

4. Aristotle, *Metaphysics: Books VII-X,* trans. Montgomery Furth (New York: Hackett, 1985), Zeta 3, 29a36.

5. Bertrand Russell, "On the Nature of Acquaintance," in *Logic and Knowledge: Essays 1901–1950,* ed. Robert Charles March (London: George Allen & Unwin, 1956), 127–74, 162.

6. *Oxford English Dictionary,* s.v. "object (*n*.), sense I.5," March 2024, https://doi.org/10.1093/OED/1643131996.

7. To be sure, the specific metaphysical details of the earlier idea characterized by the related notions of *substantia* and *inherentia* as a distinction in "real being" and the concerns that accrued to them are largely abandoned. For a full discussion of this, see Bettcher, *Berkeley's Philosophy of Spirit.*

8. While the *Oxford English Dictionary* has sense I.5 of *object* originating in 1651, it also recognizes older "senses relating to the presentation of something to the sight, senses, understanding, etc." For instance, "Originally: something placed before or presented to the eyes or other senses. Now (more generally): a material thing that can be seen and touched" (circa 1398). Here, the *Oxford English Dictionary* distinguishes the original sense that requires presentation to the senses and a current one that does not (presumably, something like "spatiotemporal entity" or "physical object"). My own sense of *object* is akin to the original. *Oxford English Dictionary,* "object (*n*.), sense I.1.a," March 2024, https://doi.org/10.1093/OED/1021962303.

9. I think this example was suggested to me by Guy Rohrbaugh about a million years ago when we were graduate students at UCLA.

10. David Hume, *A Treatise of Human Nature,* ed. David Norton and Mary Norton (Oxford: Oxford University Press, 2000), 1.4.6, 164.

11. Immanuel Kant, *Critique of Pure Reason,* trans. and ed. Paul Guyer and Allen W. Wood (Cambridge: Cambridge University Press, 1998).

12. Ludwig Wittgenstein, *Preliminary Studies for the "Philosophical Investigations," Generally known as The Blue and Brown Books* (New York: Basil Blackwell, 1958), 66–67.

13. Wittgenstein, *Preliminary Studies,* 66–67.

14. Sydney S. Shoemaker, "Self-Reference and Self-Awareness," in *Self-Knowledge,* ed. Quassim Cassam (Oxford: Oxford University Press, 1994), 80–93.

15. To be sure, one could be wrong that one is standing. The issue here is not incorrigibility. The issue, rather, is that the basis on which such statements are made does not involve identification.

16. Gareth Evans, "Self-Identification," in Cassam, *Self-Knowledge,* 184–209, 198–201.

17. Evans, "Self-Identification," 199.

18. We might add hearing as well. Thanks to Jules Wong for this.

19. Grammatically, *person* is "a category used in the classification of pronouns, possessive determiners, and verb forms, according to whether they indicate the speaker, the addressee, or someone or something spoken of" (*Oxford English Dictionary*, s.v. "person [*n.*], sense III.8," June 2024, https://doi.org/10.1093/OED/6205189904). And, further, various points of view are distinguished in literary narration. These include the first-person, the second-person, the third-person omniscient, the third-person restricted, and the third-person objective.

See Hubert J. M. Hermans, "The Dialogical Self: A Process of Positioning in Space and Time," in *The Oxford Handbook of the Self*, ed. Shaun Gallagher (Oxford: Oxford University Press, 2011), 654–80. In general, my account of the second-person stance is very different from most of this literature. See, for example, Stephen Darwall, *The Second-Person Standpoint: Morality, Respect, and Accountability* (Cambridge, Mass.: Harvard University Press, 2006).

20. David Chalmers, "Consciousness: The First-Person and Third-Person Views" (unpublished manuscript, December 30, 1987), 1, available at David Chalmers's website, https://consc.net/papers/oxford1.pdf.

21. Chalmers, "Consciousness," 1.

22. José Luis Bermúdez, "Bodily Awareness and Self-Consciousness," in Gallagher, *Oxford Handbook of the Self*, 157–79, 158.

23. I recognize different forms of dissociation. The one in this case arises from a need to distance from oneself due to dysphoria. It does not necessarily lead to a commitment to fungibility. By contrast, the commitment to fungibility invariably leads to a distancing from oneself. This latter sort will become plain in our discussion of "the subject."

24. Thanks to Michael Nelson for pressing me on this.

25. John Locke, *Second Treatise*, in *Two Treatises of Government*, student ed., ed. Peter Laslett (Cambridge: Cambridge University Press, 1988), sec. 27, 287.

26. Jean-Paul Sartre, *Being and Nothingness: A Phenomenological Essay on Ontology*, trans. Hazel E. Barnes (1956; repr., New York: Washington Square Press, 1992), 401–70.

27. Henry S. Rubin, "Phenomenology as Method in Trans Studies," *GLQ: A Journal of Lesbian and Gay Studies* 4, no. 2 (April 1998): 263–81, 271.

28. This matters with regard to Sartre's notion of the Look (*Being and Nothingness*, 340–400). For while the experience of oneself as an object for another (as subject) is important in Sartre's system, it is important only because it is his own account of how intersubjectivity is possible. It does not, however, provide for the very nonthetic awareness of oneself as a point of view that grounds his "being-for-itself." On the contrary, the latter figures independently, in some ways prior to being-for-others, which then itself appears out of nowhere.

Had Sartre reversed this, there would have been no problem of intersubjectivity to be solved in the first place.

29. Patricia Hill Collins, "The Sexual Politics of Black Womanhood," in *Black Feminist Thought: Knowledge, Consciousness, and the Politics of Empowerment,* 2nd ed. (New York: Routledge, 2000), 123–48, 138–39.

30. C. Riley Snorton, *Black on Both Sides: A Racial History of Trans Identity* (Minneapolis: University of Minnesota Press, 2017), 18–19.

31. Hortense J. Spillers, "Mama's Baby, Papa's Maybe: An American Grammar Book," in *Black, White, and in Color: Essays on American Literature and Culture* (Chicago: University of Chicago Press, 2003), 226.

32. Spillers, "Mama's Baby, Papa's Maybe," 206.

33. Amber Jamilla Musser, *Sensual Excess: Queer Femininity and Brown Jouissance* (New York: New York University Press, 2018), 7.

34. Spillers, "Mama's Baby, Papa's Maybe," 206.

35. Andrea Warmack, "We Flesh: Musser, Spillers, and beyond the Phenomenological Body," *Puncta: Journal of Critical Phenomenology* 5, no. 4 (2022): 106–24, 114.

36. Spillers, "Mama's Baby, Papa's Maybe," 206.

37. Spillers, 206.

38. Aníbal Quijano, "Colonialidad del Poder y Classification Social," *Journal of World Research System* 6, no. 2 (Summer/Fall 2000): 342–86, 343.

39. Consider Locke, who writes, "The *Idea* of Heat and Cold, Light and Darkness, White and Black, Motion and Rest, are equally clear and *positive Ideas* in the Mind: though, perhaps, some of *the causes* which produce them, are barely *privations* in those Subjects, from whence our Senses derive those *Ideas*." John Locke, *An Essay Concerning Human Understanding,* ed. Peter H. Nidditch (Oxford: Oxford University Press, 1975), 2.8.2, 132.

40. I would imagine the same is true of a queer phenomenology. See Sara Ahmed, *Queer Phenomenology: Orientations, Objects, Others* (Durham, N.C.: Duke University Press, 2006).

41. María Lugones, *Pilgrimages/Peregrinajes: Theorizing Coalition against Multiple Oppressions* (Lanham, Md.: Rowman and Littlefield, 2003), 58.

Conclusion

1. Aníbal Quijano, "Colonialidad del Poder y Classification Social," *Journal of World Research System* 6, no. 2 (Summer/Fall 2000): 342–86, repr. in *Aníbal Quijano: Cuestiones y horizontes—De la dependencia histórico-estructural a la colonialidad/descolonialidad del poder* (Buenos Aires: Latin American Council of Social Sciences, 2014): 285–327, 287.

Index

abuse, 17, 86, 187, 246, 249, 250;
blended instances of, 25, 27;
racist, 66; sanctioned, 28; sexist,
66; sexual, 26, 28, 114; systemic, 42
access, 1, 54, 231; boundaries and,
46–47, 50; first-person, 236;
sensory, 19, 47, 236; third-person,
236, 237; visual, 93, 95, 235
Adam and Eve, nakedness of, 187–88,
189
affective account, 123; defined, 257
affective makeup, 135; defined, 257
agency: denial of, 244; intimate, 249;
self-display and, 45–46; social, 3;
structural, 81
agent object, 4, 45, 47, 48, 56; defined,
257; ontological pluralism and,
80–86
agents, 82; appearance of, 83;
structural role of, 81
Alarcón, Norma, 31
almost-object, 144
always-already claim, 154; reanimation and, 155–59
animals, 82–83, 191; objects and, 243;
precultural, 274n39
animation: defined, 257; dialogical
presence and, 56; phenomenon of,
156; world-travel and, 164
anticipatory vulnerability, 85; defined,
257
Anzaldúa, Gloria, 142, 145, 146, 147;
experience/struggle and, 140–41;

Indigeneity and, 282n34; on
Mexican Indians/mirrors, 140;
mirror experiences and, 121
apparitional, 23, 121, 144, 147
apparitional liminality, 284n45;
defined, 257
appearance, 59, 251; intimacy and,
134; sensory, 44, 47, 55, 165, 237;
sex-differentiated, 99. *See also*
intimate appearance; proper
appearance
appearance–reality contrast, 18, 121,
157, 161, 163, 169, 197; BTBA and,
162; WBA and, 159, 162
Araujo, Gwen, 115
Aristotelianism, 191, 193, 211, 214,
218, 220, 247
Aristotle, 193; friendship and, 218;
Locke and, 211–12, 219, 220;
reasoning and, 219
Arteaga, Alfred, 84–85
Arvan, Marcus, 272n27
Ashley, Florence, 280n9
"as-if" behavior, 106, 116, 117, 284n39
aspirational account, 123; defined, 257
attention, 38, 106; defined, 257
autobiography, 170; textualization of,
152–53; transsexual, 152–53, 155,
158
avowals, 47–48, 56; first-person, 166
awareness, 48, 52, 57, 83, 227, 230,
238, 240; bodily, 235, 236; forms
of, 234, 248; kinesthetic, 232;

260; existential depth and, 54;
imputation of, 55, 57; original,
155–56; self-declaration and, 162;
sex-differentiated, 99; theory and,
169
interpersonal objects, 2, 38, 42–48,
54, 55, 62, 132, 133, 173, 183, 190,
194, 197, 201, 225, 228, 229, 237,
238, 239, 249, 255; access to, 231;
capacity of, 48; defined, 260; man/
woman as, 76, 246; moral sex and,
77–80; nonpersonal objects and,
49, 245; perception of, 43, 58; sensory perception of, 49; subsumption of, 56; understanding, 45
interpersonal sentiments, 52–53, 124,
146, 168, 237, 243; causal role of,
136; defined, 260; gender phoria
and, 132–37; vulnerability and,
50–52
interpersonal space, 22, 38–42, 46, 59,
183, 195, 196, 239, 255; colonial/
modern, 197; concept of, 32;
defined, 260; supremacy of, 41–42;
universe of, 201
interpersonal spatiality, 1, 2, 21, 35,
41, 43, 54, 61, 62, 91, 117, 164,
171–72, 173, 180, 186, 196, 201,
202, 230, 242, 247, 253; abusive
system of, 66; account of, 59, 60;
appeal to, 124; contests assumption, 4; defined, 260; discussion of,
80; features of, 58; forms of, 145;
hypothesis, 165–66; interpersonal
object and, 239; native system of,
53; negotiation of, 83; networks
of, 119; practices of, 191; self-
awareness and, 238; systems of,
58, 66, 136, 183, 184; theory, 3–4,
37, 38, 49, 137, 199, 220, 228, 236,
240, 241, 251; works of, 145. *See*

also folk system of interpersonal
spatiality
interpersonal spatiality hypothesis,
75–77, 79; defined, 260
intersectionality, 24–26; reality enforcement and, 26–29
intersex, 113, 179, 202
intersubjectivity, 59, 250, 299n28;
subjectivity and, 177, 195
intimacy, 13, 18, 20, 53, 119, 120, 167,
173, 187, 196, 254; acts of, 92, 107;
alternative movement of, 106;
appearance and, 134; calamities
of, 21, 22, 103; distance and, 66;
emotional-romantic, 98; eroticism
and, 97; failure, 85; foreclosure
of, 105; negotiation toward, 165;
practices of, 134; public and, 21;
self-intimization and, 45; sexual,
21, 55, 98, 105; trans people
and, 103; values of, 42. *See also*
calamities of intimacy; complex
intimacy; gesture of intimacy;
intrinsic intimacy
intimate appearance, 4, 90–93,
99, 104, 106, 158; defined, 260;
disclosure of, 102, 112; genital
status and, 89; naked body and,
94, 100, 101; nakedness and, 92;
proper appearance and, 93, 111,
165; sex-differentiated, 34; social
situation and, 102; strip and, 97
intimate cognition, 92, 93, 94, 105,
106; defined, 261
intimate deadening, 51, 135; defined,
261
intimate disregard, 40; defined, 261
intimate gestures, 44, 53, 55, 106, 167,
170; arrangement of, 45
intimate hemorrhaging, 51, 135;
defined, 261

oppression, 14, 18, 30, 65, 114, 137,
178, 254; blended, 24, 25; categories of, 15–17; disability-based, 138;
forms of, 15, 23, 68; interlocking
of, 267n14, 267n16; privilege and,
24–25; racial, 24, 29; resistance
and, 25, 171; sexist, 15, 24, 25;
vectors of, 26
ordinary notion of personhood, 33;
defined, 262. *See also* personhood
orientation, 169; gender, 156–57;
same-sex, 197; sexual, 69, 73
overworld, 68, 161, 164, 165–66, 171;
dialogical interaction in, 251;
underworld and, 62
Ozturk, Burkay, 287n37

Palóu, Francisco, 196, 291n52
Paris Is Burning (film), 117
passive presence, 46; defined, 262
pathways, 39, 45, 98, 107, 134; defined,
262; network of, 106
people, 222; person and, 77; term, 2,
33, 77, 204, 273n30, 273n32
people-as-folk, 33, 60; defined, 262
people-as-human, 33, 77; defined,
262
person, 5, 6, 11, 80, 92, 255; colonial
legacy of, 35; concept of, 34, 59,
60, 202, 219; farewell to, 33–35;
folk and, 77, 194; human and, 222;
man and, 217, 220; multicultural,
84; notion of, 59, 60, 202; people
and, 77; philosophical, 2, 32,
34, 60, 202, 205, 215; scholastic
treatments of, 203; self and, 3,
33, 200, 223, 238; technologies of,
28; term, 1, 2, 3, 4, 32, 33, 34, 58,
59, 60, 77, 124, 177, 199, 202, 203,
204, 205, 206, 207, 208, 209, 215,
218, 220, 222, 223, 225, 251, 253,

254; understanding of, 81. *See also*
physical person
personhood: autonomy and, 200;
exclusion from, 219; presumption
of, 206; technology of, 134; threshold for, 200; uniform of, 133. *See
also* folk personhood; Lockean
personhood; ordinary notion of
personhood
phalloplasty, 128, 276n17
phantom limb, 126, 130
phenomenology, 38, 109, 121, 122,
123, 238, 239; erotic, 105; trans,
248
philosophical conversations, 6, 253,
255
philosophical methodology, 5, 7
philosophical model, 242, 251
philosophical problems, 5, 203, 274n7
philosophy, 5, 7, 33, 202, 221, 231,
246–51; Aristotelian, 226; spirit
of, 255
phoria, 135, 231; framing, 129; localized, 155; positive/negative valences of, 124, 126, 132, 139; sensitivity
to, 128. *See also* gender phoria
physical person, 2, 4, 89, 90–107, 121;
defined, 263; deployment of, 240;
as moral entity, 240; possessing,
134; reality enforcement and,
99–107
physical strip, 91, 97; defined, 263
Pitts, Andrea J., 31
plantation thesis, 208–9
playing along, 20, 21, 75; defined, 263
pluralism, 67, 76, 77, 204. *See also*
ontological pluralism
plurality, 77, 204
politics, 5, 70, 163, 221; Indigenous,
282n34; intersex, 179; transgender,
3, 30, 179, 253

make-believe contexts for, 141;
multiplicity in, 146; phenomenon
of, 137–41; pretransition, 23, 121,
230, 231, 241; realization of, 147;
transition, 240
self-revelation, 55, 150, 157, 167,
169–73, 187; intimate, 98; self-
sharing, 40, 85, 135, 155, 239; trans
requirements of, 170
self-subject equivalence, 230–38, 242,
247
semantic contextualism, 67, 69–71, 72,
74, 271n21; misgendering and, 75
semantics, practice and, 62
sense of self, 170, 204, 282n25
sensory presence, passive/dialogical,
46
Sepúlveda, Juan Ginés de, 218
Serano, Julia, 106–7, 125; gender dysphoria and, 130; on subconscious
sex, 129, 131
sex: anatomical, 18; assigned at birth,
270n10; biological notion of,
79; centralization of, 73; characteristics, 69; commercial, 29;
conferred, 113; gender and, 18,
122, 192, 278n56; hiding, 220–23;
homosexual, 117; invariance of,
111; material, 158; morphological,
159; pretense and, 73–75; race and,
223; resistance to, 147; subconscious, 126, 129, 131; wrong, 21
sex category, 13, 129
sexism, 24, 26, 114, 136, 178, 190;
racism and, 25
sexology, 5
sex-representational system, 19, 33,
34, 89, 99, 100, 160, 290–91n34;
defined, 263
sexual aggression, 26, 178, 185
sexual desire, 132, 185; female, 96;

male, 96, 97; naked body and,
106
sexual dimorphism, 178, 179, 190, 191
Sexual Ethics (Michels), 185
sexuality, 32, 99, 245; alignment of,
278n61; Chicana, 31; false views of,
96–97; female engagement in, 187;
gender and, 30; mythology of, 190;
nakedness and, 95–96; natural,
96, 98; representing, 190–91;
restrained, 186; taken-for-granted
form of, 178; trans women and,
105; unrestrained, 186
sex work, 267n21; trans, 27, 28, 29,
118, 268n22
Shaftesbury, Earl of, Anthony Ashley
Cooper, 209
shame, 50, 134, 138; experiencing, 52;
feeling, 135
Shoemaker, Sydney S., 232
Singer, Peter, 201
singular mode, 93; defined, 263
slavery, 6, 29, 32, 207, 209–10, 242,
294–95n36, 297n58; colonial, 219;
defense of, 210; English, 34, 209,
220; escape from, 30; hereditary,
294n32, 295n37; justification for,
199–200; natural, 218, 219; racial,
186
slaves, 191, 219; slavemasters and, 24
Snorton, C. Riley, 30, 32, 68, 186, 246;
on fungibility, 244
social activity, 16, 56, 83
social agents, 47, 56
social construction, 42, 64, 78, 90,
129, 130
social context, 62, 63, 75, 110
social existence, 177, 288n2
social phenomenon, 65, 90; nakedness as, 100–101
social practices, 22, 23, 56, 61, 94

Talia Mae Bettcher is professor of philosophy at California State University, Los Angeles.